• • The Devil's Emissaries • •

••The Devil's Emissaries••

By
Myron J. Quimby

South Brunswick and New York:
A. S. Barnes and Company
London: Thomas Yoseloff Ltd

Library of Congress Catalogue Card Number: 71-81183

A.S. Barnes and Company, Inc.
Cranbury, New Jersey 08512

Thomas Yoseloff Ltd
108 New Bond Street
London W1Y OQX, England

ISBN: 0-498-06764-5
Printed in the United States of America

This book is respectfully dedicated
to all officers of the law, federal,
state, county, and city. It is their
willingness to lay their lives on the
line, in defense of our laws, that
keep this country from becoming a
jungle.

Contents

Acknowledgments

To Saundra Shuler, Reference Department, Oklahoma County Libraries, Oklahoma City, Oklahoma, whose invaluable help made this a much better book than I had hoped was possible.

To Miss Jerry Nelson, Aladdin Book Shop, Oklahoma City, Oklahoma, for the book, *The Story of Clyde Barrow and Bonnie Parker.*

To Mr. Coy Burroughs, *The New Era*, Hot Springs, Arkansas.

To the Editor of *The Ocala Star Banner*, Ocala, Florida; and in particular to Mr. Jim Twitty, reporter, for his assistance in the research of the shootout between Ma and Fred Barker, and the FBI, at Oklawaha, Florida.

To the Libraries in Memphis, Tennessee; Little Rock, Arkansas; Tulsa and Oklahoma City, Oklahoma; Joplin and Kansas City, Missouri; St. Paul, Minnesota; and St. Petersburg, Florida. These libraries, well stocked with microfilm records, old newspapers, and staffed with dedicated employees made researching this book a pleasure.

To three "old timers" in Sallisaw, Oklahoma, who shall remain anonymous to protect them from their friends. Their absolute refusal to give me requested information regarding Pretty Boy Floyd, a local hero, resulted in an argument among themselves. The result was a wealth of information, unwittingly given.

To Major H. C. McCormick, Boley, Oklahoma, whose graphic account of his killing of George Birdwell, and the bank holdup in Boley, Oklahoma, and its aftermath added a splendid story to the chapter on Pretty Boy Floyd.

Foreword

The people I have written about in this book were a strange lot, and the activities in which they engaged were equally strange. I have tried to eliminate the legends and myths that have grown up around them, and tell it like it really was.

Kate "Ma" Barker and her four sons presented an almost unbelievable picture as an American family. George "Machine Gun" Kelly, with his deadly-sounding name, was really the clown of the underworld. Clyde Barrow and Bonnie Parker are almost indescribable, and quite beyond belief. Yet they did exist, and the title of their chapter, "The Thrill Seekers," is, perhaps, the best description of them.

Charles "Pretty Boy" Floyd, John Herman Dillinger, and Alvin Karpis robbed and killed strictly for money, while George "Baby Face" Nelson stole for money, but killed for the sheer pleasure of the killing.

Prohibition made many of the gangsters of this era, and the inadequate prison systems schooled them in the finer points of their chosen profession. Also, the lack of adequate laws to cope with these criminals conspired to insure their longevity.

The eighteenth amendment to the American Constitution, which made prohibition a national law, went into effect in several phases. It was passed by the Congress, and submitted to the various states for ratification, December 18, 1917. A little more than a year later, following its ratification, on January 16, 1919, it became law. Still, its legality was questioned by many until the United States Supreme Court, in 1920, in a unanimous decision sustained the validity of the amendment. There were few provisions made to enforce the law, however, and it would be a while before it became effective.

Up in Norfolk, Virginia, the Reverend Billy Sunday held a funeral service for "John Barleycorn." At a meeting gathered around a horse-drawn, 20-foot coffin, over 10,000 people gathered and

cheered, as he shouted, "Good-bye, John. You were God's worst
enemy. You were Hell's best friend. The reign of tears is over!"

But in spite of the high hopes held by the "Blue Noses," who
rammed the eighteenth amendment and later the Volstead Act
through the Congress, it really ushered in an age of lawlessness
that has never been equaled. It became known as "The Roaring
Twenties," the age of the bootlegger, rumrunner, moonshiner,
smuggler, gangster, hijacker, racket man, corrupt politician,
crooked doctor, crooked lawyer, and crooked cops. It introduced
into this young nation a whole new set of moral standards, and
very few of them were improvements.

People who had never before taken a drink suddenly developed
a terrible thirst, and an entire nation seemed to go on one big
binge. Booze, bathtub gin, and home-brew flowed like water in
every state in the nation, and hip-pocket flasks became status
symbols. Speakeasies operated openly, and some of them were
located right across the street from the local police station.

Then there were the people who would make a big business
of furnishing booze and beer to the thirsty Americans. In Chicago,
perhaps the best known were "Big Jim" Colosimo, Dion O'Banion,
Hymie (The Polack) Weiss, George (Bugs) Moran, Al Capone,
and Johnny Torrio.

Clubs sprang up around the nation, sporting such names as the
Four Deuces, the Hotsie Totsie Club, the Merry-Go-Round, and
the Club New Yorker. These clubs were really speakeasies, and
issued membership cards which could get you into other speakeasies.

Suddenly bootlegging and rum running became the largest
single source of money for the underworld. Soon fights would
start over territories, while hijackings and running gun battles
between rival gangs would become commonplace. The average
citizen would take a "so-what" attitude as long as gangster killed
gangster in their wars of expansion.

Undoubtedly these events, and events like the St. Valentine's
Day massacre in Chicago, on February 14, 1929, in which seven
men were brutally machinegunned down in a Capone attempt
to rid himself of a competitor—George (Bugs) Moran—would
profoundly affect many people. Among these would be the ones
documented in this book, who, at an early age, began to get the
idea that human life was cheap and gangsters were romantic
heroes.

The citizens of this country, which was settled primarily by

Europeans, were loath to give their federal government the necessary laws to combat this crime wave. They still remembered
the lessons learned in Europe, where their forefathers had given
too much power to a centralized government, and the people had
lost their freedom. There would be no American secret police
here, they vowed.

And so it was that the Federal Government, through the Department of the Treasury and the Department of Justice, undertook to fight the criminal and organized crime. The Treasury Department tackled Alphonse Capone, among others, and eventually
sent him to a federal penitentiary for eleven years, on a charge
of tax evasion.

Then the Federal Bureau of Investigation, the investigative
branch of the Department of Justice, attacked the bank robbers,
kidnappers, and killers who were terrorizing the country almost
at will. However, they were forbidden to carry weapons, except
on special occasions, and had limited authority of arrest.

Their biggest weapon was the Dyer Act, or National Motor
Vehicle Act, which prohibited the transport of a stolen motor
vehicle across a state line. This was their "foot in the door," in
the Dillinger case, among others.

During those strange days, if a bank official were to embezzle
a sum of money from a Federal Reserve Bank he violated a federal statute, and the FBI could, and would, track him to the ends
of the earth. On the other hand, the Barker-Karpis gang could
enter through the front door of the same bank; steal two hundred thousand dollars; machinegun down employees, police and
customers, and then flee, without breaking federal law.

As soon as the gang passed the city limits, the city police lost
their authority to pursue them any further. Now they came under
county and state jurisdiction.

The county sheriff's office was usually an overworked organization, with little help. The state police were all too often paper
units. Many times their file clerks and typists outnumbered the
men in the field. Vigilante groups were often poorly organized,
and frequently fought among themselves over leadership. Once
the bank robbers crossed the state line, all pursuit stopped.

In all too many cases the gangsters and the hoodlums were far
better armed and organized than the police. Police pay was poor
at best; their risks were great, and most men had to buy their own
equipment, and even furnish their own transportation. Under
such circumstances it was a wonder that there were any police-

men at all. Only men dedicated to a high and mighty purpose, the enforcement of law and order, would have stayed with such a thankless job.

The crooked cops, while widely publicized, were really a minority, and the majority of good cops, honest cops, and brave cops rarely got their names into print, unless it was in the obituary column. It is because of this that I have chosen to dedicate this book to them.

MYRON J. QUIMBY

September 15, 1967
St. Petersburg, Florida

· · The Devil's Emissaries · ·

• •**1**• •

The Hip Pocket Bootlegger

i

At exactly 12:01 A.M., July 16, 1920, the sale or possession of intoxicating liquors—except for medicinal purposes—became illegal in America. The great experiment had begun, and Prohibition was now the law of the land. It was an experiment that introduced into America an era known as the *roaring twenties*, with its flappers, its hip flasks, its speakeasies, and its bootleggers. The term *bootlegger*, it is said, originated during the Civil War, when peddlers sold illicit whiskey to Union troops. These peddlers kept their wares hidden in their cowhide bootlegs, and were referred to, contemptuously, as bootleggers.

This chapter is about a bootlegger of the roaring twenties, who kept his whiskey hidden in his hip pockets, thus becoming known as *the hip pocket bootlegger*. He worked real hard at his trade, and later—with the help of his second wife—graduated into a big-time operator, known as *Machine Gun Kelly*. Newspapers, books, and movies referred to him as a "Western desperado," "gimlet-eyed killer," and "lusty badman." Even to this day, he is still given credit for naming agents of the Federal Bureau of Investigation *G-Men*. As the story goes—and it has been told so many times that it is no longer a story—when the FBI fell upon Machine Gun Kelly, in Memphis, he cowered in a corner, and cried, "Don't shoot, G-Men, don't shoot!" And it is from this bit of rhetoric—we are told—that agents of the FBI soon became known as "G-Men." Alas, for such a splendid story, that's just about what it was.

Who was Machine Gun Kelly, whose very name, it is said,

caused brave men to quake with fear, and gave bank presidents nightmares? Well, this is his story, and you may read it, then decide for yourself.

ii

Born in Memphis, Tennessee, on July 18, 1895, Machine Gun Kelly's real name was George Kelly Barnes. He was the son of a prosperous insurance representative of the New York Life Insurance Company, and lived at 2080 Linden. This address, in a highly respectable neighborhood, was known as part of the Cowden-Rembert District. George attended Central High School, then entered Memphis State University, where he majored in agriculture. He was a student here when World War I broke out, but received a deferment because of a heart condition. It was the doctor's considered opinion that any undue excitement, like a world war, would be injurious to George's health. Also in 1918, his mother died; and the following year he quit college and went to work for the 784 Taxi Cab Company. It was while driving a cab that George began a profitable little sideline—selling booze to some of his customers. When he found out how thirsty the people of Memphis were, he quit the Cab Company and became a full-time bootlegger.

The relationship between George and his father had never been good, and it deteriorated badly with the death of his mother. When his father remarried, the father-son relationship ceased completely. It was also in 1919 that George married Geneva Ramsey, daughter of a prominent Memphis levee contractor. All went well until the children—George, Jr., and then Bobbie—were born. Suddenly, George began to feel the unfamiliar and heavy hand of responsibility on his shoulder, and he didn't like it. Gone were his happy-go-lucky ways, and soon he began to brood. Fights with Geneva were frequent, until the marriage, at last, settled down into one long, unending battle. Geneva stood all she could, for the sake of the children, but she finally sued for a divorce. He, of course, offered no objections, and when it was granted, he once again became his old happy-go-lucky self.

By now George was well-known to the Memphis police as *the hip pocket bootlegger*. He earned this unpleasant title by hanging around the front of the old Peabody Hotel, at Main and Monroe Streets, hawking his hooch to passers-by. With a pint of booze in each hip pocket, hidden by his coat, he would slip a customer a bottle in the flick of an eye, then scurry off to his cache for more. Business was great, and George was prospering; moreover, he was doing something he really enjoyed.

Former Captain of Detectives Walter Haylo remembered arresting him at least twice for peddling whiskey in front of the Peabody. George was also well-known to other members of the Memphis police department, who arrested him, from time to time, on the same charge. The usual punishment was a small fine—promptly paid by George—and he very seldom spent more than a few hours in a jail cell. His many arrests were only inconveniences to him, and served no useful purpose as a means toward rehabilitation.

Near disaster came to George on May 30, 1924, when he, Frank Stuhl, and a character known only as "The Commodore" were arrested on a charge of bootlegging. Scared, George gave the police an alias (G. K. Bonner), but he was far too well known to get away with this.

The three of them had been selling whiskey from a small farmhouse two miles north of Ridgeway. They thought they had a good thing going, as business was booming, but their many customers actually proved their downfall.

For two weeks Deputies A. E. Baety and Brill Willis had been watching the busy little farmhouse with increasing interest. Attracting their attention were the large number of automobiles that made this spot a regular stop. Finally, under the cover of darkness, they moved in and arrested George and his pals. They also confiscated three cases of whiskey.

Their trials were not heard until October 10, 1924, in the court of Judge Harsh. Frank Stuhl and "The Commodore" were no strangers to the judge, and he had a fair acquaintance with George. He decided to live up to his name, and gave them the maximum sentence: six months in jail and a fine of $500. The three men were shocked, and all filed appeals immediately.

As soon as Frank Stuhl was released on bail, he spooked and fled the state. "The Commodore" entered a series of appeals, and eventually his case was *nolle prosequi*. George got unwanted help from his father, and his case went all the way to the Governor's mansion in Nashville. Because of the Governor's influence, George's case was also given sympathetic treatment, and he was pardoned.

However a short time later he was arrested again, on a burglary charge. He was accused of breaking into the Van Fleet home and stealing some very fine red whiskey. He was released the following day for lack of evidence, and was politely told that Memphis could well do without his presence. With this gentle urging, George left his home town and headed West.

On March 14, 1927, he was arrested in Sante Fe, New Mexico; the charge, of course, was bootlegging. Here, his luck failed him, and he was sent to the state penitentiary for a few months. As soon as he was released, George fled the state, and went to Reno, Nevada, where, thanks to connections made while in the penitentiary, he got a job as a chauffeur for some of the local hoods. It was also here that George heard himself some big talk, and saw some big money changing hands; but there seemed to be none for him. Disappointed and disgusted, he left Reno and headed for Oklahoma. One can only imagine his chagrin when the Tulsa police arrested him for vagrancy, then showed him the city limits and told him to "get!"

It was July 1927 when George arrived in the bustling metropolis of Oklahoma City—a city that would one day give him a big name and then later whittle him down to size. He had heard of "Little Steve" Anderson while doing time in New Mexico, so he looked him up and asked for a job. Anderson was one of Oklahoma's most successful bootleggers, and he and George hit it off right away. Soon, George was running illegal alky to Tulsa for Little Steve, and the money was rolling in. But once again George and the Tulsa police locked horns—this time for bootlegging—and they jailed him, fined him, drove him out of town, and told him never to come back. He fled back to Oklahoma City, where he told Little Steve what had happened. But his boss just shrugged his shoulders and told him not to worry; he would give him a territory in the big city.

Little Steve kept his word, and George began to take on an air of respectability, making his deliveries of booze in a fine leather briefcase to his equally fine customers. No longer just a hip pocket bootlegger, he began boasting—dimly hinting of a lurid past, and speculating about a great future. He told everybody about his exciting experiences in the war as an expert with automatic weapons. His favorite gun, he boasted, was the machine gun. Of course, there was no one here who knew that these experiences had been limited to the front row center of the Strand Theatre in Memphis.

George was a large man, with a round face and blue eyes, who was always grinning when he wasn't boasting. He was not exactly handsome, but women found him attractive, and he did have a natural air of good humor about him. His one big failing was his mouth. He could never keep it closed. This flaw in his character would hound him all the days of his life. He was actually a big blusterer who eventually came to believe his own lies.

George wasn't around Oklahoma City long before he attracted the attention of Kathryn Thorne, Little Steve's girl friend. She liked his good nature, his free-spending, and his carefree manner, but it is doubtful if she ever believed most of his boastings. Still, in spite of his loud braggadocio, she believed she saw in him an opportunity to get out of petty crime and into the big time. She put on her charms, and before long had an adoring George following her everywhere. Enamored by her good looks, he also fell for her phony but sophisticated manners, and her flashy clothes, which clung to every curve of her body. Love seemed to blossom, and with almost complete abandon they openly courted each other. Just what Little Steve thought of all this is unknown, for he gave no outward sign that he even knew what was going on.

When Kathryn had gained George's full confidence, he confessed to her that he really didn't know one end of a machine gun from the other. He told her, too, about his bad heart, and his dislike for violence. She watched as he talked, but most of the time she wasn't listening. She had made up her mind to take this loudmouth bootlegger, and make him into a bad man in spite of himself.

Following a precise plan—which was true to her nature—Kathryn bought him a machine gun and drove him into the Oklahoma countryside where she made him practice. Under her careful tutelage, he eventually reached a point where he could actually fire the gun without dropping it, and with his eyes open. This done, she then began gathering up the spent shells from his gun, and handed them out to some of her hoodlum friends. "Here's a souvenir for you," she would say. "It's a cartridge from Kelly's gun—that's *Machine Gun Kelly*, you know." He liked the name, and it soon became a permanent part of his incessant boastings. Years later, news stories about him would attribute his nickname to the fact that he could write the name KELLY on the side of a barn with his machine gun. Kathryn's training and her publicity campaign were so successful that "the hip pocket bootlegger" now became George "Machine Gun" Kelly!

Just as this romance was about to blossom into something more permanent, Machine Gun Kelly was arrested for selling whiskey on a nearby Indian reservation. This was a serious federal offense, and on October 11, 1928, the government put Kathryn's burgeoning badman in Leavenworth for a three-year term. She was mad—raving mad—and suspected that he had been fingered by Little Steve Anderson; but she could prove nothing. Seething with frustration and anger, she packed her clothes, stole Steve's big motor car and his pekingese dog, and drove off to Fort Worth, Texas.

iii

Kathryn Thorne was born in 1904, in Saltillo, Mississippi, and christened Cleo Brooks. Her father, J. E. Brooks, was a hard-working farmer; her mother, Ora Coleman Brooks, was a one-time bank employee, who could type, and occasionally wrote articles for farm periodicals. She was an only child, spoiled and pampered from birth.

Cleo had just finished the eighth grade when she was suddenly sent to visit with her grandmother, Mrs. T. M. Coleman, in Stratford, Oklahoma. A short time later, word filtered back to Saltillo that Cleo, only 15, had been married.

Two years passed. Then, one day Cleo Frye came home to mother, bringing with her a daughter named Pauline. She had unkind things to say about her husband, and with the help of her mother she filed a suit for divorce.

By the time the divorce had been granted, her own parents were squabbling. At the end of one particular violent spat, Ora packed her things, and with daughter and granddaughter in tow, she moved to Coleman, Texas. This town, primarily agricultural in nature, was a logical choice for Ora, as it was peopled by many of her relatives. With their help, and with some money of her own, Ora opened a small hotel. In a strict sense of the word, this was the beginning of Cleo's criminal education, for Ora's place soon attracted a motley collection of smalltime hoods and bootleggers. Cleo, now 17, helped her mother by serving home-brew to the customers, as this was the era of Prohibition.

Young, pretty, and very very bored, Cleo started making trips to nearby Abilene, and then on to Fort Worth. In these cities, she began collecting a curious group of friends. Most were prostitutes, bootleggers, and petty thieves—members of the lower rank of the underworld. She got a job as a manicurist, and worked at it for a while; but it didn't pay enough to finance her expensive nights on the town so she quit. She was subsequently arrested several times in these cities, and charged with prostitution, shoplifting, and other crimes; but she was never convicted of any charge.

It was her underworld friends who gave her the name Kathryn; she would use this name from that moment on. By now she was spending more and more time in Fort Worth, and her trips back to Coleman became fewer and fewer. Now Pauline saw very little of her mother, and the job of rearing her was left to her grandmother. Of course Ora was busy with her "hotel," her farm articles, and with securing her divorce from Kathryn's father, but she still found time for her granddaughter.

Kathryn's chosen career of crime eventually brought her into contact with a hoodlum-bootlegger named Charlie Thorne. He had good outlets in Coleman and Fort Worth, and seemed to be a big spender. This, of course, interested Kathryn, so she set her cap for him. Attractive and poised, she captivated Charlie and they were soon married. Anxious to please her, Charlie, who already had an apartment in Coleman, built a house for Kathryn in Fort Worth. Unfortunately this "dream" marriage was destined to end in tragedy.

Time passed, and jealous misunderstandings severely tested and strained this marriage. Fight followed fight, and both would become drunk and violent. They fought in Coleman, they fought in Fort Worth, and they even fought in the streets.

One evening, in Fort Worth, Kathryn stopped her car at a familiar gas station, and appeared greatly agitated. The attendant, who knew her, noticed her obvious impatience to be on her way, and asked, "Kathryn, where're you headed for?"

She shot him a startled glance, then, without much thought, she said, "Where am I headed for? I'm headed for Coleman to kill that bastard, Charlie Thorne, that's where I'm headed!" With this, she jumped into her car, and it roared off into the night.

The following day, Charlie Thorne was found in their apartment, with a bullet in his head, and a gun in his hand. On his dresser lay a typewritten note, with no signature. It read: "I can't live with her or without her, hence I am departing this life." Strange and eloquent language for a hoodlum-bootlegger who didn't even own a typewriter! The coroner's jury, however, saw nothing unusual about this, and they ruled Charlie's death a suicide.

Only 23, Kathryn was single again, with a nice house in Fort

Worth—a town she had grown quite fond of. Now, she spent most of her time here, occasionally making "fun trips" to Abilene and Oklahoma City. Then, her mother, Ora became a mail-order bride, and moved to Paradise, Texas, taking Kathryn's daughter Pauline with her.

Kathryn took little or no notice of this, as she was busy with her hoodlum friends in Fort Worth and Abilene. By now, she was well-known to the police in both these cities, and her Mulkey Street address was often under surveillance. Her own family didn't help her reputation any, for by now, her mother was a bootlegger and a hideout operator; she had an aunt who was a prostitute, an uncle under suspicion for counterfeiting, another uncle on his way to Leavenworth for auto theft, and a cousin who operated a still. Because of the heat placed upon her by the police, Kathryn began making long trips to Oklahoma City, where she was still an unknown. It was on one of these trips that she met and became involved with Little Steve Anderson. This romance would last until George Kelly hit town, then she transferred her attentions to him. It was probably the first time she had ever been in love. When he was arrested, she couldn't stay in Oklahoma City, because of Little Steve, so she returned to her Mulkey Street address, in Fort Worth.

For the entire term of Kelly's imprisonment, Kathryn managed to live in comfort and luxury, with no visible means of support. She was arrested many times, but only on suspicion. In one such case, the Abilene police, investigating a fur robbery, secured the description of the suspected burglar and his female accomplice. The description of the woman matched that of Kathryn, who was well-known to the Abilene police. They advised the Fort Worth authorities of their suspicions; a warrant was granted, and detectives raided Kathryn's home. Here, they found the burglar, the furs he had stolen, and Kathryn. She, of course, denied any part in the theft, denied any knowledge of the furs, and denounced the burglar. He, true to the code of the underworld, supported all her denials, and she went free. The burglar wasn't so lucky; he drew a five-year prison sentence.

iv

At Leavenworth, George Kelly had met such interesting people as Frank "Jelly" Nash, Francis Keating, and Thomas Holden—all mail train robbers. He had also made friends with a few bank robbers like Harvey J. Bailey and Albert Bates. They impressed him greatly, and he would listen in rapt silence as they told of their many accomplishments. For the time being, Kelly had dropped his ferocious nickname "Machine Gun," and had learned to curb his empty boastings.

Kelly's behavior as a prisoner was exemplary and his education was a cut or two above that of the average con, so he was given a job in the records room of the penitentiary. When, on February 28, 1930, Thomas Holden and Francis Keating—both serving 25 year sentences for mail robbery—escaped, using trustee passes, suspicion fell heavily upon Kelly. These passes were kept in the record room, and could have been stolen by him. Still, suspicion was one thing and proof another, so no official black mark was placed against his record.

With time off for good behavior, George Kelly was released from Leavenworth late in 1930. He wired Kathryn, in Fort Worth, and they made a date to meet in Minneapolis. They were married there a short time later.

From the moment Kelly said "I do," Kathryn took over as head of the family. She had made big plans for Kelly, and now she put them into action. Once again she started her promotion of "Machine Gun" Kelly among her underworld friends. She worked long and hard at this task, and Kelly did all he could to help. Most of the hoodlum gangs, however, just couldn't take either him or his deadly name seriously. Once, when Kelly had boasted long and loud, he managed to rile two train robbers. These men, exasperated, told Kelly, "We're going to take you out into the woods and use that damn tommy gun on you, if you don't shut up!" This so unnerved Kelly that he fled to Kathryn, and reported it. She knew what to do; she wrote a letter to the police telling them where they could find the two bandits. The police came and took the hoodlums away, the Kellys breathed a sigh of relief, and Kathryn continued her publicity campaign.

Soon, she had ingratiated herself with some of the ex-cons Kelly had met in Leavenworth. She also made friends with their wives and girlfriends. She started a mail-drop for them, keeping files of telephone numbers, and generally became an information center for the hoodlum element. All this she did in the hope that one gang or another would eventually accept Machine Gun Kelly into their ranks. She had about lost hope when Albert Bates, a bank robber Kelly had met in the pen, became so desperate for help, that he gave Kelly his first big chance. He helped them loot the bank in Tupelo, Mississippi, and didn't do too badly, so they took him along when they held up the bank in Denton, Texas. Then followed the bank in Blue Ridge, Texas, and soon the Kellys had more money than they had ever seen before. Kathryn lost no time in investing most of it in jewels, furs, and a 16-cylinder car. Most of the banks had been small, the gangs large, and Kelly's cut middling; but he was now a full-fledged bank robber, and he was happy.

Off they drove to Paradise, Texas, and met Ora's new husband— a little man with a big name. Robert K. G. Shannon was known as the "boss" of Wise county. He was not a gangster, but merely a political hack who delivered votes on demand. Ora, however, had been busy, and she soon turned the comfortable ranchhouse into a hideout for hoods. Kathryn appraised the place with a professional eye; she liked it. They were here when Kelly got a call from Bates, and soon they were speeding toward Tacoma. Edward Wilhiem Bentz, master bank robber, was planning to hit the bank in Colfax, Washington, and had asked Bates to round up a couple of men. Bentz didn't know Kelly, and had never heard of his nickname, "Machine Gun," so everything went well. During this robbery, Kathryn lolled about in a luxurious apartment they had rented in Tacoma. When her boisterous husband arrived with his cut of the bank booty, they left immediately for Chicago.

On long trips, as they tooled about the country robbing banks, the Kellys usually carried Kathryn's daughter, Pauline, with them. It was their theory, and with justification, that the police would hardly be suspicious of a couple with a small child in tow. When a job was finished, they would return her to Ora's care, in Paradise, Texas.

The early thirties were good days for bank robbers, but they were even better for kidnappers. This fact did not go unnoticed by the Kellys, and Kathryn had long been after her husband to try one. He got another bank-busting hood interested, and they decided to enter this lucrative but complicated business. Driving to South Bend, Indiana, they checked into a sumptuous hotel, and began searching the newspapers—particularly the society pages— for the name of a likely victim. They chose a local businessman, who seemed to have plenty of money. Then they shadowed him, making notes of his habits, schedule, and activities. Kelly later remarked that this had been fun—almost like playing God, as only they knew what was about to happen to the poor sucker.

When these preliminaries were finished, they drove up beside their victim, and snatched him right off the street—nothing complicated. He was then bound and gagged, and taken to a suburban hideout, where Kelly prepared the ransom note and mailed it to the man's wife.

The first Kelly kidnapping was a failure from start to finish. They had picked a victim who had a fine local reputation, but very little else. Their demand of $60,000 ransom left the man's relatives completely flabbergasted. They couldn't even raise $600 let alone $60,000, so the Kellys begrudgingly had to release the terrified fellow. Still, they wouldn't give up, and they secured a solemn promise from their victim that he would raise the money and send it to them. It was silly, but they believed him.

Since they had used Kathryn's big 16-cylinder car for the snatch, Kelly became nervous. He was sure that it would soon be identified. Kathryn was disgusted and disappointed, but for once she agreed with her husband, and they fled to Kansas City. Still, they hadn't given up hope, so they began sending threatening letters to their Indiana victim. He merely turned them over to the police. At last, the Kellys admitted defeat, and wrote him off as a business loss.

With this adventure over, they returned to Kathryn's address in Fort Worth. They still had a chunk of bank-loot money left, so Kathryn decided to give a party for all of her old friends. Included on her guest list were two local detectives, J. W. Swinney and E. Weatherford. She had the idea of bribing them for information and help. Ironically, having pegged her as a blabbermouth, they accepted, hoping to gain information.

To the delight of the detectives, Kathryn soon got a snootfull, and her tongue began to wag. Hustling Swinney and Weatherford off to one side of the room, she made them a startling proposition. She said that she and her Machine-gunning husband and decided to kidnap Guy Waggoner, son of a rich Texas family. She wanted their help! Startled, they both declined the offer as graciously as they could. They explained that a caper such as this would be too risky.

Kathryn pondered this for a moment, then brightened and said, "Well—maybe so. O.K. Well, then, if Kelly or Albert [Bates] gets into trouble will you two wire that they are wanted here? Make up some charge, you know, like a bank job, or something, and come and get them. O.K.?"

They immediately agreed, trying to humor her, certain she would remember no part of the conversation when she sobered up. This assumption was wrong, for she not only remembered, but later told Kelly and Bates of the arrangement.

The would-be victim was a thousand miles away, on vacation, and the detectives hurriedly notified the local authorities there of the danger. Waggoner and his family were kept under secret surveillance for several weeks, but nothing happened. Then it was dropped, and the matter forgotten.

When Kate "Ma" Barker and her gang kidnapped William A. Hamm, Jr., in St. Paul, Minnesota, June 15, 1933, and got the staggering sum of $100,000 in ransom, Kathryn sat up and took notice. That settled it. That old woman and her gang had gotten more money in one job than a dozen or more "Kelly-type" bank robberies could ever hope to produce. Here was the way to get rich in one quick, well-planned move, she told Kelly and Bates. They both agreed with her that the profits were grand.

Methodically, Kathryn began preparing for the biggest caper in their lives. She went to a pawnshop, in the Fort Worth slums, and purchased a machine gun. Then she shopped around, picking up the necessary ammunition and drums for the gun. Next she made a trip to the Shannon ranch, in Paradise, and talked over her plans with Ora. Determined not to make this kidnapping the fiasco the first one had been, the Kellys and Bates did a thorough research job.

They were so busy with all this activity, that they took little or no notice of a new federal law Congress had enacted. It was called the Lindbergh Kidnapping Law, and made it a *federal* offense to kidnap a person and take him across a state line. The punishment provided was life imprisonment, and the Kellys would have done well to ponder upon it, for this law would have a profound effect upon their future.

v

At 11:25 P.M., July 22, 1933, Charles F. Urschel and his wife Bernice sat playing bridge with their neighbors, the Walter Jarretts. They were on the sun porch of their home at 327 Northwest 18th Street, in Oklahoma City. One minute later, the back door of the porch opened slowly, and two men, both masked, entered and approached the table. One was carrying a machine gun and the other a revolver, but only the thug with the machine gun spoke. "Stick 'em up!" he thundered, "We want Urschel. We mean business, so don't bat an eye, any of you, or we'll blow

your heads off. We want Urschel. Now which man is Urschel?"
Instructions and questions poured from the man in a torrent. The
two families sat staring, in perfect silence, shock, and disbelief.

The big man waved his machine gun, apparently nervous at
their silence. "All right then," he swore, "we'll just take the both
of you!" With that, both Urschel and Jarrett got to their feet,
and followed the gunmen to the door. There, the big gunman
hesitated, then turned and told the women. "You don't move
until you hear a car start out of the driveway. If you reach for a
telephone before then, I'll blow your brains out!" Then all four
men left by the door and disappeared into the dark, hot night.

When Bernice Urschel could finally move her legs, she motioned to Mrs. Jarrett, and they fled upstairs. They took refuge
in a bedroom, and Bernice quickly bolted the door. Then she
snatched up the telephone, and asked the operator to give her
the police. Chief Watts was summoned to the phone, and he
assured her he would put out an immediate alarm, and come
right out. "In the meantime," he told her, "I want you to call
Director J. Edgar Hoover, in Washington. He is head of the
Federal Bureau of Investigation, and he'll want to know about
this right away. The number is National 7117."

She placed the call, and though it was early morning in Washington, she was soon talking to Mr. Hoover. He assured her the
Bureau would enter the case at once.

This time the Kellys had picked themselves a real winner.
Charles F. Urschel was trustee of a $32 million oil estate, and his
wife Bernice, widow of Tom B. Slick, was a millionaire in her
own right. But Kelly and Bates still had one little problem at
the moment. They had to sort out their two victims and establish
which one was Urschel.

At the edge of town, Bates pulled Kathryn's big car over on to
the shoulder of the road. Then Kelly began to search each man.
He checked Urschel first, and identified him as the one they
wanted. They knew nothing about Jarrett, himself a rich man,
so Kelly took $51 out of his wallet, and told him to get out of
the car. He was a little slow obeying the command, expecting to
be shot, so Kelly gave him a push with his foot, slammed the door,
and the car roared off down the road. Jarrett was a little dazed,
but otherwise unhurt; so he immediately headed back toward
town. When he got to a phone he notified the police as to his
location, and they came and took him home.

From the descriptions given by the Jarretts and Bernice, the

FBI was sure they knew who the kidnappers were. When all three of them identified Kelly and Bates from a mug book, all doubt faded.

For years the FBI had been compiling an interesting file on Machine Gun Kelly, Kathryn Thorne Kelly, and Albert Bates. Agents were doing this for most known criminals, but they could only take action when a federal law had been broken. The new Lindbergh kidnapping law now gave the FBI the chance it had been waiting for.

The bureau was still a small organization, so Special Agent Gus T. Jones was flown in from Missouri, where he had been heading the investigation into the Kansas City Massacre, to take charge of the Urschel kidnapping case. Most FBI activities were curtailed pending the release of the victim. This was in response to a request by Mrs. Urschel. One move they could and did make was to have Kathryn's house in Fort Worth placed under close surveillance.

Brutal events followed the Urschel kidnapping, and inevitably follow any kidnapping in which a great deal of money is involved. There were any number of crank telephone calls, and a large number of phony cards and letters received. The police and the FBI had to investigate each and every one of these to make certain they were not overlooking the genuine article.

One such letter was postmarked Venus, Texas, and dated July 25. It was obviously written by a person who had little knowledge of the case, and very little education. It demanded only one thousand dollars, and gave detailed instructions for an ad to be placed in the *Dallas Times Herald,* and the *Fort Worth Star Telegram.* The letter went on to say that "Mr. Urschel is faring well, but don't sleep much, a trifel [sic] nervous." It seemed apparent that the letter was from a crank, but the ads were placed, just to be on the safe side. Nothing came of them.

Wednesday morning, July 26, a Western Union Telegraph boy in Tulsa delivered a large manila envelope to the home of John G. Catlett, a friend of the Urschels. Inside this envelope were three smaller ones. These were addressed to Catlett, Arthur Seeligson, Bernice's father, and E. E. Kirkpatrick, a friend and associate of Urschel's. Catlett read his letter at once. It instructed him to deliver the enclosed letters, and warned, "Do not contact the federal or police authorities." Then, in Urschel's handwriting, a postscript added, "When later contact is made party will have my identification card. Please give the enclosed letters to Bernice,

Arthur or Kirk." Catlett drove at once to Oklahoma City, where he delivered the letters.

The letter to Kirkpatrick was typewritten, and contained the ransom demand of $200,000, in used twenty dollar bills. "It will be useless for you to attempt taking notes of the serial numbers," the letter warned, "or making up dummy package or anything else in the line of attempted double cross." When the money was ready, the letter instructed Kirkpatrick to enter the following ad in the *Daily Oklahoman:*

> For Sale—160 acres land, good five room house, deep well. Also cows, tools, tractor, corn, and hay. $3750.00 for quick sale. Terms. Box ——

This ad was to run for one week, and they were to await further instructions regarding delivery of the ransom. The ad was placed immediately, and the rush was on to get the money ready. Gathering together $200,000 in used twenty dollar bills was no small job, and was performed by the First National Bank. The monumental task was the recording of serial numbers. The money was old, and not in series, so each number had to be recorded, and in an orderly manner. It was hard, back-breaking work, but it was done, with bank employees, the FBI, and the Oklahoma police working together. Altogether they handled 10,000 separate pieces of money.

On July 27 an unsigned special delivery letter was received by the *Daily Oklahoman.* It contained Urschel's identification card, and instructions for Kirkpatrick. He was to take the Sooner Katy Limited train to Kansas City the following night. He was instructed to ride on the observation platform, and when he saw the second of two successive bonfires along the track, he was to heave the money overboard.

It also provided an alternate plan, in the event something should go wrong. In this case, he was to continue on into Kansas City, take a room at the Muehlebach Hotel, register as a Mr. E. E. Kincaid of Little Rock, and wait until contacted.

Kelly said later that car trouble prevented them from reaching the points where they had planned to build the fires.

Both Kirkpatrick and Catlett boarded the train at 10:00 P.M., July 28. Kirkpatrick said he didn't want to go alone. Throughout the long night, they watched from the observation platform, but saw no fires. They arrived in Kansas City, the next morning, tired,

worried, and nervous. Following the alternate plan, they went to
the Muehlebach Hotel, where Kirkpatrick and Catlett registered;
then they settled down to wait.

At about 10:00 that same morning, a telegram arrived at the
hotel, addressed to Mr. E. E. Kincaid. It read:

UNAVOIDABLE INCIDENT KEPT ME FROM SEEING YOU LAST NIGHT WILL
COMMUNICATE ABOUT 6:00 O'CLOCK. E. W. MOORE.

Six o'clock came and went. Nothing. Night arrived, and the
two troubled men, exhausted from the previous night's vigil, slept
fitfully until dawn. Sunday morning came and went, but still no
word. Sunday was a long, long day, as they stayed in the hotel
room waiting for a telephone call, or a rap on the door. By afternoon, they were sure something had gone wrong, but they didn't
know what to do. If they left they might miss an important
message from the kidnappers, yet if they stayed on too long, the
kidnappers might get away. They wanted to discuss the situation
with Special Agent Jones, but they were afraid to leave. Just then
the telephone rang. The time was 5.40 P.M. A voice on the other
end of the line asked: "Kincaid?"

"Yes," Kirkpatrick answered.

"You take a taxi to the LaSalle Hotel," the kidnapper instructed.
"Don't go in. From there you walk west with the money satchel.
Just keep walking until you are stopped."

Kirkpatrick asked if he could bring his friend along. "Hell no!"
he was told. "We know about your friend. You come alone, and
come unarmed."

A moment after he arrived at the LaSalle Hotel, Kirkpatrick
began the long walk down Linwood Boulevard. He saw no pedes-
trians, but did notice two big automobiles on the far side of the
street. There were three men in each car, but they paid no
attention to him so he kept on walking.

Suddenly, a large man stepped toward him. He had been standing just out of sight in a doorway. It was Machine Gun Kelly,
though Kirkpatrick didn't know this at the time. He seemed to
be very nervous, and kept looking behind Kirkpatrick to see if
anyone had followed him. "Quick," he said, "I'll take that money
satchel."

Kirkpatrick hesitated, and Kelly snapped at him, "All right,
hurry up! I haven't got all day."

"How can I be sure you are the right party?" Kirkpatrick asked,
almost pleadingly.

Kelly shifted nervously on his feet, his turned-down Panama hat moving in the slight breeze. "You know damn well I am! Don't argue with me, the boys are waiting."

Kirkpatrick sat the satchel down, then turned and walked back the way he had come. He told the FBI later that he had expected to get a bullet in the back, but kept walking straight ahead, just a little faster with each step. Never once did he look around. He also told them he never had a doubt that the man who took the money was one of the kidnappers.

vi

Kelly and Bates had the $200,000, so they headed back to Texas, and the Shannon ranch house, where Kathryn was waiting for them. A few miles from the ranch was the rundown farm of Armon Shannon, "Boss" Shannon's son. Here Urschel was being held in chains, and guarded by the Shannon family.

Charles Urschel had a most frightening experience when the Kellys and Bates gathered at the Armon farmhouse, and began discussing him as if he were a side of beef. They were having an argument as to what they should do with their victim. He could hear the whole thing from the next room, and was completely helpless. Clearly and coldly he heard Kathryn Kelly voice the opinion that they would be complete idiots to turn Urschel loose. "If we kill the son-of-a-bitch," she told them, "we won't have any trouble from him."

Kelly and Albert Bates argued against such an action. They told her that every law officer and FBI agent in the country would hunt them down and never quit until they were found. This argument didn't impress Kathryn too much, but when Kelly added that killing Urschel would be bad for future business, she began to listen. "We'll spoil it for everybody, if we kill him," Kelly told her, "and we'll have no friends anywhere." This reasoning won out, and she agreed to let them have their way. Urschel breathed a sigh of relief.

Blindfolded, Urschel was taken to a point just north of Norman, Oklahoma, where he was released. Kelly gave him ten dollars and a new Panama hat. The night was dark, and the weather was terrible. Kelly told Urschel the hat was to keep his head dry. Actually it was a plant, for the label inside the hatband read, "Newmans—Joplin's Greatest Store." The FBI would later disregard it. "Too much Joplin," they would say.

It was about 9:00 P.M., July 31, when a wet, disheveled, but most thankful Charles F. Urschel arrived at his home. Within the hour he was undergoing interrogation by the FBI.

Special Agent Jones had hardly begun the questioning when he realized that the Kellys had goofed again. Oh, they had picked a rich victim all right, and they had collected a $200,000 ransom, but their victim turned out to be a walking, talking memory machine. Urschel began reciting the facts of his kidnapping, as he recalled them, and the agents were stunned.

He told how his eyes had been taped shut, but he could remember the crossing of a rattling bridge, he estimated to be about a half-mile long. He couldn't identify the bridge, but he did remember the noisy crossing. A short time later, he told agents, the car had become stuck in the mud, as it was raining very hard. Still later, the car had stopped for gas. Urschel was down on the floor in the back of the car where he could not be seen. He could hear very well, however, and he told the agents of the conversation. "One of the kidnappers," he said, "asked a woman attendant at the gas station if the rain would help the crops. 'No,' she had replied, 'They's all burnt up, but it may help the broom corn some.'"

"We drove on dirt roads most of the time," Urschel continued, "and they warned me that I was not to see or hear anything on the trip and that if I did, I would never come home. They would kill me."

Eventually, Urschel adjusted to his frightening situation. Then he began to concentrate on getting as much information as he could about his captors. He recalled hearing roosters crowing, and from this he knew that daylight was approaching. He was kept down on the floor of the car, covered with a blanket. "Later," he said, "they drove into a farm yard, where they placed a Panama hat on me, and covered my taped eyes with a large pair of sun glasses. Then, they allowed me to sit on the back seat."

He told them how they had driven into a garage, where they stayed until it was dark. Then they took him into a house, and chained him. Here, his guards referred to each other as "Boss," and "Potatoes," and kept throwing such phrases at him as "way down in Oklahoma," and "way down in Texas." He thought it was an effort, on their part, to mislead him, and make him think he was being held north of these states.

He told the FBI about the squeak of the well pulley, when water was drawn for drinking, and about the very strong mineral taste it had. He also told them that he had gone out of his way to plant his fingerprints all over the room where he had been held. He described the voices of the people who had guarded him, and told about the sounds made by the livestock.

FBI agents were writing all this down as fast as they could, but the best was yet to come. He told them that he had noticed the sound of an airplane almost directly overhead, every day. He couldn't see his watch, so he counted slowly to himself, until he thought five minutes had passed. Then he would ask one of his guards what time it was. This way, he hoped to prevent them from becoming suspicious. Apparently they didn't connect the two events, and would give him the time. Over a period of days he was able to reckon that the planes were passing over the farm each day at 9:45 A.M. and 5:45 P.M. He said that there was one day when the planes failed to come over at all. The wind had been blowing hard the day before, and on the day the plane failed to appear it had rained very hard. He believed that the planes had been diverted because of the bad weather.

When Urschel had finished, Special Agent Gus Jones told him, admiringly, "If there were more like you, the kidnapper would soon be out of business."

The FBI went right to work with this information, and soon the long rattling bridge Urschel had described so vividly was identified as the one that crossed the Canadian River, between Lexington and Purcell. This was south of Oklahoma City, so they began to look southward. Scanning meteorological reports and weather charts, an area was located in Texas where a recent rainfall had broken a long drought. The rain had saved some of the "broom corn" in Wise County, Texas.

Their big break came when they found that American Airways had a plane that made the Fort Worth-Amarillo, and the Amarillo-Fort Worth trip each day. The planes always passed over a point near Paradise, Wise County, Texas, each day between 9:40 and 9:45 A.M., and 5:40 and 5:45 P.M. On Sunday, July 30, the flights had been rerouted, because of a storm front.

Swinney and Weatherford, Dallas detectives, filled in a few details about Kathryn Thorne Kelly. They knew about her mother's new husband, and the ranch in Paradise, Texas. With all this information, there was little doubt left that this is where Urschel had been taken and held during his long period of captivity.

Just before dawn on August 12, three FBI agents led by Gus Jones, a deputy sheriff from Oklahoma City, six policemen, two detectives from the Fort Worth-Dallas area, and Charles Urschel stopped just short of the Shannon ranch house. A quick discussion was held, and an agent and some of the policemen continued on to the Armon farmhouse. Agent Jones and the rest moved cautiously toward the Shannon ranch house on foot. Agent Jones had noticed someone sleeping on a cot in the back yard. As they drew nearer, they also saw a new Ford V-8, which was completely stocked and ready for instant flight, near the cot. Jones and one of the agents gave their attention to this man, while the rest deployed around the house.

The man was rudely awakened by the prodding muzzle of Agent Jones's machine gun. He sat up and rubbed his eyes, then grinned rather sheepishly. "Well! It looks like it is too bad, doesn't it?" he remarked.

"Yes. It is too bad for you," Agent Frank F. Blake agreed. "If any shooting starts, we are going to kill you first."

The man assured them that he was the only one there who would be likely to do any shooting. "And," he added, "it doesn't look like I'm going to do any of it." Agent Jones later admitted that this man was one of the coolest customers he had ever arrested.

They had hit the jackpot, for the sleeping man was none other than Harvey J. Bailey, eagerly sought for his part in the Kansas City Massacre. He was also an escapee from the Kansas State Penitentiary, at Lansing. He had led the Memorial Day, 1933, escape, taking ten others with him. He was innocent of the Kansas City massacre, as well as any complicity in the kidnapping of Charles F. Urschel, but he was also a loser.

The Kellys had loaned him $500 of the Urschel kidnapping money, and Bates had given him another $500. Beside him on the cot, Bailey had placed a machine gun, an automatic rifle, and an automatic pistol. A search of him would turn up $1200, of which $700 proved to be Urschel kidnap money. He would protest his innocence loud and long, but it would fall on deaf ears.

The agents, police, and detectives arrested Armon "Potatoes" Shannon, his wife Oleta, and her father Earl Brown. From the ranch house they also flushed Robert K. G. "Boss" Shannon, a hooked-nosed, balding old man, and his wife, Ora Shannon. Unfortunately the Kellys and Bates were not there. The Kellys were in Chicago, and Albert Bates was in Denver.

Bailey and "Boss" Shannon were chained to a post in the back yard, while the agents tore the house apart looking for the $200,-

000 ransom money. Armon, Oleta, Earl Brown, and Ora Shannon were kept under armed guard on the porch while the search was being made. They later found two youngsters in the house, but they required no attention. They were Pauline Fry, Kathryn's 15-year-old daughter, and Shannon's 15-year-old daughter by his first wife, Ruth Shannon.

Just two days before his capture, Harvey J. Bailey had held up the bank at Kingfisher, Oklahoma. Part of his loot had been in half-dollars and quarters. Searching agents now found a money cache of $50 hidden in Ora's bread box. The money was in halves and quarters. Ora's violent denial of any knowledge about this money brought smiles from everybody. From Bailey it brought a loud guffaw, for he had given her this money to hide him out for a while.

Then Ora saw Armon talking to FBI agents, and she shouted at him, "Armon, you keep your mouth shut. Don't tell them a damn thing!" It was too late, however, for poor, slow-witted Armon had already told them everything he knew.

vii

As soon as they had released Urschel just north of Norman, Oklahoma, Bates and the Kellys headed for Omaha. They stayed there a few days, then drove on to Chicago, and finally to Minneapolis. They were searching, by way of underworld contacts, for buyers for their ransom money. This is a transaction whereby ransom money is bought and sold at a large discount. The buyers are usually underworld characters who have contacts outside the United States. They give the kidnappers 50 cents or less on the dollar, and then exchange it for its face value abroad. Bates and the Kellys were quite willing and happy to swap $200,000 in hot money for $100,000 in safe bills. Such money transactions were, however, very complicated, and took a great deal of time.

Buyers were found in Minneapolis, and the Kellys managed to trade some of their hot money for the kind they could spend. While Bates stayed on in the town to arrange for larger transfers of money, the Kellys went on a spending spree.

In Cleveland, Kathryn bought lots of expensive clothes, more diamonds, and another automobile (a twelve-cylinder model). Since delivery would be delayed a few days, Kelly merely made a downpayment.

Back in their hotel room, Kathryn was modeling her new

clothes and admiring her latest diamonds, while Kelly had begun reading the morning paper. The news from its pages leaped out at him: the money changers in Minneapolis had been arrested by the FBI! He showed the paper to Kathryn, who was singularly unimpressed. "That's their hard luck," she said. Kelly was really worried, but Kathryn calmed him down. She told him they had nothing to worry about as long as the FBI didn't know where they were. Kelly dropped the subject, for the moment, but he was far from happy about the whole deal.

In the late afternoon, they received a telegram from Albert Bates. It read:

DEAL HAS FELL THROUGH. JACK AND TOM HAVE LEFT. COMMUNICATE WITH ME AT BOX 631—GEORGE

Bates, eluding the FBI and police, had fled to Denver, where he kept a post office box. In his telegram he was telling the Kellys they could reach him there. But the message was just too much for George "Machine Gun" Kelly, and this fearless bad man, this Terror of the Western Plains, hit the panic button. He told Kathryn they would have to leave Cleveland right away. "They'll find out we bought that big car. They know how you love big cars, and they'll trace it right to us."

Kathryn absolutely refused to be stampeded, and insisted that they wait until morning. Then, on August 12, they went to Chicago, where hoodlum friends helped them purchase another automobile. They were here when the newspapers announced the arrest of Harvey J. Bailey and the Shannons. Now it was time for Kathryn to push the button. Up until this moment, the Kellys were sure that the ranch was above suspicion.

They had to digest this news fast, for the evening papers had more for them. Albert Bates had just been arrested in Denver, Colorado, where he had been posing as a Mr. George L. Davis. Broke except for some of the kidnap money, he had tried to cash some stolen American Express checks. The police arrested him, and when he was searched, they also found $660 in Urschel kidnap money. It hadn't been identified yet, and Davis was still not connected with the kidnapper, Albert Bates.

A silly phase of the case happened when Bates, remembering the supposed arrangement between Kathryn and her two Fort Worth "friends," Swinney and Weatherford, wired them. He told them he was wanted in connection with a Blue Ridge, Texas, bank robbery. He said he would waive extradition, and for them to please fly to Denver at once, and get him. He signed the wire, "George L. Davis." The wire was immediately turned over to the FBI, and agents there took him into custody on a charge of kidnapping.

By mutual consent Kathryn and Kelly packed their clothes and fled from Cleveland to Davenport. Here they bought local license plates for their car, then drove to Des Moines, where Kathryn raved and ranted. She cried and wailed, as she nagged her cold-eyed and ruthless husband, Machine Gun Kelly. He, in turn, guzzled gin to give him the courage he needed, and to drown out the sound of his wife's wailings and gnashings of teeth. Eventually he got drunk enough to agree to a proposal Kathryn had made. She wanted him to give himself up to the Attorney General, in exchange for the release of her "poor, old, innocent mother." The entire idea was idiotic, and conceived in a moment of panic by Kathryn. It would eventually become an obsession with her, and replace all reason.

On August 18, Kathryn fired off a letter to the Assistant Attorney General, Joseph B. Keenan, in which she offered "to put George Kelly on the spot for you, if you will save my mother, who is innocent of any wrong doing." She also babbled on about getting herself arrested for some minor offense. This was so that she would not be suspected of taking any part in "the terrible slaughter that will take place in Oklahoma City, in a few days."

The offer in the letter was, of course, considered ridiculous, but grave attention was given to the part about "a coming terrible slaughter." The Kansas City massacre was still too fresh in their minds to overlook this threat. Kelly was considered a prime suspect in this bloody affair, and if he were capable of that, he would be capable of anything.

The Kellys then fled to the home of Kathryn's grandmother, in Stratford, Oklahoma. They hid out here while waiting an acceptance of Kathryn's weird offer. The Attorney General's Office lost no time in publicly rejecting any such swap.

With this announcement, the Kellys agreed to split up for awhile. Kathryn decided to go to Fort Worth, and try and arrange for the swap through her attorney. Kelly said he would head south to Brownsville. Agents later found that he had purchased some camping equipment here, apparently intending to camp out until the heat cooled down.

Just about now, this bold bandit was beginning to see an FBI

agent, or a policeman, behind every clump of sagebrush. Unable
to stand it anymore, he now fled to the ranch of Cass Coleman,
and begged Kathryn's uncle to hide him. Cass, himself a bundle
of nerves—with the kidnap money hidden on his place—took the
steel-nerved killer to the ranch of a neighbor, Will Casey. He
paid him to hide Kelly in a one-room shack.

All alone in this shack, with no radio and no newspapers, Kelly
nearly went out of his mind. With the silence, he began to hear
all kinds of sounds. At last, he couldn't stand it any longer, so he
packed again, left word with Casey to tell Kathryn to meet him
in Mississippi, and drove to Biloxi.

Before Kathryn could get to Biloxi to join him, he thought he
had spotted a suspicious-looking character in the lobby of his
hotel. Without further ado, he checked out, and fled back toward
Texas. Somewhere along the line, Kathryn and Machine Gun
Kelly passed each other without knowing it.

Unable to find her husband in Biloxi, Kathryn correctly guessed
that her ruthless man had probably backtracked to Texas, so she
wheeled around and headed after him. On her way, she stopped
in a small Texas town, and visited with her former Negro maid.
She rested here for a while, and made discreet inquiries, but no
one had seen her *now blonde* husband.

Certain now that Kelly was on his way back to her uncle's
ranch, Kathryn borrowed some old clothes from her former maid.
She also acquired an old Ford pickup truck, and a red wig. Then
she headed toward Fort Worth, still hoping to see her attorney,
and negotiate a trade of Kelly for her mother.

On the approach to Hillsboro, where the highway forked west
to Fort Worth and east to Dallas, she spotted three forlorn-look-
ing people, hitchhiking. They were Mr. and Mrs. Luther Arnold,
and their 12-year-old daughter, Geraldine. They were migrant
workers, broke and hungry. The sight of them gave Kathryn an
idea, and she stopped and picked them up.

viii

One innocent pawn in this whole kidnapping affair was Harvey
J. Bailey, alias J. J. Brennon, alias "Big Tom" Brenner. Though
innocent of any complicity in the kidnapping of Charles F.
Urschel, as both Machine Gun Kelly and Albert Bates would
later testify, he was guilty of many things.

Bailey was born in 1885 on a Sullivan County farm in northern
Missouri. He had served in the World War, and this not only

taught him the use of many weapons, but allowed him to travel abroad. When the war was over, Bailey decided he didn't want to go back to the little old farm in the clay hills of Missouri. So he went to Chicago where he worked as a rumrunner. When he had accumulated a little money, he bought his own farm in northern Wisconsin. This farm soon became a cooling-off place for Chicago mobsters. One of his best customers was Fred "Killer" Burke. At the time, "Killer" Burke was known as "America's most desperate criminal." This was, of course, before the phrase "public enemy number one" had been coined. Burke was a prime suspect in the St. Valentine's day massacre in Chicago. He was captured on Bailey's farm, and subsequently given a life sentence in the Michigan State Penitentiary for killing a policeman. With his capture, Bailey fled and gave up his unique method of farming.

Bailey had been arrested in Omaha, Nebraska, March 23, 1920, for hijacking, but was later released for lack of evidence. He was identified as the leader of the Lincoln Bank and Trust Company robbery, of September 17, 1930. This job netted the bandits over $2 million in cash and negotiable securities. The real brains behind this robbery had been Edward W. Bentz, and it became known as the world's largest bank robbery.

Bailey, Ed Davis, Jim Clark, and Bob Brady were convicted, on August 17, 1932, of robbing the Fort Scott, Kansas, bank of $32,000. The Barkers, Frank "Jelly" Nash, and Alvin Karpis had also been in on this robbery, but they were still free. The FBI, hot on the trail of Thomas Holden and Francis Keating, also arrested Bailey as he was playing golf with them in Kansas City, July 7, 1932. He was turned over to Kansas authorities, and subsequently given a sentence of 10 to 50 years in Lansing State Penitentiary. On Memorial Day, 1933, Bailey and Wilber C. Underhill, leading nine other prisoners, kidnapped the warden, Kirk Prather, and two guards. Using them as hostages, they fled Lansing. They released them at the Oklahoma border, unharmed. Bailey had remained free until the FBI caught him on the Shannon ranch, August 12.

It was now September 5, 1933, and Harvey J. Bailey—outlaw, escapee, bank robber, suspected kidnapper and killer—was securely locked up in the Dallas County Jail. Between him and freedom were seven barred doors, and numerous armed guards. Sheriff Smoot Schmidt, of Dallas County, had posted extra guards to prevent any jail delivery of Bailey by his pal Machine Gun Kelly, and gang. His bail was set at $100,000.

Only Bailey and Kelly himself knew how ridiculous the rumors were that Kelly might round up "his gang" and break Bailey out of jail. The newspapers were full of reports and rumors, as most of the nation—including the police and the FBI—awaited Kelly's next move.

Bailey knew that if he were to get out of jail he would have to do it himself. With his glib tongue, and the promise of $500, he managed to buy the services of Deputy Sheriff Thomas L. Manion, a jailer. Manion, in turn, persuaded Grover C. Bevill, of Dallas, a civilian, to purchase the necessary hacksaws, and a revolver for him to slip to Bailey.

With these instruments, Bailey sawed and chopped his way through the bars of his ninth-floor cell door, then used the revolver to take keys away from a guard. It was 7:10 A. M., when Bailey slipped down the stairs to the sixth floor. There he surprised two more guards and locked them in a cell. He then rode the elevator to the main floor, where he took Deputy Sheriff Nick Tresp hostage. They sped away from the jail in Tresp's four-year-old sedan.

Since Bailey was a prime suspect in the Kansas City massacre, hundreds of officers and many FBI agents were thrown into the man hunt. Six airplanes from Love Airfield took to the air, and the entire operation was directed from Washington, D. C., by Assistant Attorney General Joseph B. Keenan.

Now Bailey's 115-mile dash to Oklahoma was nearing its end. Sheriff Sam Randolph of Love County, Oklahoma, sighted Tresp's car on the highway just south of Marietta. He hurried to a phone and called Police Chief Hale Dunn, of Ardmore, and told him Bailey was headed his way.

Chief Dunn, with Detectives Raymond Shoemaker and Bennet Wallace, immediately drove out of Ardmore to search the incoming highway. A short distance from town, on U.S. 70, they spied Bailey at a gas station. He was busy having his tank filled, but he saw them too. Jumping into the car he tore away from the station, jerking the gasoline hose from the tank.

Bailey headed directly into Ardmore, then turned into a residential district. The police car was just behind him, and gaining ground all the time. The detectives fired at the car, but they had to be careful not to hit an innocent bystander. They had no idea who Tresp was, but naturally assumed he was a fellow escapee.

Down Washington Street—a main thoroughfare—they roared, then Bailey, in a desperate move, took a corner too close. The car smashed into a curb, and the right front wheel collapsed.

In a moment he was covered by three pistols and made no move to pick up his own. Bailey had been at liberty a little less than four hours.

By now Deputy Sheriff Tresp was on the verge of collapse. He had been kidnapped, taken on a wild ride, and now, before his horrified eyes, he was being handcuffed to Bailey. "But, I'm a jailer!" he protested in a weak voice. A call to the authorities in Dallas confirmed this claim, and Tresp was released. By now he had begun to recover enough of his composure to talk with reporters. According to him, Bailey had talked very little on the 115-mile trip. He had promised Tresp that he would return his car, and then give him some money to get back to Dallas. "But he never did say where he was going, though," Tresp added, thoughtfully. When captured Bailey had only three one dollar bills on him.

As Bailey sat in the Ardmore jail, smoking a cigarette and reflecting upon his situation, he had only one thing to say to the reporters, "Well! I got out, didn't I."

Curiously, a few week before Bailey's arrest on the Shannon ranch, he and five of his gang sent a letter to the *Daily Oklahoman,* in which they confessed robbing a Black Rock, Arkansas, bank. Another gang had been jailed for this. They had authenticated the letter with their fingerprints. Authorities speculated that the confessions were an attempt by the gang members to establish an alibi for themselves during the Kansas City massacre. The bank at Black Rock, had been robbed on June 17, 1933—the same day the massacre took place.

ix

When the Arnolds had finally settled down in the truck, Kathryn became a talkative and obsequious person. She asked the Arnolds all about themselves, and based upon their responses, she made a quick decision. That night she bought them supper, then put them up in a tourist camp. She also told them her name was really Kathryn Kelly, the woman desperado the entire country was looking for.

The Arnolds were nomads, constantly shifting from job to job and place to place. They had no loyalties to any particular place, nor were they beholden to any particular group. They had been hungry and broke, and this woman had fed them. Now she was offering them more money than they could hope to earn in a year of hard toil. She asked for, and got, their pledge of aid and assistance.

When they arrived in San Antonio, Kathryn rented a house at 160 Mahncke Court. Then she gave Luther $500 and a note to her Fort Worth attorney, and sent him on his way. When he returned, he brought bad news. The government still had no interest in a trade. They had vowed to search out and prosecute everyone connected with the case, no matter how remote that connection might be. This information should have frightened off the Arnolds, but it did not.

Suddenly Kathryn turned her attention toward the Arnold's daughter, Geraldine. She told them she would truly love to take her on a little trip. "It won't be a long one," she assured them, "only about 250 miles, or so."

By now the Arnolds were fully committed to this woman, and Luther had $300 in his pockets. They agreed to let their daughter go with this female kidnapper, provided the trip was a short one. It was incredible, but that was the agreement. So, with little Geraldine as a cover, Kathryn now drove to Coleman, Texas, where she picked up her blonde badman; then the three of them drove on to Chicago.

Here, in a rented apartment, Geraldine penned a note to her parents, while the Kellys prepared one for their former kidnap victim, Charles F. Urschel. The trial of Kathryn's mother was to begin today, September 18, and she wanted Kelly to make one last desperate effort to get her mother free. That Kelly was very drunk when he wrote the letter is reflected by its contents:

Ignorant Charles—
Just a few lines to let you know that I am getting my plans made to destroy your so-called mansion, and your family and you immediately after this trial. And young fellow, I guess you've begun to realize your serious mistake. Are you ignorant enough to believe the Government can guard you forever . . . . if the Shannons are convicted look out, and God help you for he is the only one that will be able to do you any good. In the event of my arrest I've already formed an outfit to take care of and destroy you and yours the same as if I was there. I am spending your money to have you and your family killed—nice—eh? You are bucking people who have cash—planes, bombs and unlimited connections both here and abroad. . . . . . I don't worry about Bates and Bailey. They will be out for the ceremonies—your slaughter.
Now say—it is up to you. If the Shannons are convicted, you can

get another rich wife in hell, because that will be the only place you
can use one.

Adios, smart one.

Your worst enemy.
George Kelly

I will put my fingerprints below so you can't say some crank wrote
this.

[SMUDGED PRINTS HERE]

Give Keenan my regards and tell him maybe he would like to meet
the owner of the above.

See you in hell.

When Kelly awoke the following morning, the gin had worn
off, and he had that insecure feeling again. He began to fret about
the possibility of the FBI tracing their car. He carried on so badly
that Kathryn was forced to take desperate measures. She took
her gimlet-eyed killer to the movie theatre nearest their apartment, and dumped him in a dark corner. Then she went out and
rented another apartment, and at nightfall she returned and took
him to their new home.

The trial of the Shannons, Bailey, and Bates was now entering
its third day, and the newspapers were filled with details. From
the papers and the radio Kathryn soon learned that her "poor, old,
innocent" mother might get life for her part in their little caper.
She began nagging Machine Gun Kelly. The more he listened
to her rave and rant, the more he drank, and the more he drank,
the more malleable he became.

Soon, at Kathryn's behest, Kelly was writing more threatening
letters. He wrote to the judge, the witnesses, and others, and
always put his fingerprints on the letters. The FBI was most
grateful for his cooperation in this regard.

While Kelly was writing his dire threats, Kathryn was penning
a few letters of her own. She wrote to Urschel, telling him of her
innocence, and of the innocence of her family. "The entire blame
for this horrible mess," she wrote, "is squarely on the shoulders
of Machine Gun Kelly."

When all these protestations and claims of innocence had no
apparent effect, even Kathryn began to feel the strain on her
nerves. At midnight on September 21, she and Machine Gun Kelly
packed up and fled to Memphis.

A week before, the Arnolds had received a letter from Kathryn
instructing them to go to Oklahoma City, and rent a room at a

place she specified. They were to wait there for further word
from her. They did as they were instructed.

On September 14, FBI agents broke into the Mahncke Court
address in San Antonio. They had missed Kathryn by only one
day, and the Arnolds by only a matter of hours. Drawn to Chicago
by the stream of Kelly letters sent from there, the FBI again
missed them by only one day.

x

When they arrived in Memphis, Machine Gun Kelly called
Langford Ramsey, at 1830 Mignon, and asked his help in finding
suitable quarters for a hideout. Ramsey was the brother of Geneva,
Kelly's first wife. He responded at once, and took them to the
home of John C. Tichenor, at 1408 Rayner.

Tichenor was a good friend of Ramsey's, and he frequently held
all-night drinking parties at his home. He told Kelly he was sure
his friend would be more than willing to hide them for a price.
John Tichenor was a crippled, semi-paralyzed automobile mechanic, and he was very hard up for money. He and Kelly agreed
on a price, and he also promised to run a few errands for him.

The first thing Kelly wanted him to do was buy a pistol for him.
He told him he didn't want a machine gun, in spite of his nickname, just an automatic pistol. Tichenor said he would be happy
to get one for him, but mentioned that it might be a little expensive. Kelly made no comment about this.

The next day Tichenor contacted a Memphis automobile dealer
he knew, and purchased a Colt 1911 model automatic. He paid
the dealer ten dollars for the gun, and then sold it to Machine
Gun Kelly for $17.50, skinning this terror of the Western Plains
out of $7.50. When he saw Kelly's hesitation, he got worried and
hastily added that he had unsuccessfully tried to get a cheaper
one from a Beale Street pawnbroker.

Kelly's hesitation was not because he suspected any skuldug-
gery, but because he was running out of money—in fact he was
just about broke. But there was plenty of money buried on a
ranch in Texas, so Kelly again called Ramsey, and made him a
proposition.

That night, September 23, the Kellys and Ramsey got roaring
drunk at the Tichenor home. Later on they made a deal. Ramsey
agreed to drive to Santa Anna, Texas, using Kelly's Chevrolet. He
was to take Geraldine along for use as a guide and for identification purposes. When he arrived in Santa Anna, Geraldine was to

direct him to the ranch of Kathryn's uncle, Cass Coleman. Ramsey was then to tell Coleman, "I want those fox furs which Kathryn left here. That party wants to see you." The term "fox furs" was hoodlum talk and meant money. He was also to instruct Coleman to drive to a point five miles west of McGregor, Texas, on Highway 7, the night of September 28. Kelly was supposed to meet him there, but if he failed to come, Coleman was to be told to repeat the trip nightly for one week. With this done, Ramsey was then to drive Geraldine to the rooming house in Oklahoma City. There he was to ask for Mrs. E. L. Moore, a code name for the Arnolds. Then he was to pick up Kathryn's clothes, which she had left in the Arnold's care, and return to Memphis. He was also instructed to bring Geraldine back with him.

Ramsey did as he was told, and when he reached Santa Anna, Geraldine showed him the way to the Coleman ranch. But then things began to go awry. Coleman was badly frightened, and he refused to give Ramsey any "furs," refused to agree to any meeting with Kelly, and ordered Ramsey off the place. He told him his ranch was surrounded by machine gunners, who were out to get him. Coleman had evidently seen some of the FBI agents who were keeping his house under close surveillance.

Frightened, Ramsey left at once. When he arrived at Fort Worth, on September 25, he wired Kelly:

DEAL FELL THROUGH. TRIED TO GET LATER APPOINTMENT BUT PROSPECT WAS AFRAID. IMPOSSIBLE TO CHANGE HIS MIND. DON'T WANT TO BRING HOME A SAD TALE.

The phrase "Don't want to bring home a sad tale" meant that Ramsey was afraid of being trailed back to Memphis.

Before they left Fort Worth, Geraldine, tired of riding around in the automobile, begged to be allowed to go on to Oklahoma City by train. Ramsey was having enough troubles as it was, so he agreed. He put her on the Rock Island to Oklahoma City, then wired Luther to meet the train at 10:00 P.M., Monday. He signed Geraldine's name to the wire, then drove on to Gainesville, Texas. Here, by prearrangement, he picked up Kelly's reply to his telegram. It read:

PROCEED WITH TRIP AS INSTRUCTED. MOTHER IS FINE. JACK

The remark "Mother is fine" meant that things were all right with the Kellys in Memphis. Encouraged, Ramsey continued his trip to Oklahoma City.

When he arrived, Ramsey drove to the rooming house, and asked for Mrs. E. L. Moore. He was told that she was out at the moment. Just then, an FBI agent walked up and told Ramsey the Arnolds could be found at a nearby restaurant. Ramsey didn't have the slightest idea who the man was, so he thanked him, and proceeded to the restaurant. There he found the Arnolds and Geraldine having breakfast. He asked for Kathryn's clothes, but the Arnolds said no. They told him they owed a $200 board bill, and they were going to hold on to the clothes until they got their money. In a manner of speaking, Kathryn would have to ransom her clothing from the Arnolds.

By now, most of the fight had gone out of Ramsey, and he didn't even argue with them. He gave them an address in Memphis, and told them to express the clothing there later on. The address he gave them was neither his nor Tichenor's. He wasn't that stupid. But it didn't really matter, for the FBI had already gotten the Kelly's address from little Geraldine.

When Ramsey asked if he could take Geraldine back to Memphis, the Arnolds again said no, so he left without her. What Ramsey didn't know, was that his and Kelly's telegrams had been intercepted and read with great interest by the FBI. They had located the Arnolds in Oklahoma City, before he arrived, and the Arnolds were now cooperating with the government.

xi

At the crack of dawn on September 26, 1933, FBI agents and members of the Memphis police surrounded Tichenor's home. On a given signal, Detectives A. O. Clark and Floyd Wiebenga, and Detective Sergeant Bill Raney, crashed through the front door.

George "Machine Gun" Kelly, whose very name made brave men quake with fear, stuck his blonde head out of the bedroom door to see what all the fuss was about. In his hand he held his expensive automatic. Then Detective Sergeant Raney, flanked by Clark and Wiebenga, pushed his sawed-off, double barreled shotgun about an inch into the ample stomach of this cold-eyed killer, and barked an order for his surrender. Meekly, Kelly opened his hand, and the automatic slid to the floor. If he said anything about "G-Men" to Raney, Clark, or Wiebenga, they didn't hear it. Kelly seemed much too relieved that the long chase was now over.

Meanwhile, the FBI had rounded up Kathryn, still half asleep from an all-night gin party. They also arrested John C. Tichenor and his brother-in-law, Seymore E. Travis. Everybody was immediately handcuffed, and bundled off to the police station in Memphis.

Now that the fright of being hunted day and night was over, Machine Gun Kelly became his old blowhard self again. "Machine Gun Kelly does not sleep at night, and has not slept at night since the nation-wide search for him was started," Kelly proudly told FBI agents, and delighted reporters. "I didn't think you fellows had the nerve to come after me in the day time. I usually slept in the day and stayed awake at night," he crowed. This is why he had been so slow-witted the morning of his capture. He had been up all night, drinking his nerve tonic (gin). and had just retired to bed.

Later in the day, warrants for their arrest were read to the Kellys by Elman Jester, United States Deputy Marshal. Kelly complained that he couldn't hear what Jester was saying. With that, Commissioner Brenner took the warrants, and reread them in a voice loud enough to be heard out on the street.

Kelly was in his cell, looking through the bars, but Kathryn— who had been brought down from the woman's section upstairs— was standing outside, dressed in a chic black outfit with a smart hat pulled down over one eye. When a photographer snapped her picture, Kathryn screamed, "Wait a minute," then she turned fiercely to the photographer, posed, and said, "I'll give you a good picture."

After the warrants were read, Kelly snapped at Commissioner Brenner, "No! I won't sign that."

"You don't have to sign it, that's the charges against you," FBI Agent John M. Keith explained, trying hard to conceal a smile.

"How do you plead?" Commissioner Brenner asked Kelly.

"Not guilty," he said, firmly.

"And how do you plead?" he asked, turning to Kathryn.

"Not guilty," she answered demurely, all the while eyeing the photographer with a smile.

"The bond is set at $100,000," Brenner told them. "Can either of you make bond?"

They both answered that they could not, and he remanded them back into custody.

Just then the photographer tried to get a picture of Machine Gun Kelly, but he refused to pose. He was now in a vile mood, and told him, "You've snapped enough of those damn things today!" Then he turned and stalked back into his cell and wouldn't talk to anyone.

At 5:40 that same afternoon, Machine Gun Kelly and Kathryn were transferred from the city jail to the county jail. It was just a short distance to the corner of 2nd Street and Washington, so they walked. Kelly was so proud he actually strutted, for guarding them were ten FBI agents, armed with sub machine guns, and seven police officers. With such an impressive entourage he now felt he was bigger than Pretty Boy Floyd, John Dillinger, and all the rest.

The government, the police, the press, and the public all thought this windy, boastful, two-bit hoodlum-bootlegger was a deadly killer. He was still suspected of having played a part in the Kansas City Massacre, though there was no proof. He was also given credit for leading a gang of five bandits in a Chicago bank messenger robbery, and of killing Miles Cunningham, a patrolman.

What the world still didn't know was that George "Machine Gun" Kelly had never killed anyone. He had never even fired his machine gun at anyone in anger. In fact the only thing Kelly ever shot with deadly accuracy was that big mouth of his.

It is easy now, to make light of such elaborate precautions, but at the moment it was happening, everyone thought it was necessary. Machine Gun Kelly, with his ferocious nickname, and his deadly threats, lent credibility to these beliefs. And now that he was safely behind bars, Kelly played his part in the drama to the hilt. He growled, he snarled, and he tried the best he knew how to imitate the typical Hollywood gangster. Kathryn Kelly had invented him; newspapers and detective magazines had told the world what a terrible bad man he was; so Kelly was now playing his expected role. It was really sad, and a little pitiful, for every time he opened his mouth, he aided the prosecutor of his coming trial a little more. He was almost childish in his actions, and couldn't seem to understand the irrevocable damage he was doing to his own case.

A heavy guard watched over Kelly, and held him virtually incommunicado. Under these conditions, Kelly showed the quick changes of temperament normally expected from a small child. One moment he would be wisecracking with his guards; the next he would be snarling at them.

"Watch them popguns on your laps," he would say jeeringly to his guards, as he eyed the machine guns they held pointed at him. "You'd feel like hell if one of the damn things went off and killed you." With this, he would laugh loudly.

When Chief Deputy Sheriff Garibaldi came into his cell, with shackles for his legs and a chain to link them to his bunk, Kelly blazed into anger at the very idea. "Do you think I'm going anywhere with these guards watching me, and with these bars?" he demanded.

The deputy, quiet, and unimpressed with Kelly, snapped the leg irons on, and then looked up at him. "Not going far, especially with these on," he told Kelly, with a smile. In just a few moments, Kelly was again joking with his guards, apparently having the time of his life.

xii

Langford Ramsey read with horror of Kelly's capture, then stared with disbelief at the story that a warrant was out for his own arrest. He drove back to Memphis in a state of stunned shock. When he got there, he headed straight to the Shelby County Jail, where the Kellys, Tichenor, and Travis were being held. It was 5:15 A.M., September 27 when he arrived, but he couldn't get in. The front of the jail had been closed, and all visitors were discouraged. His efforts did rouse Lee Miller, a watchman. He led Ramsey around to the rear of the jail, where he surrendered himself to the night jailer, Albert Hodges. Hodges immediately turned him over to Detective Sergeant Ernest Wattam, who notified his superiors and the FBI. The process of getting oneself arrested seemed quite complicated to Ramsey.

A series of confessions began, starting with Tichenor's. He had broken down, admitting he had bought Kelly a gun. He also admitted he had known Kelly's identity from the first, and had helped him and Ramsey in their efforts to get the ransom money out of Texas. He admitted sending telegrams to Ramsey, and of remarking to Kelly, "That just goes to show that if you want something done right, you had better do it yourself," when Ramsey failed in his task.

Tichenor's confession completely incriminated Langford Ramsey, scion of a highly respectable Memphis businessman. Then Ramsey broke down, and spilled the entire story to the FBI. He told them of his trip to the Coleman ranch, and of his failure to get the money. The FBI already knew much of the story, but Ramsey's confession filled in small gaps.

It was midnight, September 27, when FBI agents arrived at the ranch house of Cassey Coleman. They placed him under arrest, and he too broke down and confessed. Following his directions, the agents went directly to a lone mesquite tree growing in the center of a cotton patch, just about a half-mile from Coleman's ranch house, and began to dig. In one hole they found a jug which contained $46,000 in twenty dollar bills. Then they dug up a molasses can, which contained $27,200 in twenty dollar bills. Machine Gun Kelly had buried the loot there, and only he and Cass Coleman knew where it was.

When all this evidence was placed before Kelly, he dramatically confessed. "You've got me right on the kidnapping job," he boasted, "but you can't pin a thing on me in that Chicago killing." He also denied any knowledge of the Kansas City Massacre, but then spilled the beans on his old buddy, Albert Bates.

At first, Kelly threatened to fight extradition to Oklahoma, but later changed his mind. He said he would go without a fight if Kathryn, who even now still wore the pants in the family, would also agree to go. She wanted to go to Oklahoma City right away, "where I can tell the truth and get my poor, old, innocent mother freed."

But the government decided to hold the Kellys in Memphis until the trial of the Shannons, Bailey, Bates, and various money changers was over. They were still afraid that the presence of the Kellys might intimidate their witnesses.

Kathryn was in a vile mood when she found out they wouldn't be rushed to Oklahoma City for an immediate trial. Now wallowing in the luxury of nation-wide publicity, she wanted to make a grandstand play, and save her mother.

George Kelly lapsed into a morose mood, often jerking at the Oregon boot on his leg that kept him chained to his cot. He spent most of his time sleeping, or just glowering at his guards; and they sat there with machine guns and glowered right back.

Albert Bates, Harvey J. Bailey, Robert K. G. (Boss) Shannon, Ora Shannon, Armon (Potatoes) Shannon, and his wife Oleta, were indicted on August 23 for participation or complicity in the kidnapping of Charles F. Urschel.

Now, new indictments were issued against George Kelly, Kathryn Kelly, Cassey Coleman, Will Casey, John C. Tichenor, Langford Ramsey, Clifford Skelly and Barney Berman. The charges were kidnapping, conspiracy to kidnap, harboring a criminal, giving aid to a fugitive from justice, and the illegal changing of

known kidnap money. Seymour E. Travis, brother-in-law of John
C. Tichenor, was released without indictment because of insufficient evidence.

xiii

The trial of those indicted on August 23 began on September
18, 1933. It was held in the Federal Building, in Oklahoma City,
and was the first to be held under the new Lindbergh Kidnapping
Law. Because of this, the whole nation was watching the proceedings with great interest. Precedents would be set in this,
and the trial that was to follow, that would be the guidelines for
future prosecutions.

A dramatic moment came on the second day of the trial, when
Charles F. Urschel walked over to Albert Bates and pointed his
finger at him. "That's one of the men," he told the court, "he's
one of the two who kidnapped me at the point of a gun, and later
guarded me at the Shannon farm." Bates, his arms folded, looked
straight ahead and said nothing.

Albert L. Bates, alias George Bates, alias George L. Davis, alias
George Harris, alias J. B. King, etc., was sentenced on March 28,
1916, as J. B. King. He was given one to fifteen years for burglary
at the state penitentiary in Carson City, Nevada. He was paroled,
November 13, 1917. As Albert Bates, he was arrested in Salt Lake
City, and given six months for petty theft. As George Davis, he
was arrested by the sheriff of Ogden, Utah, April 22, 1920, for
burglary. Sent to the penitentiary August 3, 1921, he escaped on
October 27, 1926. As A. L. Bates, he was sent to the Colorado
State Penitentiary, at Canyon City, Colorado, May 10, 1927, for
three years on a burglary rap. He was released on July 15, 1930.
As A. L. Bates, he was arrested by the state police at Paw Paw,
Michigan, for a minor offense, and given thirty days. He was also
wanted for bank robbery in Lincoln, Nebraska; Colfax, Washington; Denton, Texas; and Wheaton, Illinois.

On the eighth day of the trial, Robert Shannon, in an attempt
to save his own neck, turned on two of his co-defendants. He
testified that he and his family had been forced to keep Urschel
on the farm. He also told the court that his family had been under
constant threat of death by Bates and Bailey. At this, Bailey managed a strained smile; Bates remained calm.

The jury hearing the case was made up of twelve small-town
businessmen, and they listened with great attention. Technical-

ities were swept aside, as the trial neared its final stages. Motions by the defense for a directed verdict of "not guilty" were entered, and denied by Judge Edgar S. Vaught.

The drama of fear hung over the trial, as precautions were taken to preclude any reprisals by the underworld. Kelly's letter to Urschel had threatened that he had "cash—planes, bombs, and unlimited connections both here and abroad." The FBI kept the Arnolds under heavy guard, and the entire court area itself took on the look of a military camp. Everyone, including the participants, was thoroughly searched before being allowed into the courtroom. Earlier in the trial, a small plane had flown low over the courthouse, and everyone ducked, including the judge. When the Kellys were captured on September 26, the atmosphere of fear cleared just a little, but it never completely disappeared.

Then it was suddenly all over. "So say you, so say you all?" Judge Vaught asked, as he queried the jury about the verdict they had just handed him. It was a sweeping verdict of "guilty, as charged" against all the defendants.

Before pronouncing sentence the judge had George and Kathryn Kelly brought before the bench. Then he asked for their pleas. They entered an official plea of "not guilty."

The prosecutor was stunned, for the Kellys had previously agreed to plead "guilty" and throw themselves on the mercy of the court. That had been the reason for the interruption; the judge was prepared to sentence them along with the others. Now there would have to be another expensive trial, so the Kellys were seated in the court, and the judge turned his attentions, once again, to those who had just been declared "guilty."

As the four principals in this case stood before him, Judge Vaught's words rang harshly in their ears. "I sentence you and each of you to spend the rest of your natural lives in a federal penitentiary!"

The Shannons, a middle aged farm couple, appeared dumbfounded when told by the judge that they must now spend the rest of their days behind the grim walls of a prison. Bates and Bailey, however, were more hardened, and they took the judge's sentence with a kind of stoical indifference.

Then, Armon (Potatoes), 22-year-old son of the Shannons, and his wife Oleta Shannon were brought before the judge. He had been advised that Armon was a none-too-bright but obedient son, and had only done as he was told. Accordingly, he and his wife were given ten-year suspended sentences, upon the condition of their future good behavior. Now, these two were free to return to the empty ranch and farm, in Paradise, Texas. Oleta's father, Earl Brown, was not prosecuted.

Edward Berman and Clifford Skelly, both of Minneapolis, were convicted as money changers in this case, and they received five-year sentences in a federal penitentiary.

Cassey Coleman and his friend Will Casey would be tried later, in San Angelo, Texas, and ultimately received sentences of a year and a day and two years, respectively.

xiv

The really big trial was yet to come, and thousands of people milled in the streets just outside the Federal building, in hopes of getting a glimpse of the great Machine Gun Kelly and his wife Kathryn.

The selection of a jury began on October 7, and the Kellys were taken to and from the courtroom during these proceedings. The very first day in court, Kelly began to feel that his crown of fame was slipping. He had the feeling of being ignored, and apparently decided to do something dramatic to get the public attention back where it belonged—on him. As he and Kathryn were being taken back to their jail cells, Kelly suddenly turned to Urschel. He drew his index finger across his own neck (in a throat-cutting gesture) and shouted at him, "You'll get your's, you bastard!" Urschel, by now, was used to Kelly's idiotic threats, and he simply ignored him. To Kelly this was the unkindest cut of all.

Another drama occurred the following day, when the Kellys were being brought back into the courthouse. Just as she was about to enter the elevator, in the Federal Building, Kathryn paused to kiss her father, J. E. Brooks. Special Agent J. C. White, aware that this was just another move on her part to get publicity and attention, gave her a shove. Kathryn immediately turned and slapped him on the face, and screamed that she would do it again if he dared to push her.

This attracted a lot of attention, and Kelly saw this as an excellent opportunity to do something chivalrous, so he raised his manacled hands above his head in a menacing manner. Agent White was quicker, however, and he gripped his pistol by the barrel and pounded Kelly on the head several times. Then Kathryn got into the act, with one eye on the reporters, and screamed, "Don't, don't!" Whereupon their guards pushed both of them on to the elevator, and the act was over.

With blood trickling from his flattened head, Kelly entered the courtroom in a somewhat subdued manner. From this moment on, he would lose some of the bluster and the braggadocio that had become such a part of his character.

Once they were seated, Kathryn apparently forgot all about her husband and his bleeding head. Soon she was smiling and cheerfully chatting with Agent White.

One venireman introduced a little laughter into this otherwise serious trial when he asked to be excused on the grounds that he was an undertaker. Judge Vaught excused him with the wry remark, "We don't need an undertaker here just yet." Everyone in the courtroom laughed—even Machine Gun Kelly.

In his opening statement, District Attorney Herbert K. Hyde declared that two figures had played the lead in the kidnapping of Charles F. Urschel. Then he pointed at the Kellys, and shouted: "They sit in this courtroom now! Their names are George and Kathryn Kelly!" He went on to tell the jury that the government would prove Kelly, with a machine gun swinging from under one arm, was the scowling companion of Albert Bates the night Charles Urschel was kidnapped. "He guarded the millionaire captive on the Shannon ranch, near Paradise, Texas, and he took the $200,000 ransom money from E. E. Kirkpatrick, on a Kansas City street. Kathryn," he continued, "will enter the picture at Stratford, Oklahoma, at the T. M. Coleman farm home, where you will hear her saying, the day of the kidnapping: 'We're going to make some money,' and you will hear Kelly saying: 'There's going to be a kidnapping tonight.' "

Hyde then swung into the threats which had marked the first trial. "Kathryn Kelly wrote two or three letters to the Urschel family, threatening them with violence and destruction. And now we have ten or fifteen witnesses to testify that, in this very courtroom, last week, George Kelly stopped in front of Mr. Urschel and said, 'You'll get your's yet, you bastard.' "

Then Hyde took on Kathryn's attorney, John V. Roberts, declaring, "We'll show that Roberts made the statement to Kathryn Kelly, in jail, that Verne Miller, a fugitive from justice and an outlaw, and Wilbur Underhill, an outlaw and a fugitive, 'will take care of Arnold if he testifies in this case.' "

The first witness for the prosecution was Gay Coleman, son of Cassey Coleman. The 18-year-old farm boy pointed at Kelly and said he was the man he heard boast, "There will be a kidnapping tonight." But then he claimed he could not remember some of the incidents he had previously testified to at the first trial.

Prosecutor Hyde angrily interrupted his questioning of this witness, and demanded of him, "Who's been talking to you since the first trial?" This remark struck George Kelly as funny, and he laughed loudly. Judge Vaught looked at him, from his high perch, but said nothing.

Mrs. Luther Arnold was the next witness, and she told how Kathryn had virtually kidnapped her 12-year-old daughter, Geraldine, and used her as a blind in their flight from the law. "I let her have my baby for a little ride," Mrs. Arnold said, "She told me she would be back the same day. It was two weeks before I saw her again. Luther was in Fort Worth, consulting with a lawyer of Mrs. Kelly's and getting information."

She then went on to tell how her little family had been befriended by Kathryn, while she was traveling near Waco, in an old truck. In telling of Kathryn's remarks about Urschel, Mrs. Arnold said, "I can't use the words Mrs. Kelly used."

"Speak right out," the judge urged.

"Well—Mrs. Kelly said they ought to have killed the er—bastard—and that she wished she could do it herself. She was referring to Mr. Urschel," Mrs. Arnold explained.

Then Geraldine took the stand, and sketched the picture of her wild dash about the country with the Kellys, while posing as their daughter. She detailed their subsequent travels, which ended in Memphis, and then told how the Kellys had sent her to Texas with Langford Ramsey. She also testified that Kelly had threatened to kill the judge, the prosecutors, and Urschel. Then she told the court that it was Kathryn Kelly who had written those lurid threats about "wiping out the Urschel family," and that she had talked Kelly into signing them.

"That's a lie," Kathryn told her attorney in a stage whisper heard all over the courtroom. "I wrote a letter to my mother, but I didn't write the other!"

D. C. Patterson, a handwriting expert, took the stand, and testified that a note airmailed from Chicago to Urschel during the first trial, was apparently in Kathryn Kelly's handwriting.

J. Klar, a Fort Worth pawnbroker, testified that he sold a machine gun to Kathryn Kelly for $250. "She came in alone and bought it from me," he said. The machine gun was later found in the possession of Harvey J. Bailey.

"He's lying!" Kathryn again told her attorney, in a loud voice, and Judge Vaught rapped for order as the courtroom buzzed, following her outburst.

It was now apparent that the government was trying to put the big lie to Kathryn's contention that she had been forced into any wrongdoing by her husband.

In swift succession, the daughter of Robert K. G. Shannon, and then his son, Armon, were brought to the witness stand. They both told of Kathryn's activities in Fort Worth, and on the farm, some forty miles away.

"Kathryn came to the farm," Ruth Shannon—Kathryn's half-sister—testified, in a low frightened voice, "and she asked me to go to Fort Worth with her. That was Sunday [July 23] the day Urschel was brought to the farm." She then told that she, and Pauline, Kathryn's daughter, and Armon's wife, Oleta, were kept in Kathryn's Fort Worth house all the time Urschel was being held on the farm.

E. E. Kirkpatrick, Urschel's business associate and friend, took the stand, and dramatically pointed to the slouching Kelly as the man who had taken the $200,000 ransom satchel from him on a Kansas City street. With this Kelly slouched just a little further, and chewed a little harder on his chewing gum.

Then, the prosecutor put the victim of the kidnapping, Charles F. Urschel, on the stand, and he immediately identified Kelly as one of his kidnappers. He also testified that Kelly had later acted as one of the guards, while he was being held at the farm house.

With this, and with a demand for a conviction, District Attorney Herbert K. Hyde rested his case for the prosecution.

Now the defense took over, and the big moment of the trial arrived when Kathryn Kelly took the stand. She was completely at ease as she walked to the witness chair. She then took the oath, and sat down, carefully crossing her legs. Then she smiled demurely at the judge, the jury, and the spectators. She started her story at the Stratford, Oklahoma, farm of her grandmother, Mrs. T. M. Coleman. Reluctantly, she told of her two previous marriages, and of her marriage to George Kelly. She testified that she and Kelly had been married in Minneapolis in 1930, three months after he was released from Leavenworth.

"He deceived me," she told the court, "I didn't know he made his money dishonestly." Then, holding her black hat in her lap, and tearfully blinking her brown eyes, the auburn-haired Kathryn Kelly began to portray herself as the innocent pawn of a machine gun packing husband. Crying softly to herself, she declared that Kelly had threatened to kill Urschel, during his captivity on the Armon farm, and that she had warned him, "If you do, I'll tell on you, even if you kill me."

When the prosecutor began his cross-examination, Kathryn began to lose some of her cool. As the clash between her and District Attorney Hyde progressed, her voice rose sharply, and her eyes began to flash with the fire of hatred. Still, he couldn't shake her contention that she had been forced into the kidnapping caper by Machine Gun Kelly. When he asked her if she loved her husband, she replied that she still loved him, but she didn't believe in him anymore.

Then the defense, in rapid succession, called Kathryn Kelly's daughter, Pauline Frye, and her father, J. E. Brooks, but they could contribute nothing to the case but their unshakeable belief in the pureness of her character.

During the entire trial, not one word was spoken in the defense of George Kelly. As he sat, slouched in his chair, chewing on his gum, he heard his wife, the witnesses, and even his attorneys, placing all the blame on him. He had agreed with her attorneys (and his), before the trial, to take the full blame for everything, and spare the woman he loved.

Arguments were made by both counsels, and were climaxed by District Attorney Herbert K. Hyde's plea for a conviction, under the new Lindbergh Kidnapping Law. He also asked for a sentence of not less than life in prison for the both of them.

Judge Edgar S. Vaught had understood only too well what was transpiring in his court. He knew that there had been some kind of agreement between George and Kathryn. Because of this, he decided to put his two cents worth into this case, in his charge of the jury: "The court would feel it had been cowardly and derelict in its duty if it had not pointed out its conviction that the defendant, Kathryn Kelly, was not wholly truthful. This court will not hesitate to tell you that Kathryn Kelly's testimony, concerning her removal of the little girl from the Shannon farm, near Paradise, Texas, on the day Mr. Urschel was brought there, did not sound convincing." With this, the jury, consisting of four farmers and eight businessmen, leaned forward and listened more attentively. "Her conduct," the judge continued, "at the Coleman farm, near Stratford, Oklahoma, not only is a strong circumstantial point, but is convincing to the court that Kathryn knew about the kidnapping and knowingly participated. Other testimony from this defendant is utterly convincing to this court that Kathryn Kelly had criminal knowledge of the abduction conspiracy. However, you can ignore my remarks altogether. They are not binding upon the jury."

Though the judge's remarks were not binding upon the jury,

they were very impressive. Twenty-five years later, he would be called to account for them in an appeal issued by Kathryn.

The jury took only three hours to reach its verdict, but it was too late to deliver it, so the verdict was sealed in an envelope for the night. The jury then left the Federal Building, around 8:45 P.M., and were taken to their hotel.

October 12, 1933, the jury filed into the jammed courtroom at 9:35 A.M., and while hundreds of women fought with guards outside, trying to get a look at the defendants, the sealed verdict was opened and read. The defendants were found to be "guilty as charged!"

The two prisoners were then brought up before Judge Vaught for sentencing. "Do either of you have anything to say before I pronounce sentence upon you?" he asked them.

"No," Kathryn replied.

Kelly just shook his head, but made some remark out of the corner of his mouth to Kathryn.

"The jury has found you guilty," the judge continued, "and the court concurs in their verdict. It is therefore the judgment and sentence of this court that you and each of you be taken to a federal penitentiary, and there to remain for the rest of your natural lives."

Kathryn tried to smile, as she sat down, but it was more of a grimace. "My pekingese dog would have gotten a life sentence in this court," she muttered. Then she rose to be taken to the county jail. There she would stay until her transfer to the Federal Detention Jail at Milan, Michigan.

As Machine Gun Kelly, "Western desperado, gimlet-eyed killer, and lusty badman," was being led from the Federal Building, he heard newsboys crying, "Read all about Pop-gun Kelly!" He lunged at one of the boys, but the lad leaped deftly aside, grinning widely. Now he'd have something to tell his grandchildren about.

xv

Kathryn Kelly, still trying to make deals, told newsmen, at an impromptu news conference: "I'll go stark raving crazy if they separate my mother and me. If they send us to the same place where I can watch over her, I'll be good. They know I've got plenty of friends who will come and get me if I say the word. But, if I'm with my mother, I won't want to escape."

This was actually an empty boast, for the only friends Kathryn had left were two-bit hoodlums, and a few cheap thugs. Not a one of these had either the nerve or the inclination to try to help her. Their ideology was that she had made her bed and now she could lie in it. Kathryn knew this, but she wanted to impress the government with her powers.

The following day, Kathryn Kelly kissed her husband through the steel bars of her cell, and told him, "Be a good boy."

"I will," Kelly replied, glumly. Then he was led to a barred, bullet-proof special coach, which had been attached to the north-bound Katy passenger train.

The government was still convinced that George Kelly Barnes, alias George Machine Gun Kelly, alias Pop-gun Kelly, was the bad man he pretended to be. And Kelly? Why, he played the roll of the tough machine gunning desperado right up to the bitter end. Eight FBI agents, each carrying a machine gun, rode with George all the way to the penitentiary. He entered Leavenworth, October 14, 1933, and remained there until he was transferred to Alcatraz, when it opened in September 1934. He didn't belong with the case-hardened criminals Alcatraz was built for, but he stayed there nearly 17 years. During this time, Kelly's hair took on its final color, grey. He also turned into a kind of prison "bible-toter," and wrote heart-rending letters to his former victim, Charles F. Urschel. *"Nothing,"* he lamented in one of his letters, *"could be worth what I am going through now!"*

Charles F. Urschel, however, could never forget nor could he forgive Kelly's many other letters, and his former threats. He would remain cold and aloof to Kelly's plaintive cries for forgiveness.

Kelly was returned to Leavenworth Penitentiary, in June 1951, where he was employed in the furniture factory. He had suffered from a heart condition most of his life, and at 7:30 P.M., July 17, 1954, he suffered a heart attack. He died in the prison hospital of a coronary thrombosis at 12:20 A.M., July 18, 1954.

••2••

The Phantom of the Ozarks

Pretty Boy Floyd, who left a bloody trail of murders, bank robberies, and kidnappings throughout the Southwest, was born Charles Arthur Floyd on a farm in the northern part of Georgia, February 3, 1904.

In 1911, Mr. and Mrs. Walter F. Floyd packed up their large brood of children and moved to the Cherokee Indian Territory of Oklahoma, where the Floyds hoped to find their fortune. Instead, they found hard work, just like the kind they had left behind in Georgia.

Here, shadowed by the verdant Cookson Hills, the Floyd family settled on a small farm, near Akins, about eight miles from the larger village of Sallisaw, Oklahoma.

Sallisaw is known as Floyd's home town, because of its proximity to Akins. It was once a trading post and camp site, named "Salaison" by French trappers, because of its large salt deposits. The early Oklahomans soon changed the name to the more pronounceable "Sallisaw."

In Akins, Mr. Walter F. Floyd also opened a small grocery store to supplement his meager income from the farm. It was here that Charles attended school with his four sisters and three brothers. Academically Charles showed no great promise; but he managed to keep up his grades, and offered no important behavior problem to his teachers.

Possessed of a vivid imagination, he was greatly influenced, in his younger years, by the local folklore, and by his surroundings. Old timers spinning their tales of Belle Starr, Bill Doolin, Cherokee Bill, Mont Cookson, and the Kimes Brothers, wove their gossamer spell of magic upon him. He would sit patiently for hours, listening to their every word, never questioning; never doubting. Here, then, might be the greatest single clue as to what would, eventually, mold him into one of the bloodiest outlaws of the Southwest.

The Cookson Hill country of southeastern Oklahoma, and the nearby Ozark country of Arkansas is rich in traditions and beautiful to look at, but they give forth little in material wealth to their poor but hardworking residents.

Floyd's father worked long and hard to feed his large family, and his mother was quiet and active in the local church activities. His viciousness and evident dislike for all types of labor were certainly not inherited, but of his own making.

Floyd's first noticeable movement into a life of crime came in 1922 when he was arrested in Akins for looting the post office of $350 in pennies. Before he could be brought to trial, the evidence disappeared, and the case was eventually *nolle prosequi*.

This brief brush with the law tempered Floyd for a while; and in January 1924 he married the 16-year-old daughter of a Bixby sharecropper. Her name was Ruby Leonard Hargraves, and she was tall, dark-eyed, with auburn hair and a nice face. In 1925 she bore Floyd a son, whom he promptly burdened with the name Jack Dempsey.

Things didn't go at all well for the Floyd family, and from the first Floyd felt the heavy hand of responsibility. This was a duty Floyd was ill prepared to accept, and Ruby took a disgruntled attitude toward his increasing interest in crime and criminals. They separated by mutual agreement in 1925, with Ruby seeking the divorce and Floyd leaving Akins for the brighter lights of St. Louis.

In St. Louis, Floyd found the going hard, and the easy money always in the hands of others. Without friends or money, he had to throw aside his hatred for work, and take employment in a bakery. Here he labored as a cleanup man and errand boy, so that he might eat.

It was during this period that he met up with members of a holdup gang; they were older men. They made light of his labors in the bakery, and told him they were about to pull a big job that would net them a lot of money. It took little persuasion on their part to get him to join in the operation.

The "big job" they pulled was one of utter disaster for Floyd. In a September 1925 highway robbery, they held up a paymaster and took $5,000. As luck would have it, of the five members of the gang the only one the paymaster would remember was "a young fellow, about twenty or twenty-two, with a round, kind of pretty face."

This description rang a bell for the patrolman who pounded a beat where Floyd worked in the bakery. He went straight to Floyd's place of toil, and returned him to headquarters. The paymaster identified him at once, and he was booked as St. Louis prisoner Number 22318. Floyd was on his way.

He was subsequently tried on a charge of highway robbery, given five years, and on September 16, 1925, he entered the state penitentiary at Jefferson City, Missouri, as Number 29078. Typical of that strange era in American history, Floyd was released on December 8, 1926, after serving less than one year and three months.

Somewhat disturbed by this experience, Floyd then returned to the Akins-Sallisaw area, where he found that his father had been killed. A neighbor of theirs was on trial for the killing, and Floyd attended the trial, listening to every word. The jury found the neighbor innocent—Floyd didn't.

He vowed vengeance upon the killer of his father, and word soon got around that Floyd was on the rampage. It is doubtful that his vow of vengeance was done out of love for his father, for there had been little love between them. Most likely it was forced upon him, as a "code of the hills," the kind of "eye for an eye" justice that still prevails in some parts of America.

Whatever Floyd's reasons were, the neighbor disappeared a few days later, and was never heard of again. And though there was no shred of proof, most of his friends swore that Floyd took him into the rugged Cookson Hills, where he killed and buried him. If he did, this would have been the first of his many murders.

Rather than subject himself to possible investigation, Floyd left Oklahoma, and drifted from job to job. He seemed to have no singular purpose in mind, except to exist. In Kansas City, Missouri, on May 6, 1927, he was arrested for vagrancy and suspicion of highway robbery, becoming Number 16950. He was released the following day for lack of sufficient evidence.

While in Kansas City, Kansas, on March 9, 1929, he was picked up and booked as Number 3999. This was for investigation for possessing an automatic pistol. He was released the same day, but the gun was confiscated.

Still drifting, and this time further west, Floyd was again arrested, in Pueblo, Colorado, May 9, 1929, for vagrancy. He became their Number 887; here his luck failed him. He was fined $50, and when he couldn't pay he was sent to jail for two months.

March 8, 1930, he was arrested in Akron, Ohio, as Frank Mitchell, his favorite alias. Arrested with him were John King and Bert Walker, two well-known criminals. Found in their hideout were machine guns, revolvers and nitro-glycerin.

They were held under a charge of killing Harland F. Manes, a traffic officer, and Floyd became Akron's Number 19983. But the evidence against Floyd and King was inconclusive, so they were turned over to Toledo authorities, May 20, 1930. The less fortunate Bert Walker was tried, convicted, and executed November 10, 1930.

In Toledo, Floyd and King were booked on suspicion of robbing a bank at Sylvania, Ohio, and he became Number 21458. Later they were both convicted for this crime, and Floyd received a 10 to 25 year sentence.

December 10, 1930, while enroute to the Ohio State Penitentiary, Floyd escaped by leaping through an open window of the train, while only ten miles from the prison gates. From here on out, Charles Arthur Floyd would never again see the inside of a jail or a prison.

Floyd didn't stay inactive for very long, according to Kansas City authorities, for on March 25, 1931, he and William (Bill-The-Killer) Miller, a Missouri outlaw, murdered William and Wallace Ash.

The Ash brothers were smalltime Kansas City hoods, who were well known in both Kansas and Missouri. Their bodies were found in a ditch beside a burning automobile. Both men had been shot in the back of the head with a single bullet. The reputed motive for the gangland-type execution was Floyd's desire for Wallace Ash's wife Rose, and Miller's interest in her sister, Beulah Bird. Substance was given to this accusation a few months later.

Following a bank robbery in Kentucky, Floyd and his companions were recognized by Patrolman Ralph Castner while they were passing through Bowling Green, Ohio. He attempted to halt the vehicle, and they killed him. With Floyd at the time were his pal William Miller, Mrs. Rose Ash (the bereaved widow of Wallace Ash), and Beulah Bird.

Settling down in Kansas City for a while, "Pretty Boy" Floyd, as he was now called, decided to try his hand at bootlegging. This was a favorite occupation for many hoodlums during this period. The risks were not too great and the profits could be high.

Floyd's career in this field was to be short lived, however, for on July 21, 1931, he fatally wounded a Federal Prohibition Officer, Curtis C. Burke, and seriously wounded three other persons. The shootings took place during a raid on a flat over the Noto-Lusco Flower Shop, at 1039 Independence Avenue. A pedestrian was also shot, and John Calio, a northside gunman, was killed in an attempted shootout with Lieutenant E. L. Nelson of the Kansas City police. Floyd made his getaway from the shooting scene in a green Chevrolet sedan and fled the state.

With his promising career as a bootlegger turned into a fiasco, Pretty Boy Floyd had to look elsewhere for money. So, on November 6, 1931, he held up the Citizens State Bank of Strasburg, Ohio, getting $50,000. For him this was a fabulous sum of money, and he decided to head back to Oklahoma for a while.

Back in the Cookson Hill country, Floyd lived like a returning emperor. He doled out money here and there, buying friends right and left. A $50 tip to a hill farmer, trying to grub out a living during these days of a deep depression, was a small fortune. As the easy money flowed from Floyd's pockets, even his estranged wife, Ruby, began to see the error of her ways. Soon the divorce was forgotten, and they were seeing more and more of each other.

ii

When Floyd met a kindred soul by the name of George Birdwell, an immediate partnership was born. Birdwell was a tall, lanky Oklahoman, with adventure and greed in his heart, and murder in his soul. At the time of their meeting, Birdwell had been credited with over ten killings, and countless bank robberies. He was described as an expert gunman, killer, and bank robber, and as having pure snake venom flowing through his veins.

By now Floyd had also built up something of a reputation as an expert gunman, killer, and bank robber. Consequently they struck up a fine relationship that was to last until Birdwell's sudden death later on.

Neither Pretty Boy Floyd nor George Birdwell could be accused of having a superior intellect, but Floyd was undoubtedly the smarter of the two. Because of this, Birdwell willingly accepted the lesser role in their partnership, and became known as Floyd's lieutenant.

This partnership, from 1931 until late 1932, rolled up a list of crimes that staggers the imagination. For two busy years, this pair held up so many banks, and kidnapped so many people, that the Oklahoma insurance rates became the highest in the nation. In fact Oklahoma hadn't seen the like of this since the days of Al Jennings and the Daltons.

Acting as a team, Floyd, driving a fast automobile, would roar up to the door of a bank, leaving Birdwell to man a machine gun in the car. Inside he would compel the employees and customers to lie on the floor, while he scooped up all the money in sight.

Then, kidnapping the banker—and sometimes other employees —for hostage, he and Birdwell would make good their escape. Later on they would dump their hapless victims at the edge of town, though they usually didn't harm them.

They hit banks in Seminole, Maude, and Earlsboro—all booming oil towns—and then headed back to their hideouts. Sometimes, needing a third man, they were joined by other young hoodlums. Among these was a lad from Tulsa named Fred Barker.

Floyd and Birdwell repeatedly slipped through the roadblocks set up by the law, to reach hideouts in the mountains of western Arkansas, where Floyd was soon known as "The Phantom of the Ozarks," or in the Cookson Hills, where they called him "The King of the Bank Robbers." They would also successfully disappear into the Seminole Oil Fields.

One prime factor in their successful evasion of the law was Floyd's reputed habit of giving part of his loot to the indigent mountain and hill people where he hid out. Even today, Charles "Pretty Boy" Floyd is still revered in Akins and Sallisaw, Oklahoma. People on the streets will tell you what a fine man he was, and that he didn't do half the terrible things attributed to him.

They remember how good Floyd was to children and old ladies. With misty eyes, they will tell you stories of how he helped many old people, who were about to lose their farms to heartless bankers. The one who did all the killings, they will assure you, was mean, old, cold-blooded George Birdwell, who scared the devil himself.

The legend grew, as legends grow, and Floyd became a modern Robin Hood, who stole from the rich and gave to the poor. This was pure myth, for the record clearly indicates that Floyd stole from everyone. He killed indiscriminately, whenever it served his purpose, and gave money only to those who would hide and protect him. He literally bought fame and legends with stolen money.

Other legends grew: Pretty Boy once penned a note to the Sheriff of Sallisaw, telling him, "I'm coming to see my mother.

If you're smart you won't try to stop me." The Sheriff was smart.
Then there is the time Pretty Boy robbed the bank at Sallisaw,
because the banker had said he wouldn't dare. Afterwards he
rode around town, with complete impunity, sprinkling the money
out of the car windows, while the poor people in town grabbed
it up. He had, of course, only robbed the bank to prove to the
banker that he could do it, and to show his utter contempt for
the law. One wonders what George Birdwell must have thought
of his generosity.

Then there is the time Birdwell's father died in a small Oklahoma town. The word quickly spread that he and Pretty Boy were
coming to view the body. The Sheriff sent five deputies to watch
for him, but Pretty Boy got the drop on them and Birdwell paid
his respects to his father; then they left.

And so the stories went, new legends spun by the myth makers,
successors to the ones of Floyd's childhood. Now their tales were
about him, and Floyd's ego grew to an enormous size. Perhaps
some of the wide-eyed youngsters who listened to the tales about
him are robbing banks of their own today.

Few of the Cookson Hill people, or the Ozark Mountain people,
ever had enough money to put into a bank, and they were simply
delighted with Floyd's method of taking it out. As the tales about
him grew more ludicrous, he became more and more generous to
keep them alive. Because of this he never had to worry for a
place to hide from the law, or fear that some law-abiding citizen
would turn him in. Too many of them believed that laws were
made only for the rich.

While Pretty Boy Floyd's friends in Oklahoma and Arkansas
were calling him "The Phantom of the Ozarks," the newspapers
were reporting, with increasing regularity, the latest depredations
of "Pretty Boy" Floyd.

It is obscure whether the nickname "Pretty Boy" was a newspaper invention, or if it had its source elsewhere. It might have
originated in St. Louis, where he was arrested from the description of having "a kind of pretty face." Many attributed it to a
fond nickname given to him by Rose Ash, the woman he killed for.

Whatever the reason for Floyd's nickname, a good, close look
at his photographs failed to give much weight to this description.
He was a large hulk of a man (weighting over 200 pounds), but
he moved with agility. He had a round face, topped by a shock of
black hair, which he parted in the center. His complexion was

ruddy, and he had a small, hard mouth, with a rather large nose. Attractive as a child, he soon lost his angelic looks, as his career in crime deepened and his murders increased in number.

iii

In January 1932, Floyd rented a house at 512 East Young Street, in Tulsa, Oklahoma. He used the name of Jack Hamilton, and was soon joined by his estranged wife, Ruby, and son Jack Dempsey. Jack was now seven years old, and they enrolled him in the nearby John Burroughs school. Then Floyd made a half-hearted stab at being a family man, between robberies.

Acting on a tip, on February 7, 1932, Sergeants George Steward, Wade Floor, Williard Wilson, and Lon Elliott, all of the Tulsa police department, sighted Floyd and Birdwell in a coupe, parked at the curb of a side street. They drove up beside the car, and three of them piled out, calling for Floyd's surrender.

But surrender was the furthest thing from Floyd's mind, and he opened up with a machine gun, sending a barrage of bullets into the police car. The shots tore off the steering wheel, splattered most of its glass, and wounded Detective Williard Wilson. As the rest of the officers scurried for cover, Floyd and Birdwell sped away from the scene.

Later, one of the officers reported that he had fired six shots into the seat Floyd was sitting in. He said he saw the bullets rip through the back, but they had no apparent effect. Floyd was wearing a steel vest at the time, and the bullets did little more than pound him on the back.

After this encounter all the officers in Tulsa were on a kind of "Pretty Boy Floyd-George Birdwell" lookout. Then on the night of February 9, 1932, Detectives Homer Myers and Roy Moran, of the Auto Recovery Squad, noticed two men in a souped-up, V-8 Ford, near Fifth Street and Harvard Avenue. When they recognized one of the men as Floyd, they fired at the car with a sawed-off shotgun, and Floyd returned the fire with his pistol. (Their machine gun was out of ammunition.) On the chase went to Utica Avenue, then it sped into a dead end at 15th Street, alongside the Katy tracks; there they ditched the car and took off on foot.

Detectives R. B. (Blackie) Jones, and Earl Gardner had been assigned to "prowl on foot," and at about 2:00 A.M., February 11,

Gardner saw two men come from the Midland Valley right-of-way, near Apache Street. They worked their way southwest, and the officers followed. At one time they were only 50 feet behind them, but they held their fire. When the two men entered a residence at 512 East Young Street, the detectives called in to the station and reported.

Later that same morning, Detective Sergeant Lon Elliott, heading a team of 20 policemen and detectives, surrounded the house. The team had been put together hurriedly, but were armed with tear gas, shotguns, and rifles.

At the time the Tulsa Police Department had one machine gun in stock, but someone had misplaced the key to the ammunition container. It took over an hour to find the key and rush the gun to the scene, but by the time it arrived it was not needed. One officer at the scene found out later that he had a 12 gauge shotgun, and ammunition for a 20 gauge.

A tear gas bomb ripped through one of the windows, and almost immediately the front door was thrown open. Out raced Ruby Floyd, clutching the hand of her son. They raced down the stairs, across the lawn, and down the street. Some of the officers took up the chase, and the two were apprehended.

Officers stationed at the rear of the house were astounded to see Floyd and Birdwell walk down the stairs and exit from the back door, a pistol in each hand. For some unexplicable reason not a shot was fired, and they made good their escape.

Ruby and Jack were taken to the police station, where Ruby denied even knowing Floyd. She was, she steadfastly maintained, Mrs. Jack Hamilton, and nothing and no one could make her change her story. Even though the truth was known, there was no evidence on which to hold her, so she was released and returned to her residence on East Young Street.

News of this near capture of Pretty Boy Floyd and Birdwell reached the ears of Erv D. Kelley, former sheriff of McIntosh County. Floyd had held up the bank in Eufaula, Oklahoma, while Kelley was sheriff, and the lawman had sworn to get him if it took the rest of his life. So he and a few others took up a vigil outside the house in Tulsa, and patiently waited.

On April 8, 1932, the surveillance paid off, as Ruby Floyd and her son left Tulsa and drove to the house of Cecil Bennett, a mile south of Bixby, Oklahoma. Nearby was the home of her father, William Hargraves, and her two younger brothers. Here she was to rendezvous with Pretty Boy Floyd.

Erv D. Kelley and William Counts, who was a former Eufaula deputy, followed them to the Bennett farm house, and then sent word to other possemen. At 8:30 P.M., Friday night, six armed men were lining the only road to the Bennett farm house. At 2:15 A.M., Floyd still hadn't shown, and four of the possemen decided to go to Bixby for a cup of coffee. The weather was cold, and the long vigil in the brush had stiffened and numbed them.

Kelley and Counts decided they would remain behind, and it was only five minutes later that a Chevrolet approached the farmhouse. It was 2:25 A.M., when Counts, who was about 500 feet away, near a school, heard seven shots. They were the single spaced shots of a pistol, and not the rapid fire of a machine gun.

At the approach of the Chevrolet, Kelley stepped into the center of the road, his outline clearly shown by the headlights of the approaching car. He lifted his machine gun, and started firing, but only soft sound issued forth, as the silencer muffled its bark.

Floyd saw Kelley immediately, and opened the door on the driver's side, firing through the window. He hit Kelley five times, with his .45 caliber automatic. Floyd didn't escape unharmed, however, as he took two bullets from Kelley's machine gun, in his hip and thigh. This would retire him to the Cookson Hills for a while.

As soon as Counts heard the shooting, he knew the bullets hadn't come from Kelley's machine gun, so he jumped into his car, and sped toward the place where Kelley had been hiding. He saw the tail lights of Floyd's car as it disappeared down the road. He also saw Kelley, sprawled across the road, dead with five of Floyd's bullets in him. Kelley had fired 14 shots from his 21 bullet clip, and Floyd's car was a mess.

Cecil Bennett disclaimed any knowledge that Bill Hargraves was Floyd's father-in-law. He said he had heard the shots, but didn't know what they were, and sure wasn't going to leave his warm bed to find out. "Sure," he said, "I know Bill Hargraves, he works for me. So what?"

Ruby Floyd was interviewed at her father's shack that morning, by a reporter from the *Tulsa Sun*. He asked her, "Do you know that your husband knocked off Erv Kelley?"

"Well, that's fine," she smiled, and then she asked, "Did anyone else get killed?"

"No," the reporter replied, "no one else."

"Too bad," she sighed.

Still the reporter persisted, "Did you know Kelley trailed Pretty Boy for three months before he caught up with him, this morning?"

Ruby laughed, "Well, the son-of-a-bitch won't trail him any longer, will he."

Kelley was 46 years old when Floyd cut him down, and he left a widow and five children. The State Peace Officers' Association presented his widow with a check for $50, and the State of Oklahoma put a $6,000 reward on Floyd's head, dead or alive.

Pretty Boy and Birdwell had another close shave with the law, near Stonewall, Oklahoma, June 1932. Floyd was still recovering from his wounds, and they had holed up in a farm house here. A dozen officers, acting on a tip, caught up with them. But again, the criminals' luck held, and they escaped in a hail of bullets.

In the early part of September 1932, Floyd and Birdwell decided to hit the bank in Sallisaw. They had tired of hearing the banker's boast that neither Floyd, nor anyone else, could rob his bank. At least this is the reason given in a Floyd legend.

The robbery wasn't legend, however, and early one morning a car drew up in front of the bank. Floyd, still favoring his game leg, remained in the car. Birdwell and Ossie Elliott, an 18-year-old escapee from McAlester Penitentiary, entered the bank, where they grabbed all the money they could find.

Now, according to legend, Floyd then drove around town throwing the money out of the car window. Since George Birdwell was never known for his generosity, and Ossie Elliott hadn't come along just for kicks, and Floyd didn't kill the both of them, it is highly improbable that any great amount of money was disposed of in this manner.

At 12:25 P.M., November 7, 1932, a car drove up to the front of the bank in Henryetta, Oklahoma. Ossie Elliott stayed at the wheel of the car, while Pretty Boy and Birdwell entered the bank. Once inside, they both drew pistols, and ordered the three customers to line up against a wall. Pretty Boy then handed a sack to A. D. Diamond, Jr., the bookkeeper, and told him, "Put the money in that sack, and if any of you give an alarm, I'll kill you."

They netted $11,352.20 in this robbery, even bothering to take more than $100 in nickels and dimes. The entire operation was over in minutes, and they took two of the employees as hostages, putting them on the running boards of the car.

The hostages were later released unharmed on the edge of the small town, and the bandits were more than a mile away before the first alarm was sounded back in Henryetta.

With this money, Floyd decided to take a little trip to Ohio, to see "some of the boys," and have a little relaxation. Birdwell had other ideas. He wanted to rob the bank in Boley, before they took a vacation. Floyd vetoed the idea, and told Birdwell he would do well to stay clear of that place. "I've been tipped, by friends, that the bank isn't as helpless as it looks. You could get yourself killed, if you're not careful." What wonderful words of wisdom these were.

Boley, Oklahoma, was a small, but progressive town, enjoying an unusual prosperity for these depression days. It stood unique from most other Oklahoma towns in that the entire population was Negro. It had been founded by slaves freed from one of the Oklahoma Indian tribes.

Pretty Boy and George Birdwell sometimes used the home of C. C. Patterson, in Kiowa, Oklahoma, as a hideout, so Birdwell persuaded him, and another hoodlum, a Negro bandit named Johnny Glass, to join him. They drove to Boley to case the bank.

Boldly, they drove right up to the bank, and Birdwell went straight to the teller's cage, where he asked to cash a five dollar personal check. As he had expected, the teller explained that they couldn't cash personal checks without proper verification. Birdwell wasn't really listening, as he took mental pictures of the inside of the bank, and the number of employees. He muttered a "forget it," and left the bank.

One week later, Tuesday, November 22, 1932, the trio again drove up to the front of the Farmers' National Bank of Boley, and this time all three entered. The president, C. Turner, was busy at his desk and the teller was in his cage when Birdwell, waving a nickelplated .45, announced the holdup.

Both Turner and the teller raised their hands without being told to. Then they stared in disbelief as Birdwell paraded back and forth, spinning his .45 automatic on his trigger finger, western style. Apparently he was trying to make an impression, and he did.

Back in the vault, a pair of interested eyes were watching his antics, as they peered through the half-closed door. They belonged to the assistant cashier and bookkeeper, H. C. McCormick. From his vantage point in the vault, he had a clear view of the holdup, by looking between the crack formed by the door and the wall. Silently he picked up a newly purchased shotgun, and thrust its barrel through the crack, just above one of the hinges.

Birdwell told Glass to empty the teller's cash box, and he entered the cage where he hungrily scooped the money into a bag. In the rear of the drawer was a small, neat pile of large bills, and he grabbed these. When he did this, the end of the bills, out of sight, were pulled from between two electrodes, allowing them to touch, and alarm bells clanged in the sheriff's office, and in the town's two hardware stores. Inside the bank there wasn't a sound.

Had Birdwell realized that the 22nd of November was the opening day of the *bird* season, he might have chosen another day for his bank robbery. The two hardware stores were filled with customers, who were picking and choosing among the many shotguns. When the alarm sounded, they simply slipped shells into the new guns, and stepped outside, and waited.

In the vault, McCormick couldn't find the safety catch on the new, and unfamiliar shotgun, so he threw it aside in disgust, and picked up the more familiar 32.20 Winchester rifle. Again he took aim at Birdwell and pulled the trigger.

Birdwell staggered backward, then dropped to his knees, a bullet in his black heart. But he was just down, and not yet out. He pointed his pistol at Turner, and ordered him to help him to his feet.

When Turner had helped Birdwell up, Birdwell suddenly shoved his shining automatic into Turner's stomach, and fired six times. Then both Turner and Birdwell dropped to the floor, Turner dead, and Birdwell dying.

Watching this with horror, were Patterson and Glass, and they fled to the door in panic. Glass was the first one out and he immediately received shotgun blasts from a score of guns. He was literally torn to pieces, and was dead before he hit the ground.

Before some of the "sportsmen" could reload, Patterson nimbly hopped over the prostrate Glass, and made it to the car. Then the deadly guns spoke again, and Patterson fell, his back perforated like the roll of a player piano. The only thing that saved his life was the arrival of the sheriff, who put an end to the "turkey shoot."

Turner and Glass died instantly, but Birdwell lingered on until an ambulance got him to Henryetta, where he also died. Patterson lived to serve a term in the state penitentiary at Mc-Alester. He had lost all interest in making his money "the easy way." Today he lives the quiet life in Arizona, working in a filling station, and occasionally he gets a visit from Major H. C. Mc-Cormick, and they talk about the "good old days."

The hero of the day was of course H. C. McCormick, and the grateful Governor of Oklahoma sent for him in due course. At a special ceremony, held at the capitol, he was made an honorary

Major in the state militia, and Oklahoma voted him a reward of $1,000. This was a princely sum in depression days.

George Birdwell's body was returned to his home town, where he was accorded all the honors usually reserved for local heroes. Thousands attended the funeral, and it is said that Pretty Boy Floyd was among them, dressed as a woman. One unwelcome mourner was a young buck in his late twenties, who had just been made an honorary major. He wasn't molested for he had a strong group of Boley admirers with him.

After the appropriate rituals, Pretty Boy Floyd made the required threats against the life of Birdwell's killer. He even wrote him a little note, telling him he would never live to see Christmas. When this was made public, McCormick became one of the most guarded individuals in the state.

The vigil was maintained until the end of 1932, when it then became apparent that Floyd had just made an empty threat. It was Birdwell who got the final laugh, for McCormick had been carrying Birdwell's nickelplated automatic in his hip-pocket since Floyd's threat, and now he backed into a tree. The gun, with its hair trigger, went off, sending a bullet tearing into McCormick's right leg.

This brought half the town of Boley on the run, fully armed. It is no wonder that Pretty Boy Floyd decided that discretion was the better part of valor. With this kind of protection, Floyd could have gotten himself killed.

The loss of Birdwell seemed to sap some of Floyd's get-up-and-go, and the state enjoyed a breather. In fact Floyd decided to take a trip to New York, where he enjoyed the sights, like any other tourist, and blew his whole bankroll. Before he returned to Oklahoma, however, he stopped long enough in New York to rob a bank, and get back the money he had spent.

iv

As part of a statewide move to combat the plague of bank robberies the state had suffered from for so long, many of the smaller towns formed vigilante committees. These were necessary to back up the overtaxed police authorities in the state.

Alarm systems, such as the one used in Boley, were set up between the banks and certain public places. The alarms, while signaling the vigilantes, did not sound loud enough to warn the bandits or bank robbers. Because of this, more than one bank robber came out of a bank, and found himself in a shoot-out with half the town.

On March 9, 1932, Thursday, Big Al Capone was languishing in the Cook County jail in Chicago, awaiting appeals of his eleven year sentence for tax evasion. He had just made an offer to the cops. If they would let him out of jail, he'd soon find the Lindbergh baby. He loved babies, he told them, and this kidnapping was bad.

That same Thursday, three men drove up in front of the First National Bank of Mill Creek, Oklahoma. They were a newly formed gang, and out to flex their muscles. None of them had had any real experience at bank robberies, and this was to be a disastrous one.

Adam Richetti, a Coalgate, Oklahoma, Italian, was one of the trio, and the most experienced hoodlum. He had been arrested on August 7, 1928, in Hammond, Indiana, for participating in a holdup. Turned over to the County Bureau of Investigation at Crown Point the following day, he was subsequently tried, and sentenced to one to ten years at the state reformatory at Pendleton, Indiana.

This was the same time that the then-unknown John Dillinger was also serving his time at Pendleton. It is doubtful that they ever met or took note of one another. Richetti, however, was paroled September 26, 1930, and received his final discharge a year later, on September 24, 1931.

L. C. (Blackie) Smalley, another of the trio, was from the small town of Seminole, Oklahoma, and had no previous record or experience. Fred Hammer, the final member, was from Wewoka, and had experience as the former deputy sheriff of Seminole County.

Richetti was either elected or appointed himself as wheelman and lookout, so he stayed in the car, while the other two entered the bank. It was here that the lack of experience took over the reins in this deadly game they were playing.

His hands gripping the steering wheel, until their knuckles were white, Richetti kept his eyes glued on the door of the bank. Never once did he take his eyes off that door, and he remained tense and alert for instant take off. He would have done well to look around once in a while, for then he might have seen all those well armed men, slipping up and taking vantage points around the bank.

Smalley and Hammer, equally bereft of experience, slowly

backed out of the bank, clutching a money satchel with only $800 in it. They had no hostages with them to act as a shield, and they came out with their backsides offered as targets to all those guns. This didn't go unnoticed by the members of the Mill Creek Vigilante Committee.

Fred Hammer fell to the ground, killed instantly, in a hail of bullets, and Smalley toppled beside him, seriously wounded. Richetti, stunned for a moment, gunned the car and roared out of town, with a bullet barrage right behind him. He was also wounded, and the car was splattered with bullets. He was forced to abandon it at the edge of town, and take to the fields, on foot.

Two hours later, the vigilantes flushed him from the bushes, and he was taken to Sulphur, where he was given medical attention, and booked for armed robbery.

Later Adam Richetti was sent to McAlester State Penitentiary, for safekeeping. He was received on April 5, 1932, and remained until August 25, 1932, when he was released on bond. He jumped the bond, and became a fugitive, and ran head-on into Pretty Boy Floyd.

Floyd needed a replacement for his late and lamented buddy, George Birdwell, so he asked Richetti if he would like to fill the gap. Despite his almost fatal experience with Fred Hammer and Blackie Smalley, Richetti was overwhelmed, and accepted at once.

The first real test of his new lieutenant came shortly after the start of the new year. They were caught by the law, at Seminole, Oklahoma, but Oklahoma's "will-o'-the-wisp" bandit, Pretty Boy Floyd, and his new partner shot their way to freedom. In fact Richetti acted superbly, covering their retreat with machine gun fire, while Floyd pushed the throttle of their car to the floorboards.

Neither side suffered casualties, but there was a certain amount of wounded pride on the officers' side. $6,000 had just slipped through their roadblock.

The pair proceeded to hit several small town banks, always using Floyd's proven tactics—hit hard, hit fast, and run. They were particularly fond of hitting the small, rich oil towns, just south of Oklahoma City, where money was more plentiful.

After each raid, they would flee into the Cookson Hills, or over the Arkansas border, into the Ozarks. Floyd had many friends here, and he lived like a king, handing out money for protection, left and right. And the poor hill people loved him all the more for it, and the legends grew.

With more and more vigilante committees being formed, and

more lawmen getting bolder, urged on by that $6,000 reward on his head, Floyd decided to seek safer ground. Accordingly the bandits moved their activities into the state of Missouri. Oklahoma never regretted his departure, probably wondering what took him so long.

Wednesday, June 14, 1933, Floyd and Richetti held up the bank in the small town of Mexico, Missouri. A short time later Sheriff Roger Wilson, of Boone County, and Sergeant Ben Booth of the Missouri State Highway Patrol were killed.

They had set up a roadblock at a highway intersection, on the outskirts of Columbia. They were shot when they approached a car to question the occupants.

Because of Pretty Boy Floyd's and Adam Richetti's presence in the area, they received the credit for these killings. They would be suspect until 1938, when another hoodlum confessed to this crime, and by that time it didn't matter to either of them.

v

June 16, 1933, Friday: The day broke bright and beautiful, but the morning activity in Bolivar, Missouri, held little promise of any respite from dull routine. Typical of any small town, the people here went about the same activities they had performed yesterday, and would, most likely, do again to morrow.

The Bitzer Garage, where Joe Richetti was employed as a mechanic, was one of these dull places. Joe busied himself with the usual duties that made up his eight- and sometimes ten-hour days. He was a hard worker, a good mechanic, and a respected citizen of Bolivar. Joe had a wooden leg, but this didn't affect the dexterity of his talented hands.

Present in the garage, also, were the typical worried car owners, fretting about funny noises in their cars' engines, big repair bills, and the big question of who was ahead of whom. Then there were the usual number of hangers-on, who came each day just to look.

It was a little after 7:00 A.M., when two men drove into the garage. They were fresh from a bank robbery, nervous, and driving an overworked automobile that needed immediate repairs. They were also in a desperate hurry and consequently in no mood to wait.

Emerging from their car with a machine gun and a pistol, they quickly and efficiently rounded up everyone in the garage. One of the men—the one brandishing the machine gun—was wanted in Oklahoma, Ohio and Kansas for bank robbery, kidnapping and murder. The other was wanted in Oklahoma, as a fugitive, and now in Missouri for bank robbery and murder. Their names were, of course, Charles "Pretty Boy" Floyd, and Adam Richetti.

Adam had often visited his brother here, in Bolivar, in happier days, but today his visit was one of necessity, and anything but friendly. Now he, as well as Floyd, was one of the hottest items on the nation's wanted lists.

Floyd, laying down the facts of life to Ernest Bitzer, the owner, and to the other terrified citizens, explained tersely, "This is life or death with us. We have to do this because the law would kill us if they could get us. Just line up against the wall, and if you try to get away, we'll kill you."

Joe Richetti and the other two mechanics were put to work on Floyd's tired automobile, and told "get it fixed, and hurry it up!" Floyd and Ernest Bitzer then sat down on a bench, and Floyd began to query him about the latest news, the local law, and the town's habits.

Richetti, who had just exchanged his pistol for a machine gun, wasn't as pleasant as Floyd in explaining things. He was standing guard over them, and he cursed the men, and looked and acted as if he would shoot them all, for the slightest reason. That he could be capable of such mass slaughter, he and Floyd would prove to the world, tomorrow.

Today, however, Floyd, sitting on the bench, admonished, "that liquor's getting the best of you, Eddie. Settle down." Richetti relaxed a little and the tension eased, just a bit.

William "Jack" Killingsworth, only six months in office as the new sheriff of Polk County, drove up at 7:10 A.M.; he parked his car in front of Bitzer's Chevrolet Garage, and went to see if he could get some work done. He had left his gun in the car. He later remarked, "I saw this man, and Ernest Bitzer sitting on a bench, talking, and I knew from Bitzer's face that something was wrong. I took a second look, and I knew what it was."

Adam Richetti knew Killingsworth by sight, as he had grown up in Bolivar, before moving on to Oklahoma. So when the sheriff walked in, Richetti yelled to Floyd, "There's the law!" and then spun to cover him with his machine gun. Floyd jumped from his seat, and also trained his weapon on the sheriff.

Killingsworth scowled at the two guns pointed at his middle, then scanned the faces of the hoodlums holding them. One man he recognized immediately as Adam, Joe's brother, and the other, he was reasonably sure, was Pretty Boy Floyd.

For a moment his entrance charged the air with suspense, but the contest was clearly one-sided, and the sheriff offered no resistance. Grimly Floyd and Richetti motioned, with a wave of their guns, and the sheriff joined the other prisoners.

During all the confusion surrounding the sheriff's sudden entrance, one of the customers, a salesman, managed to slip out the side door, and raced to give the alarm. He was missed immediately, and a sudden sense of urgency gripped the outlaws.

Quickly abandoning all thought of getting Floyd's car repaired, they filled the gas tank of Joe's car and forced the sheriff inside. Adam got in the rear with the sheriff, and Floyd took the wheel. "You can have my car, Joe!" Floyd yelled, good naturedly, as he raced Joe's out of the garage, with a screech of tires. They then headed northwest.

The garage emptied almost immediately, with people, frightened people, fleeing in all directions. Pursuit from Bolivar came at once, and there were times when the posse was only a mile behind, but they lost the criminals in Warsaw, Missouri.

It wasn't until the next day that they found Joe's abandoned car in Deepwater. Skirting the sleepy farm towns like Montrose, Archie, Main City, and Drexel, Floyd headed northwest. Events from this point are best described by Sheriff Killingsworth himself: "Floyd seemed as clean a fellow as I ever ran into, outside his record. He treated me nicer than I ever expected."

He explained his delay in notifying authorities upon his release by Floyd: "I promised Floyd I wouldn't tell. My action is what any man with sense ought to do. They might come back some time, and I am not going to take chances.

"These men are killers," he continued bravely, "they told me I would be safe if I would direct them to safety. Then the highway patrol got right behind us. They stuck a gun in my side, and told me to wave them back—I was more than willing. What worried me from the start was the boys would try to help me out."

The sheriff said Floyd compelled him to flag down a car near Deepwater. The driver of the car was Walter Griffith of Clinton, a real estate man, and he was driving his pride and joy, his new Pontiac. When he stopped to see what the sheriff wanted, the outlaws commandeered the car, taking Griffith prisoner.

Griffith sat up front with Floyd, while Killingsworth and

Richetti sat in the rear. Richetti kept taking long drags on a fruit jar, filled with moonshine whiskey, and was in a surly mood.

Griffith, not knowing who his captors were, nearly got himself killed fussing about his new car. He told Floyd he was driving too fast, and when they stopped, near Ottawa, Kansas, to wait for darkness, he told Floyd to be careful and not scratch the paint. Right then and there Richetti wanted to dispose of one passenger, but Floyd said no. Griffith, getting the message, shut up.

While they were resting, and waiting for the approaching darkness, Floyd seemed to be in a depressed mood. He asked the sheriff, "How would you like to be hunted day and night? How would you like to sleep with this thing [he touched the machine gun] over your knees." He brooded about this for a moment, then added, "They'll get me. Sooner or later I'll go down full of lead. That's how it will end."

Finally Floyd stood up, stretching his legs, and said, "Well, Eddie, I guess it's time to go." The four of them then loaded up, and about 11:00 p.m. they arrived in Kansas City.

It was in the Central Industrial district of Kansas City that Floyd stopped, and went into a building to make a phone call. When he came out, he drove the car to 9th Street and Hickory, where he told his two prisoners to get out.

Fear stuck in the throats of the two, as they awaited the sudden death they were sure was coming, "You wait here for five minutes," Floyd told them, "and then walk down and get into this car. You then drive home and don't call no one because we will be watching."

Then Floyd drove the car on ahead for a short distance. Almost immediately the two hostages saw another car approaching, and heard the clanking of guns as they were being transferred to the other vehicle. The car then drove away, heading in the direction of downtown Kansas City.

After waiting for a respectable period of time, Griffith and Killingsworth gingerly approached the car. There was no one in sight, and only an empty fruit jar in the back seat, reeking of moonshine, was left to remind them of their nightmare.

"Floyd told me to take the golf bags he left in the car they abandoned at the garage to remember him by. But," Killingsworth valiantly told officers later, "I told him I wouldn't need anything to remember *him* by."

vi

Friday, June 16, 1933. In Hot Springs, Arkansas, two agents of the FBI, together with the police chief of McAlester, Oklahoma, closed in on their quarry.

This was the era in American history when federal officers were not permitted to carry firearms, except upon special occasions. They also held no powers of arrest, other than those of the average citizen, and were required to secure local assistance when the power of arrest was necessary.

It was under these conditions that Special Agents Frank Smith, and Frank Lackey, dependent upon the help of Chief Otto Reed of McAlester, arrested their man, one Frank "Jelly" Nash, handcuffed him, and sped away to safety.

Nash, college bred and 49 years old, had escaped from the Federal Penitentiary at Leavenworth, Kansas, where he had been a trustee, on October 19, 1930. Shortly thereafter, he had begun to work again at his old trade of bank robbery and other crimes.

Nash had a very unsavory past. He had been involved in a murder at Hobart, Oklahoma, his home town, March, 1913, but had been tried and acquitted. He was convicted of the murder of a witness in his first trial, September 13, 1913, in Kiowa County, Oklahoma. He was then sent to McAlester Penitentiary for life, as Frank Nash, Number 4458.

On March 25, 1918, his sentence was commuted to ten years, and on July 10, 1918, after serving only four years, and seven months, Nash was granted a full pardon. He then went out and robbed the Corn State Bank at Corn, Oklahoma, by explosives and was sentenced to 25 years at McAlester.

After a little less than three years, he made application for clemency, in the form of a 60-day furlough, alleging business reasons. On December 29, 1922, the Governor of Oklahoma signed an order commuting the 25-year sentence to five years. The following day, December 30, 1922, Nash was discharged.

Less than eight months later, August 20, 1923, Nash participated in a holdup and robbery of a mail train, in Osage County, Oklahoma. This was undoubtedly the "business reasons," he had in mind when he applied for his 60-day furlough.

The mail train robbery was a federal offense, and he was sentenced in the U. S. District Court for the Western District of Oklahoma, at Oklahoma City, March 1, 1924. He received 25

years for assaulting a mail custodian. He was subsequently sent
to Leavenworth, March 3, 1924, where he remained until his
escape, October 19, 1930.

With no hope of a parole from the federal penitentiary, Nash
worked out a carefully conceived plan. He became a model
prisoner, and as such was made a trustee. Finally came the day
when he was given an outside assignment, and he just walked
away. No muss, no fuss, no bother—it had been just that simple.

After the escape, Nash had gone to Joplin, Missouri, where he
held a reunion with his old prison buddy, Herbert (Deafy)
Farmer. They were both graduates of the Oklahoma State Penitentiary.

Later Nash went to Chicago, where he owned a joint, and he
was often a visitor of another gangster buddy, Louis (Doc) Stacci,
owner of the O. P. Inn in Melrose Park, Illinois. It was in Stacci's
place that he met a good looking brunette using the name of
Frances Luce.

Nash was bald as a billiard ball, with just a dark fringe of hair
around the back of his head and over his ears. He was anything
but handsome, with his large, hooked nose, pointed chin, and
prominent ears; but no matter—it was love at first sight, and
soon they were married. Of course, Nash had another wife at the
time, but little things such as this never bothered him.

He then took extraordinary precautions to disguise his appearance. First he had a nose job in Chicago, to take a little of the
hook out. Next he grew a bushy mustache, purchased a most
handsome head of hair, and sported a pair of fancy nose glasses.
He always changed names much like some people change handkerchiefs.

Eventually he moved to Hot Springs, Arkansas, with his new
wife, and they registered at the Woodcock Apartments, as Mr.
and Mrs. Harris. They had checked out of the apartment two
weeks before he was arrested, and moved into a motel.

In Hot Springs, Nash reported to Dutch Akers, Chief of Detectives, received his orders, and then was introduced to Richard
T. Galatas, who owned the White Front Cigar Store. Galatas was
the go-between for hoodlums and Dutch Akers (and Aker's boss
was Police Chief Joseph Wakelin).

The White Front subsequently became one of Nash's favorite
hangouts, but he was also fond of visiting night clubs. He had a
fine baritone voice, and sometimes was persuaded to sing his
favorite song, "A Shanty In Old Shantytown." Always, after he

sang, he would distribute money among the members of the orchestra, which would explain, in part, why his voice was so popular.

On June 16, 1933, he drove his roadster to the White Front Cigar Store, and parked it nearby. Inside he bought a bottle of 3.2 beer, and as "Doc" Williams stood around chatting with a few buddies. At this moment Frank Nash's whole world came crashing down around his ears.

Three men walked into the store, on upper Central Avenue, purchased some cigars, and turning to leave drew pistols. They surrounded Nash, and one of them shoved a pistol into his stomach and told him, "Put the beer down, and get into that automobile," pointing to a sedan with California license plates. Then two of them escorted Nash to the car, keeping him covered, while the third remained, for a moment, looking up and down Central Avenue. He then joined the others, and the sedan sped down the street, turned left, and was gone.

As Frank Smith, federal agent out of Oklahoma City, later explained—"We pegged Nash right in front of a pool hall and race booking joint at Hot Springs. From a car, we saw him contact a couple of other fellows. Then he pulled away from them again, and we pulled up and hopped out.

"I knew he was very bald with only a fringe of hair. There was a full head of brown hair on this man. He wore a black mustache, too, and had on some nose glasses. Nash didn't resist. He entered our car, and we tore out on the highway, taking the road to Joplin so that we could throw off anyone that tried to follow.

"I pulled Nash's hair, and off it came—a toupee. Then he saw me eyeing his mustache, and he smiled at that, and assured me that it was real. 'That's a good toupee,' Nash said, 'I paid $100 for that in Chicago.'

"It was a wonder that we weren't killed when we took Nash. He had been there for some time, and was surrounded by his own gang of outlaws and criminals.

"Our method was to work fast and get him out of the country before anyone could get hold of us. Nash had been a notorious bandit, and train robber in the Al Spencer gang, and many other gangs, for years. [It was federal agents who had ended the violent career of Nash's chief, Al Spencer, when they cornered the robber and killer in the Osage hills of Oklahoma, ten years before.]

"Nash had been one of the desperate killers and bandits of the Middle West. We knew that. That's why we acted cautiously.

That's why, when I learned that Nash was in Hot Springs, I asked Chief Reed to go with Lackey and me.

"Nash had been in Chicago since his escape from Leavenworth. He told me that, on the way up from Arkansas. He had had a good set-up in Chicago, a joint up there with beer and other stuff like that. He told me he had some slot machines working there too, and making money on them."

And so it was on June 16, 1933, that two FBI agents and a police chief from Oklahoma had to sneak into Hot Springs, Arkansas, grab their man, and then run for their lives.

The main problem in Hot Springs was the Chief of Police, Joseph Wakelin, who operated his department in a very lax manner. His chief of detectives, one Dutch Akers, had established an unholy alliance between the law enforcement authorities of Hot Springs, and the underworld.

For a cut of the take, crime flourished there with complete immunity from the police. The town was also wide open for all visiting hoods, as long as they didn't try to undercut local operations. It therefore became a rest haven for such unsavory characters as New York's Lucky Luciano, Alvin Karpis, selected members of Al Capone's mob, and members of Detroit's Purple Gang.

Akers was a tall, six foot four character, slender, with stooped shoulders. As he shuffled his way around Hot Springs, in a lazy kind of gait, his large, almost owlish eyes saw no evil.

He spent a lot of time with Galatas, since they split the take on the baseball pool concession, a type of numbers racket. He also got his rakeoff from every prostitute in town, and in his spare time sold police weapons to visiting gangsters for their use elsewhere. Akers was not unique, for he had his counterparts in Chicago, Kansas City, St. Paul, and other so-called "safe cities" throughout the country.

vii

For the FBI agents and Otto Reed, the trip out of Hot Springs was a harrowing experience indeed. They had planned to drive their prisoner to Joplin, and then on to Kansas City. A series of mysterious happenings was soon to make them change their minds.

First, upon entering Benton, Arkansas, they were stopped by the local police, who had established a roadblock. They told Smith that they had received word from the police department in Hot Springs that a man had been kidnapped there, and they were checking all cars coming from that direction.

When Smith and Lackey identified themselves, the Benton police allowed them to proceed. They then telephoned Dutch Akers in Hot Springs, and reported that they had intercepted the men, who had displayed badges and claimed to be government officers, and that they had let them go.

Upon reaching Little Rock, they again ran into a roadblock, put up by Captain Martin, and Sergeants Henson, Traweek, and Easterly, all of the Little Rock Police Department. Once more they identified themselves, but refused to divulge the name of their prisoner. Satisfied that Smith and Lackey were who they claimed to be, the Captain gave them safe escort through Little Rock and out the other side, to the city limits.

They later stopped at Russellville, Arkansas, to eat, and ponder their next move. Obviously there was some sinister force at work, for their "secret maneuvers" to throw off all pursuit from Hot Springs had suddenly become a farce. They voted to continue on to Fort Smith, and formulate future plans from there.

At Fort Smith, they held a hasty conference, and decided to call Special Agent Raymond Caffrey, in Kansas City, for advice. Caffrey told them to leave the car there, at Fort Smith, and take a train the rest of the way. He, Caffrey said, would meet them at the Union Station, with sufficient reinforcements to preclude any attempt to free Nash. They took a stateroom on the Missouri Pacific, and left at 8:00 P.M., for Kansas City, Missouri.

While the FBI agents and Otto Reed were wheeling out of Hot Springs, with Nash in tow, the underworld wheels had also started to turn. The "sinister force," in the person of Richard Tallman Galatas, better known as "Dick," was the owner of the White Front Cigar Store where Nash had been apprehended. With a series of phone calls, he would set in motion forces that would eventually result in the deaths of at least nine men, and put himself behind bars.

Dick Galatas was a distinguished looking man, with greying hair about the temples, and cold steel-grey eyes. He was a heavy-set man, and had that look of respectability all confidence men must have to be successful at their trade.

Galatas, who had once been a bank clerk in Chicago, was a known confidence man, and was very successful at his chosen profession. He had worked Milwaukee, Chicago, Detroit, and even California with satisfactory returns.

Originally he had come to Hot Springs because he thought the hot baths would be good for his rheumatism. In a series of trips there he had become friendly with Dutch Akers, and by 1933 was running the White Front Cigar Store and living there permanently.

Soon his place became a rendezvous for hoodlums from all over. It was here that Dutch Akers made his contacts with the underworld, and the underworld paid for its unusual privileges.

With the arrest of Nash, Galatas first called Akers, and notified him of the "federal snatch." Dutch immediately put out an APB, together with the story that a man had been kidnapped in Hot Springs, and "taken for a ride," by unknown persons.

He asked all police officers between Hot Springs and Joplin to be on the look out for a Buick sedan, bearing California license plates, and to arrest the occupants. Just what he hoped to accomplish with this is unknown. Perhaps he had some idea that Nash would eventually be turned over to his custody, and he could either help him escape, or have him shut-up for good.

Busy Galatas then drove out to Nash's place, at the Oak Park Tourist Camp, and told the new Mrs. Nash that her husband had been abducted by the law. There, he also called Louis (Doc) Stacci at the O. P. Inn in Melrose Park, a suburb of Chicago.

Dutch Akers then called Galatas, and told him that the "Feds" apparently were taking Nash to Joplin, as they had been spotted in Benton, Arkansas. With this news, Galatas called Herbert (Deafy) Farmer, gambler, ex-con, and sometime chicken rancher, in Joplin. He told him, through Herbert's wife, Esther, of the sudden chain of events. Farmer advised Galatas to get Mrs. Nash, and fly up to Joplin; meanwhile he would handle things at that end.

Quickly Galatas gathered up Mrs. Nash, and her seven-year-old daughter, and hurried to the municipal airport in Hot Springs. There they told John Stover, the owner, their tale of woe. After some haggling over prices, Stover agreed to fly them to Joplin, for $100.

In Joplin, Stover landed at the abandoned airfield there, but was told by Harry Song, who operated a beer stand nearby, that the plane would have to be registered at the new airport, on the Webb City Road. Galatas, unconcerned about such trivia, used Song's phone, and called a cab from Joplin. When it came he, Mrs. Nash, and her little daughter climbed in, and they rushed to Joplin.

Stover, confounded by a determined Harry Song, took off and landed his plane again, this time at the new airport. Here he signed his name, in an almost illegible handwriting, as "John Stacy," or "John Stover." He gave his home field as Fort Smith, his plane as a Ryan B-1, with numbers NC 7672, and his license number as 21265. He reported his first landing at the old airport as being made at 6:00 P.M., and the second at 6:20 P.M.

The cab took Galatas, Mrs. Nash, and her daughter Darnell to a drugstore in Joplin, which was one of Farmer's favorite hangouts. Here they were met by Herbert and Esther, and they went straight to their 20-acre chicken ranch, just out of Joplin.

Shortly after 8:00 P.M., the Farmers received a call from Dutch Akers, in Hot Springs, advising them of the federal officers' change in plans. He told them the officers had left their car in Fort Smith, at the railroad station, and had taken the Missouri Pacific to Kansas City.

Mrs. Nash had been told by Frank that if anything ever happened to him she was to call Louis Stacci in Chicago. She put in a call, the second one, to the O. P. Inn; she got Stacci and told him, "The government's got Frank. He's being taken back to prison at Leavenworth."

Stacci then called Fritz Mulloy, told him what had happened, and to get in touch with Vernon C. Miller. Mulloy gave Stacci Miller's number, and Stacci called him and issued the order, "The law's got Frankie. They'll be at the Union Station in the morning. Go down there and take Nash away from them."

Vernon C. Miller was a small, five foot, eight, 160 pound fellow, with piercing blue eyes and a shock of blonde hair. His appearance belied a vicious nature, and a dark and brooding soul. He did not look, act, or even talk like a criminal. His dress was conservative, and he presented the appearance of someone who belonged to the best of society.

Miller had active memberships in respectable country clubs in Asheville, North Carolina, and Kansas City. A good golfer, he often posed as a wealthy oil man when he traveled, and made people believe it. He was also reputed to be quite a ladies' man.

He came from a good family, and his father was a respected citizen of White Lake, South Dakota. After Miller graduated from high school, the wanderlust hit him, and he became a fighter, a parachute jumper at county fairs, and at one time he even jumped from smoke-filled balloons.

When the World War came along, Miller joined up at once,

and went to France, where he was eventually promoted to sergeant. As the legend goes, he became the A. E. F. champion of quick shooting.

Upon Miller's return to his home town of Huron, South Dakota, he was welcomed as the hero of the moment. They quickly elected him Sheriff of Beadle County.

While serving in this capacity, he ran up an excellent record as a man hunter. It is said that he was very fond of shooting his initials in the rear end of automobiles filled with fleeing bootleggers.

Then everything went wrong for Miller. He was renominated for the sheriff's position, but before the election he disappeared and a shortage in his accounts was discovered.

He was arrested for embezzlement of public funds in 1923, and sent to prison for two years. He was released in 1925, and started a whole new career as a rumrunner, bringing in liquor from Canada.

He was again arrested, this time in Sioux Falls, South Dakota, and charged with bootlegging. He jumped bail, and subsequently embarked upon a career that made him one of the most feared guns in the country.

He became a member of the St. Paul gang of Tommy Holden and Francis Keating. At first, as the legend goes, Holden and Keating were skeptical of Miller, because he had once been a sheriff. He said he'd prove his loyalty, and asked the name of a hood they didn't particularly like. Then he kidnapped the hood, took him into the open country, and proceeded to break all ten of his fingers. Then he let the hood go, without killing him, and Holden and Keating were convinced: the man was a nut.

Verne Miller, Tommy Holden, Francis Keating, Harvey J. Bailey, Frank Nash, Frank Weber, and Charlie Harmon all held up the Kraft State Bank at Menomonie, Wisconsin. During the robbery they took the bank president's son as a hostage, but on their way out of town, Weber and Harmon killed him. This was considered bad taste by the rest of the gang, so they killed Weber and Harmon, dumping their bodies in a ditch.

Gus Winkler and Al Capone in Chicago came to know Miller, and had a high regard for his gun. He made buddies of Frank Nash, and Harvey Bailey, and his connections finally grew until he was a sometime member of Detroit's Purple Gang.

He was a cold-blooded killer, and completely unemotional; but he had two weaknesses. He loved whiskey, and drank prodigious amounts of it, and as Holden and Keating had found out he was a complete nut. He had to have been a mental case to do the things he would do in the next 24 hours.

While working with the Purple Gang in Detroit, Miller had met a pretty, bright and clever little blonde, who was using the name of Vivian Mathis, alias Vivian Gibson, alias Vivian Matthews. She had flashy brown eyes, beaded eyelashes, smooth skin, and a baby voice. She also had a 10-year-old daughter named Betty. When Miller left Detroit for Chicago he took Vivian with him.

Later he moved to Kansas City with his paramour and took up residence under the name of Moore, at 6612 Edgevale Road, a white, clapboard house, in the Armour Hills District. This was the place assigned to him by John Lazia, ward-heeler, gangster, and political boss of Kansas City's north side.

When a new hood came to town, the rule was "behave yourself; and keep the heat off this town. If you start some kind of racket here, we get part of the action." With this kind of alliance between the underworld, and the political forces in Kansas City Miller settled down for a few months of leisure and fun.

It wasn't long before the house at 6612 Edgevale Road had become known throughout the underworld as a safe place to rest while the heat was on.

Miller was playing golf at the south side golf club when Vivian Mathis drove up in a car and told him that Herbert Farmer had called from Joplin, Missouri. There had also been a call from Louis Stacci in Chicago, and one from Fitz Mulloy. They talked at the car for about five minutes, while his companions waited to tee off.

To understand what happened next, it is necessary to flash ahead in time to 1934. It was nearly midnight, July 10, 1934, when two men stepped from their hiding place in the shrubs in front of a fashionable apartment house in Kansas City, and riddled one John Lazia with machine gun bullets.

Tom Pendergast sent flowers to his old friend, and two of the pallbearers, doing their bit for "Good Old Johnny," were Charles Gargotta and Charles Binaggio. A few years later Charles Gargotta and Charles Binaggio would go up the underworld ladder and become bigshots in their own right. On April 6, 1950, their bullet-riddled bodies were found in the First District Democratic Headquarters in Kansas City.

Jack Gregory and Al O'Brien killed Lazia, and it was suspected by Lazia's boys that Michael Jimmy ("The Needle") LaCapra, drove the getaway car. Lazia's boys tried to kill Gregory, but only wounded him. Later Gregory was arrested on another charge, and someone immediately posted his bail. Two hours later he disappeared.

LaCapra had quarreled with Lazia over rackets, demanding a larger place of his own. He had been running a small bookie joint on the north side of Kansas City. A few weeks later he shot it out with gangsters on Independence Avenue, then ran into a post office sub station and escaped.

He later went to Augusta, Kansas, but a carload of gangsters followed him there and tried to kill him again. After a gun battle both LaCapra and the Kansas City gangsters were picked up. LaCapra was returned to Kansas City, where two efforts were made to get him released on a $50,000 bond, but LaCapra refused. He remembered what had happened to Jack Gregory and he was getting worried.

On October 10, 1934, while languishing in the Jackson County jail, LaCapra decided to turn himself over to the Federal authorities, so he pleaded guilty to a violation of the Dyer Act, taking a stolen car across a state line. Upon a promise that they wouldn't prosecute he told FBI agents what they wanted to know. He said that, on the night of June 16, 1933, Verne Miller walked through the downtown Kansas City streets, and entered the Baltimore Annex, at 1106 Baltimore Avenue, and asked for Lazia. He asked John Lazia for his help in getting Nash away from the "Feds." Lazia had vetoed the idea of using local talent, and voiced the opinion that Miller must be out of his mind to even try such a delivery.

Back at his house on Edgevale Road, Miller had made long distance calls to contacts in Detroit, Chicago, and New York, vainly seeking help. By now the idea had become an obsession with him, and he seemed almost desperate. All his contacts turned him down, with the same answer, "it's just too late to get anyone there in time."

Shortly after 11:00 o'clock Lazia had a change of heart, and called Miller to tell him that there were two nervous triggermen in town who might be interested in his proposition. Their names were Pretty Boy Floyd and Adam Richetti.

Through the good offices of Fitz Mulloy, a meeting had been set up downtown. After the meeting, Miller, Floyd and Richetti retired to Miller's house to formulate their final plans and have a few beers. Miller then put through a call to Herbert Farmer's place in Joplin, and asked to talk to Frances Nash.

Frances was still crying uncontrollably, as she poured out her sad tale of woe to Miller, who already knew the details. He consoled her, and told her not to worry. "I'll take care of things, on this end. I'll call you later."

Then he hung up and drove to the Union Station, where he laid his final plans. Around midnight, his reconnaissance trip finished, he again called the Farmer ranch, and told Frances, "Cheer up. You'll see Jelly again soon." When Frances kept up her sobbing, he hung up in disgust.

For his testimony, Jimmy "The Needle" LaCapra was released from custody, and his case was *nolle prosequi.* He immediately fled to New York, in hopes of escaping the gangland vengeance he knew would be waiting for him. A short time later his body was found along a highway in upstate New York, with a neat, round bullet hole in the forehead.

viii

The date was June 17, 1933, it was Saturday, and the time 7:20 A.M. The weather was a bright and pleasant 70 degrees. The Harvey Restaurant was filled with breakfast diners, and an event was about to take place here at the Union Station in Kansas City that would shake an entire nation right down to its apathetic boots.

It is best told by Special Agent R. E. Vetterli of the FBI, by Special Agent Frank Smith, and by Mrs. Lottie West, a travelers' aid worker—an eyewitness and later to be one of the Attorney General's star witnesses.

"I don't believe they intended to kill Nash," Agent Vetterli said in recounting the details of the massacre at the Union Station. "We went to the station to meet the officers who were bringing Nash back from Hot Springs. Raymond Caffrey and I drove to the station in his Chevrolet coach.

"The two Kansas City Detectives, Hermanson and Grooms had come in their car. There were eight of us, including Nash, and we were to enter Caffrey's car. The Kansas City detectives were to follow us in their car to Leavenworth.

"I was standing at the rear, and west side of Caffrey's car. In the back seat were Lackey and Smith, and Otto Reed. Caffrey was to drive; however Nash had sat in the driver's seat, temporarily, until the car was loaded. Then he had to move over into the other front seat, which was folded up to allow the three men to enter the rear.

"Caffrey stood on the pavement, beside Nash, on the east side of the car, waiting for Nash to slide over. Frank Hermanson, and W. J. (Red) Grooms, were standing on the west side, toward the front.

"Suddenly I heard a man say, 'put 'em up, up, up!' I looked and saw a man blazing away with a machine gun, from near the southwest corner of the car. He seemed to be standing on something, perhaps the running board of a car. I crouched under the murderous fire. I believe there were other machine guns working too.

"Hermanson and Grooms fell to the pavement in front of me, their bodies riddled. The windshield of Caffrey's car was splintered, the men inside powerless before the fire.

"I fell to the pavement. I felt a stinging pain in my left arm. When the firing ceased—and it was all over in a flash—I leveled my pump gun at the escaping car, which roared westward out of the station parking lot."

Special Agent Frank Smith, the only one to escape the slaughter without a scratch, presented this version:

"I heard 'Up, up.' The words came fast. I reached for my six shooter, drew it, and then looked up in time to see a man aiming a machine gun. It was shooting red flame.

"I don't know what all happened. I ducked as bullets splintered our car. I crouched down and played dead. It was the only thing that could be done. If the fellow had a six shooter, I could match him, but not a machine gun.

"I felt my friend Reed sag down upon me. I looked up and saw Nash had been hit. His toupee had fallen down into the car. Lackey began to groan. It was over quicker than you could imagine.

"I put my arm under Reed's head and tried to comfort Lackey. I noticed Lackey's revolver handle had been splintered. Maybe that was why he wasn't killed outright, like the others. Maybe the bullet ricocheted.

"I don't know where the machine guns were stationed, except the one I saw aimed at the car. It seemed to be in the hands of the man who had shouted, 'up, up.' He was standing up high. Maybe on the running board of one of the cars parked in the parking lot."

Mrs. Lottie West, Travelers Aid Worker, Union Station, Kansas City, presented this version:

"I saw the killers of the government agent, city detectives, the Oklahoma police chief, and Frank Nash, in front of the Union

Station this morning. They were calmly awaiting their victims to group themselves about the motor car, which was to take them to Leavenworth.

"I saw them step out of hiding and deliberately open fire. The first men to fall were the officers. Nash was one of the last to be killed.

"Sitting at my desk, I had watched the group of officers take Nash through the doors from the trains, and march him across the lobby. Two of the officers carried sawed-off shotguns, and another kept his hand on his hip, ready to draw his revolver.

"The group crossed the station, fan shaped, Nash in the center. Nash was handcuffed. 'He must be pretty bad,' I remarked to a friend. 'Maybe he is Pretty Boy Floyd.'

"I followed the group out to the station platform, watched them walk across the street, and saw them direct Nash to get in the front seat of the motor car. Some of the officers went on each side of the car. The two carrying sawed-off shotguns leaned these guns against the left-hand, front fender of the car. [Hermanson and Grooms.]

"Just at that time a large man, who would weigh about 200 pounds, stepped out from behind the lamp post, beside the concrete bus landing. He was carrying one of those guns with a cylinder on top of it. He started shooting right into the back of the two officers.

"At about the same time, two men stepped out from behind my automobile, which was parked a little west of the officers' car, and facing north. Both were small men. One had what appeared to be a shotgun, and the other a machine gun.

"They started shooting at the other officers. The officers fell to the ground, except one on the west side of the car, in which Nash was sitting. He started shooting at the two men back of my car. He was shooting right by Nash. *I believe he shot Nash.*

"There were six Catholic sisters on the platform. I called to them to run out of danger. Four did, but the other two stood still. When I looked again, I saw Mike Fanning, a motorcycle patrolman, assigned to the station, running through the station doors. 'There he is, Mike, get him!' I shouted, pointing to the big gunman.

"Fanning started shooting, firing three shots. The big man dropped to the ground, and I thought he was hit. I ran back to the station then, and did not see how the killers escaped."

Thus you have three versions of how the Kansas City Massacre took place. There were many other versions, and other variations of the same story. These were chosen because they were given by the persons who should know—the men being shot at, and by the Federal Government's star witness. The results, however, were the same.

In seconds, the deed was done, and as the smoke of the machine guns lifted, Grooms and Hermanson lay where they had fallen together. Their heads and bodies were riddled with machine gun bullets, and their hats were blown several feet away by the force of the guns, and were literally shredded to bits.

In the back seat of Caffrey's car lay Chief Reed, dead before he even knew how, or why. On the other end of the same seat, directly behind Nash, lay Agent Lackey, with two .45 bullets lodged in his spine, and a third near his pelvic bone. While he would live with these wounds, it would be a painful life, and his disability would eventually force him to retire from active service.

In the center sat Agent Frank Smith: stunned, bewildered, but by some miracle completely unharmed by the bullets. It was later thought that the gunmen might have mistaken him for Nash. He was sitting in the position most criminals are transported in.

By the door on the driver's side, slumped in death, lay Agent Caffrey, after being tossed like a rag doll by the machine gun fire. Agent Vetterli, still at the rear of the car, lay on the pavement, wounded in the arm, but otherwise physically unharmed.

And what of Nash, the man Floyd and Richetti had been hired to free? Frank "Jelly" Nash was still sitting behind the steering wheel of the car. He had lost not only his expensive toupee but an important part of the right side of his head. In short, Mr. Frank "Jelly" Nash, was very, very dead.

Remembering the words of a Missouri Sheriff, who described Floyd as being "as clean a fellow as I ever ran into, outside his record," and remembering also his admonition "I promised Floyd I wouldn't tell. My action is what any man with sense ought to do. They might come back some time and I am not going to take any chances." Remembering all this, one must then stand in awe and admiration of Mrs. Lottie West, who not only gave the full story of what she had witnessed but lated identified Pretty Boy Floyd, from rogue's gallery photographs, at police headquarters.

Picking out a picture of Floyd from the many put before her, Mrs. Lottie West said, "That's the man I saw fire on the officers with a sub machine gun! I noticed him first, sitting at my desk in the Union Station, as early as 7:00 A.M. The man left immediately when I stepped up.

"The man with the machine gun was about 30 years old. He

had a round face, ruddy complexion, wore a dark blue suit, with a white shirt, and a turned-down panama hat. I would think he weighed nearly 200 pounds."

This description would later tally almost exactly with the one furnished by the employees of the Bitzer Chevrolet garage, in Bolivar. They, however, described the suit as dark brown, and also added that he was wearing white shoes.

Robert Fritts, a cab starter, saw the entire thing from his position in the parking lot. The crime was also witnessed by Charles Moore, a cab driver, who was sitting in his car nearby. In fact there were many more people who saw the massacre; but of all these people Mrs. West would be the only one who would testify at the conspiracy trials in Kansas City, a year and a half later.

Confusion reigned supreme in Kansas City, and in Washington for many months. Positive identification by other witnesses would mark the killers as George "Machine Gun" Kelly, Harvey Bailey, Robert Brady, Wilbur C. Underhill, and others. Warrants would be issued for the arrest of these hoodlums.

All the while, the testimony of Mrs. Lottie West would be treated, by both the FBI and the Kansas City authorities, as that of questionable value. No one could conceive any idea as to why, or how, Vernon C. Miller, who was identified almost immediately, and Pretty Boy Floyd and Richetti would unite in such an action. Their paths had never before crossed, and while Miller was a personal friend of Nash's, Floyd had never even heard of him.

When the FBI eventually found Miller's place, at 6612 Edgevale Road, they were too late. Miller had long since fled, and his household goods had been moved to Fritz Mulloy's place. When they did search the house, the FBI was certain he had been one of the machine gunners, but had no idea who the other two were.

Right now, their attention was on his place, but no entry was made, for the furniture was still there. The neighbors were questioned about the "Moores." It was Joe Ann Alford, age nine, of 6621 Edgevale, who fingered Moore as Verne Miller. He was known as Mr. V. C. Moore. The girl also pointed out the driver of his car as William (Two Gun) Weissman. Joe Ann had often played with Betty, the 10-year-old daughter of Mrs. Moore (Vivian Mathis).

Other neighbors testified that cabs came and went at all hours, and that at one time they had seen cars from six different states parked at or around the residence. On the weekend of the massacre, however, the house was quiet; but Miller and Weissman returned Monday in a large Packard. A week later a truck had backed up and hauled away several items of household goods, but no furniture.

Federal agents gave several neighbors pairs of binoculars, and asked them to keep watch on the house, and its visitors, but it was too late. Vivian Mathis and her daughter had fled the weekend of the massacre, and Miller fled the following week. They rendervoused in Chicago.

Eventually FBI agents and Kansas City authorities gained entry into the house. Jack B. Jenkins a fingerprint expert for the bureau, took several empty beer bottles away with him. They had been found in the cellar of the house. He later developed three latent prints of Verne Miller on one of the bottles, and one of Adam Richetti on another.

This, the missing link that coupled Miller with Richetti, was the first real break in the case. It therefore followed that Pretty Boy Floyd couldn't be far behind. Suddenly Mrs. Lottie West's testimony took on an entirely different light.

The real story of just who killed Nash will never be known. It seems highly probable that Nash was killed by the careless machine gun fire being spewed around the scene, and hardly feasible that a trained marksman like Vetterli did it by accident.

Investigation revealed that it was Miller who demanded Nash, and that Nash attempted to pull himself out of the car. Detective Grooms then opened fire with his shotgun and someone, possibly Miller, said "Let 'em have it." The slaughter began.

In a last desperate effort to save himself, Nash had cried, "For God's sake, don't shoot *me!*" but his pleas were drowned out by the chatter of machine guns. After all the fire had stopped, Floyd peered into the car, and shouted, "They are all dead. Let's get the hell out of here!"

As a gesture of international goodwill and mourning for the slaughtered officers, General Guillermo, Chief of Police, Mexico City, on June 18, 1933, instructed his force of 4,500 men to stand at attention for one minute at 5:30 P.M. in silent tribute to the fallen officers of the Kansas City massacre. He also made an impressive radio speech in tribute to them, which was translated into English and beamed to the United States. He knew only too well that crime is an international disease which knows no boundaries.

ix

Following the Kansas City Massacre, Attorney General Homer Cummings ordered every law enforcement agency under his control into the quest for the killers. This included the FBI, which set out to bring in Verne Miller, Machine Gun Kelly, Wilbur C. Underhill, Robert Brady, Harvey Bailey, Charles "Pretty Boy" Floyd, and Adam Richetti, among others, as possible killers in the massacre.

With the massacre also came the cry of the public, who until now had viewed the battle between criminals and police authorities with a kind of detached interest. They also looked upon the criminal as a sort of underdog, battling a huge organization.

Nothing could have been further from the truth, for it was the law-enforcement agencies who fought the criminals at an extreme disadvantage. They were hampered by a lack of money, a shortage of manpower, insufficient training, crooked politicians, and an apathetic public.

Many highway patrol and state police organizations were mostly paper units. In all too many cases the clerk typists and file clerks outnumbered the law enforcement officers. Many were required to use obsolete equipment, were poorly paid, and even had to buy the bullets they fired at the criminals.

At times it was a thankless and frustrating job, for as fast as they put the criminals in the front doors of the nation's prisons, there were other forces at work letting them out the back. Coupled with the totally inadequate laws that limited the nation's police forces to city, county, and state borders, and the general "I don't care" attitude of many of the nation's citizens, you can plainly see it was the forces of the police that were the underdogs.

With powerful cars, the criminals in America robbed and killed in many states, and often traveled thousands of miles during a single raid.

Like a predatory animal, Pretty Boy Floyd emerged from his lairs to prey on the small and the unprotected. Sometimes his forays took him as far north as New York, as far south as Kentucky, and as far west as Colorado. These hit and run tactics, with people willing to help, hide, and protect him, gave longer life to his depredations.

It was an outraged Congress, urged on by its equally outraged constituents, which began to pass needed laws to combat this

crime menace. Soon the FBI was armed with the necessary powers
it had been previously denied.

Laws that made it a federal crime to strike a federal officer
while performing his duties, but only a state offense to kill him,
were changed. Federal men were given the powers of arrest and
were allowed to carry weapons to enforce this power and protect
themselves. It was with this added power that the FBI, with less
than 300 special agents scattered throughout the country, set
about to do battle with the outlaw and the killer.

Pretty Boy Floyd had been wounded in the shoulder by a shot
from Mike Fanning's gun. As a result he was taken to the West
Bottoms of Kansas City, where he moved into a hideout in a
rooming house. Then a doctor was summoned and his wounds
dressed.

There was a long discussion among Johnny Lazia's henchmen,
as to whether Floyd would be able to travel or not. Floyd, over-
hearing the discussion, walked into the room and snatched up a
machine gun, which was laying on a nearby table. He threw the
gun up to his shoulder and sighted down the barrel. "I'll be able
to travel all right," he said firmly, then grinned. That ended that
discussion.

Richetti, who had driven the getaway car from the Union
Station, was again elected driver; the fugitives were given a car
belonging to Jack Gregory, one of the later executioners of Lazia.
Lazia's men furnished an armed escort to the city limits for them;
however this was strictly window dressing.

What Floyd didn't know was that Lazia had instructed his
men to "cut out" if anything happened. That short Italian boy
wasn't going to take any chances on getting more involved in
this mess.

Floyd and Verne Miller made hasty arrangements to meet
several weeks later in Cleveland, but Floyd, who had friends in
Ohio, headed there immediately. They drove from Kansas City
to Springfield, and here Floyd mailed a poorly printed postal
card, addressed to "Kansas City Police, Kansas City, Mo." The
card was postmarked June 20, 1933, 3:30 p.m., and read:

"DEAR SIR: I—CHARLES FLOYD—WANT IT MADE KNOWN THAT I DID
NOT PARTICIPATE IN THE MASSACRE OF OFFICERS AT KANSAS CITY.
CHARLES FLOYD."

The card was printed in pencil, but was later authenticated
by a comparison of other writings and printings of Floyd already
on file.

Then they drove on to Cleveland, where Floyd's underworld friends got him medical attention. The car they drove there was later found in a Cleveland suburb, burned to a cinder, with an unidentified body in it.

This denial by Floyd was proof positive that he was running, and running scared. He had never before bothered with denials of killings, in fact he had boasted of them. Now he had the whole of the country looking for him, and he had lost some of his braggadocio.

Floyd was worried, for while it was one thing to rile the police of one state and then jump deftly into another to safety it was quite another to rile the Federal Government. Now, when you jumped into another state, they jumped in right after you, or worse, they were there already, waiting for you.

Federal agents set upon Floyd's trail, and during the ensuing months they haunted every place he had ever been. They questioned any and all persons known to have had dealings with him. In fact, they intentionally made themselves so obnoxious to the underworld that Pretty Boy Floyd became a plague upon its house.

Still Floyd needed money—even more now than ever before. He was unwelcomed by most of the underworld, and he couldn't chance trying to get back to the safety of the Ozarks or the Cookson Hills. He had to pay double, or triple, for everything he got, and he had to keep moving.

September 22, 1933, four masked men drove up behind a car on Jackson Boulevard, between Clark and La Salle Streets, in Chicago. Two Federal Reserve Bank messengers were busily transferring money from the post office to a car.

Prodding with machine guns, and hardly a word spoken, the bandits quickly made their presence known. They grabbed the money, abandoned their armored, smoke-screen belching car, ran to another and were soon speeding west on Jackson Boulevard.

While reports of the robbery were still coming into the precinct, they received news that patrolman Miles Cunningham, 35, had been killed while on duty at West Adams and South Halsted Streets. This was about a mile west of the robbery scene.

George "Machine Gun" Kelly would be given credit for this caper, for a long while, but later the credit would be placed on the already burdened shoulders of Verne Miller, Charles "Pretty Boy" Floyd, Adam Richetti, and Clifford Harback. Verne Miller was identified as the killer of Patrolman Cunningham.

Special agents in Chicago received a tip that Verne Miller was hiding in the Sherone, an apartment hotel on the north side of Chicago. With him were two women, later identified as Bobbie Moore, widow of slain New York gangster Jake Harris, and Vi Gibson, alias Vivian Mathis.

The FBI rented a nearby apartment and staffed it with two agents who had previously lived in Huron, South Dakota, and knew Miller by sight. Other agents were placed at various vantage points in and around the hotel. Peeping through a small hole punched in the door, they searched the face of everyone who used the hall.

Finally, on November 1, 1933, Verne Miller walked out of the door of his apartment, and was instantly identified. But here something went wrong; signals got mixed, and the other agents down in the lobby didn't get the message. Verne Miller, living so long by instinct alone, apparently sensed something was amiss, and skipping the elevator, he used the stairs.

He raced through the lobby before the startled agents, and jumped into a car at the curb, driven by Bobbie Moore, and they roared away. Just then the agents got the message from the other apartment, and they rushed to the door, firing at the fleeing car with machine guns. Later the car was found a few blocks away, abandoned and with 17 bulletholes in the back.

Miller had answered the fire with a few shots from his automatic, but they were fired in haste, and missed. After dumping the car, both fled on foot, Bobbie in one direction and Verne in another. Bobbie later surrendered to the police, but insisted she had not seen Miller since their narrow escape from the hotel.

That time was running out for Floyd and his companions became more evident on November 29, 1933. On this date a late stroller discovered the nude and trussed body of Vernon C. Miller, age 37, in a Detroit suburb. His head had been crushed in, and he had been stabbed nearly a dozen times in the face with an ice pick or some such small instrument.

His body was wrapped in two blankets and tied, jackknifed, by several feet of cheap clothesline. The body was stiff with rigor mortis, and the hair had been dyed a bright red. Miller was later positively identified by his fingerprints.

The underworld in general never forgave Miller for bringing the FBI down on its neck. The big wheels of crime thought the Kansas City massacre was an idiot play, and a botched mess. Miller was too hot to handle, and was one of the most wanted, and unwanted, men in America.

There was a story that Miller had been killed because he was the killer of Gus "Big Mike" Winkler. Gus had been machine-gunned to death at 1:30 P.M., on October 9, 1933, in Chicago. His bullet-riddled body was found dumped on the doorstep of the Charles H. Weber Distributing Company, at 1414 Roscoe Street.

The more educated guesses had it that Miller had popped up in the midst of the Purple Gang in Detroit—unannounced, unwanted, and unexpected. Because he was too hot to handle, and because he knew too much, his buddies got rid of him, gangland style. His had been the third gangland murder in Detroit that week. The other victims were Abe Axler and Eddie Fletcher, two small-time hoods.

Bobbie Moore, alias Mrs. Jake Harris, and Vivian Gibson, alias Vivian Mathis, were both indicted for harboring a criminal wanted by federal authorities. They were each sentenced to serve a year and a day in prison.

As ludicrous as it may sound, while all this was going on—and while Pretty Boy Floyd was being hunted throughout the country—Mrs. Ruby Floyd and her nine-year-old son were *touring* the country. She was making her kinship to Floyd pay off, for they were traveling with a company, promoting a film called "Crime Doesn't Pay."

February 18, 1934, disaster again struck the Floyd gang, when Clifton (Kip) Harbeck, 25, notorious Arkansas and Oklahoma bank robber and killer, was shot three times. Again, it wasn't the police that was chipping away at the last of Floyd's buddies. This time it was a woman.

Harbeck was living on Crystal Street in Hot Springs, Arkansas (where Dutch Akers still ruled), with a Mrs. Thomas Orvel Tackett, 35. They had quarreled, and Mrs. Tackett, alias Mrs. Frank Hays, alias Mrs. John Hayes, shot him three times in the chest. Mrs. Tackett, the former Lillian Murray, had an interesting police record.

Early in February, 1934, Oklahoma Governor W. H. Murray decided he had had enough of outlaws, banditry, and the use of the Cookson Hills as a constant hideout.

On February 17, 1934, between 350 and 400 federal, state, county, and city officers started a systematic beating of the brush. With the full cooperation of federal authorities, the Governor mobilized 1,000 national guardsmen to act as guards for all prisoners caught. The guardsmen did not take part in the actual search.

The area they were to scour was an estimated 75 to 100 square miles. The Cookson Hills had been used as a bandit hideout since the days of the James Boys, the Daltons, and the Youngers. It was hoped that the result of this search would turn up such killers as Charles Floyd, Adam Richetti, Clyde Barrow, and Bonnie Parker.

The results were disappointingly small, as they flushed out only 19 minor hoods. It hardly took 1,000 national guardsmen to control such a small catch. The news of this search, however, did discourage further use of the area as a hideout, for a while.

Details of the search was given wide news coverage, and one interested reader was Pretty Boy Floyd, safely ensconced in a house 1,000 miles away, in Buffalo, New York. With him was his faithful lieutenant, Richetti, and two women companions. Floyd could see that any thought of returning to his beloved Oklahoma hills, and the hero worship he needed so desperately now, was definitely out.

Floyd's activities are rather obscure at this point, as he didn't want any publicity, and was too busy running to stop and make trouble. With the number of gangs operating at the same time, and in the same areas, it is hard to pin down specifically who was robbing whom.

For instance, on one given date, February 2, 1934, the following took place.

NEEDHAM, MASSACHUSETTS: The local bank was robbed of $14,-500 by four men with blazing machine guns. They killed Policeman Forbes McLeod and shot Walter H. Bartholomew, the 75-year-old vault attendant, Patrolman Frank Haddock, and Fireman Timothy Coughlin. The holdup was attributed to the Pretty Boy Floyd gang.

PENNSGROVE, NEW JERSEY: Four bandits swept down on two bank employees at the Pennsgrove National Bank and Trust Company, and grabbed four packages containing $130,000 in cash. Then they made good their escape. No one was hurt in the brief but lucrative foray.

COLEMAN, TEXAS: Three masked men robbed the First National Bank of Coleman of $24,000, kidnapping six employees. The Barrow-Parker gang was given credit for this crime.

This was not an exceptional day, for in the year 1933 alone, bank robberies had increased to a rate of almost two a day. And this count was to continue into 1934, with a large majority of them pulled by gangs only vaguely identified or not identified at all.

x

By October, 1934, Floyd and Richetti decided it might be safe
to try to make their way back to the Oklahoma hills, to the sweet
feeling of security they had missed for so long. It was on October
11, 1934, that the name Pretty Boy Floyd was again splashed
across the front pages of the nation's newspapers.

Deputy Sheriff Will Owens of Cresco, Iowa, had gone to a
farmhouse to serve some papers a little over a week before. He
had seen Pretty Boy Floyd while there, but only for a fleeting
moment and did not recognize him.

Almost a week would pass before Owens would connect the
face he had seen with the name Pretty Boy Floyd. Floyd had
taken on a gaunt and hunted look, and had lost much of his
widely publicized "prettiness."

When he realized who it might be, he called the FBI in Des
Moines. Agent Haight was immediately dispatched to assist
Owens in his investigation. Due to many false leads they had
followed in the past, the Bureau wasn't too convinced that this
was really Pretty Boy Floyd. Deputy Sheriff Owens hadn't
sounded very convincing.

The Sheriff and Agent Haight drove to the farmhouse, but
Floyd had left a short time before. With nothing else left to do,
they decided to cruise the area. Before long they spotted a sus-
picious car parked near the cornfield of a farm owned by a Mr.
Bosteter, near McIntire, Iowa. Behind the wheel sat Charles
"Pretty Boy" Floyd, who also saw Owens' car.

Owens and Haight, still not sure of the identity of the criminal,
stopped their car and put together a hasty plan. Owens got out
and pretended to check out the corn field for its pheasant hunting
prospects. He also tried to get a closer look at Floyd. Agent
Haight remained in the car, and kept a watchful eye on Floyd's
car.

Suddenly two figures bolted from the cornfield, jumped into
the car, and with a grind of gears, Floyd was off. Sheriff Owens
and Agent Haight took off after them, and the race was on. Being
unfamiliar with the local roads, Floyd turned into a small country
lane, and found himself at a dead end. Spinning the car around,
he headed it back at full speed, toward the approaching officers.

When the two vehicles were close enough both criminals and
lawmen opened up with machine gun fire, but with the dust and
the excitement, all shots went wild and nobody was hurt.

Floyd now headed northeast into Minnesota, dodged further east into Wisconsin, skirted Chicago, crossed Illinois, Indiana, and headed across Ohio, in the direction of Pennsylvania. He had clearly abandoned any hope of getting back to Oklahoma.

After that close brush with the law, the third member of the Floyd gang chose to go it alone, leaving just Floyd and Richetti. The third member's identity was never established.

Having been flushed into the open, it wasn't long before Floyd and Richetti were back in the news again. Since their original decision to return to Oklahoma, they had been camping out to avoid detection. Also, the usual underworld hideouts were closed to them. Crime was a business, and it just wasn't good business to have anything to do with either Floyd or Richetti.

On Saturday, October 21, 1934, a citizen of Wellsville, Ohio— who for obvious reasons insisted upon remaining anonymous— complained to Police Chief J. H. Fultz that there were two men living in a ravine near his home. They were acting mighty suspicious, he added, and he asked Chief Fultz to check it out.

When Fultz and his deputy approached the ravine to question the two men, they were met with a hail of bullets. Now Fultz had no idea who or what he had come up against, but there was one thing he was sure of: those men were in no mood for conversation, so he and his deputy withdrew to a safe distance and called for reinforcements.

A posse was soon formed, and with the additional help Fultz once again approached the ravine; but this show of force didn't help at all. The results were the same, and a full fledged battle royal was soon in progress. The only casualties of the flying bullets were a member of the posse, Grover Potts, 35, who was shot through the arm by Richetti, and Sheriff Fultz, who received a minor wound in the foot.

Richetti soon ran out of ammunition, and the posse closed in, taking him prisoner. Floyd, however, dashed off through the tangled underbrush, and managed to elude his pursuers—temporarily.

A short distance away, Floyd flagged down the car of James H. Baum, 65. Baum, a florist, was not used to the ways of the "quick and the dead," and stopped to see what Floyd wanted, to his everlasting regret. Before he realized what was happening he was a prisoner, and they were speeding down the road with the posse in hot pursuit.

It didn't take the posse long to overtake Baum's old automobile and Floyd saw that things weren't going at all well. Near Lisbon,

Ohio, he ordered Baum to stop the car, and then told him to jump. When the old man hesitated, Floyd barked, "Jump out, you old bastard, or I'll shoot you right here!"

Baum jumped, and then Floyd jumped, running as soon as he hit the ground. The posse, confused, fired at one of the figures, but guessed wrong and shot the old man in the hip, while Floyd went loping off into the nearby woods. Once again he had made one of those miraculous escapes that had dotted his nine-year rampage of crime and terror.

xi

It was on a farm located between Sprucevale and Clarkston, Ohio, on October 22, 1934, that the long arm of the law caught up with Pretty Boy Floyd, and wrote a finish to his unhappy life.

Around noon, Floyd—tired, disheveled, and hungry—came to the door of the Cookle farm. He asked Mrs. Cookle if she would give him something to eat, and offered to pay her.

While she prepared the meal, her husband, who had recognized Floyd, raced to notify the authorities. He didn't dare take the truck, for fear that Floyd would hear it and become suspicious, so he took off on foot. The FBI had set up a headquarters in East Liverpool, and had been there ever since the capture of Richetti.

As Floyd ate, he questioned the nervous Mrs. Cookle about newspaper stories she had read regarding the recent events. Then, when he finished eating, he paid Mrs. Cookle for the meal and went outside, where he tried to persuade a farm hand to drive him into Youngstown. He hoped to lose himself in its dense population.

The farm hand told him he couldn't possibly go, and besides the truck wasn't working too well, and probably wouldn't make the trip, anyway. Floyd pondered the use of force, but thought better of it, and left on foot, without an argument.

It was nearly two hours later that the four FBI agents, led by Melvin Purvis and Police Chief Hugh J. McDermott of East Liverpool—with his three officers, Glenn G. Montgomery, Chester Z. Smith, and Herman Ross—arrived at the farmhouse. They were too late.

Frustrated, they set out to search each and every farmhouse, barn, and shed in the neighborhood. Finally at 4:10, at a farmhouse they sighted an automobile with three people in the front seat and one in the rear backing out from behind a corn crib.

When the occupants saw the approaching agents and officers,

the car pulled up behind the corn crib again. The crib, a wooden affair, was built about 1½ feet off the ground, and as they approached carefully they could see a pair of blue-trousered legs get out of the car.

Suddenly Pretty Boy Floyd bolted from behind the building and raced toward another car, parked nearby. When he saw this was a useless maneuver, he again changed directions and sprinted off across a pasture toward a distant wooded ridge.

Charging out in front was Melvin Purvis, Agent-in-Charge, Chicago office. Just three months before he had been with the group that had brought Dillinger down. Now he was after Pretty Boy Floyd, and he shouted for him to stop and surrender. Floyd never slowed down.

An order was given, and at a range of less than 200 feet a hail of rifle, pistol, and machine gun bullets reached out and pulled Pretty Boy Floyd down. At that distance it would have been almost impossible for him to have escaped.

He dropped at once, struggling to get his automatic free, but he had been hit in the right arm and couldn't get a grip on it. Purvis came up and kicked the gun out of his hand. Then he leaned over and asked Floyd, "You're Pretty Boy Floyd?"

He replied, "I am Charles Arthur Floyd." Then, in rapid succession, he demanded, "Who in hell tipped you? Where is Eddie?"

Floyd had been hit eight times and his life was fast ebbing away, so Purvis left to arrange for an ambulance. Another agent then bent over Floyd and asked him if he had taken part in the Kansas City Massacre. Floyd raised himself up and shouted obscenities at the agent, then falling back he said, "I won't tell you nothing." And true to his word, he didn't, because he died almost immediately.

Death came to Charles "Pretty Boy" Floyd, in the same violent manner in which he had dealt it out to so many others. Later, as he lay on a concrete slab in the morgue in East Liverpool, a tag dangling from each big toe, his total worldly possessions were tabulated for the records. They were his clothing, two automatic pistols with full clips, $120 in cash, and a silver dollar with ten notches in it.

Officers speculated that the notches were Floyd's record of the lives he had taken during his sordid career. He had killed at least ten human beings, five of them policemen, and one an agent of the FBI. He had also wounded many other men, some of them seriously, all of them painfully.

Charles "Pretty Boy" Floyd had inflicted upon his fellow men all this murder, robbing, kidnapping and misery just because he wanted what other people had but he didn't want to work for it.

The story of Pretty Boy Floyd cannot end with his death, however, for there was still the mess he'd left behind—a mess that would take another life, and put additional people behind bars.

xii

With only Adam Richetti left of the trio who had committed the Kansas City Massacre, national attention was focused upon the small town of Wellsville, Ohio. With so much publicity the officials of the town were loath to give up Richetti to the anxious FBI and Thomas Brash, the Sheriff of Jackson County, Missouri.

Frustrated at every turn in his efforts to get custody of Richetti, J. Edgar Hoover made a statement to the press: "The sheriff did a splendid piece of work in capturing Richetti, but I don't think he realizes that he is hampering the efforts to clear up the Kansas City massacre, by obstinately insisting that Richetti be held in Wellsville.

"Why, so far, federal agents have even been refused permission to question Richetti, much less take him back to Kansas City. The Kansas City case promises revelations that are startling, to put it mildly. We think if we were permitted to take Richetti back to Kansas City, or even to have questioned him soon after he was captured, it might have simplified our task."

In an effort to retain Richetti, on October 23, 1934, the city of Wellsville rushed the handcuffed and heavily guarded hoodlum into the court of Mayor W. H. Daugherty.

Here he was charged with carrying concealed weapons, and of shooting with intent to kill. Richetti had a stolen automatic on him when he was captured. It had been furnished him by the Lazia gang; its serial number was 483296, and it had been stolen from the National Guard Armory in Kansas City, August, 1932.

Mayor Daugherty asked him if he knew his constitutional rights, and Richetti smugly replied, "No, sir." After the Mayor patiently explained them to him, Richetti asked for permission to obtain counsel, then suddenly changed his mind. "I think I'll plead guilty to carrying concealed weapons," he said, "and not guilty to the other offense."

Mayor Daugherty then set his bond at $50,000 and asked Richetti if he could raise it. Richetti replied that he couldn't and then, dramatically, threw his handcuffed hands above his head and slowly brought them down before his face, in a gesture of utter despair.

It wasn't until early November that the FBI succeeded in gaining temporary cutody of Richetti. Agents immediately rushed him to Kansas City, to testify before the grand jury. They tried to fly him, but the plane was forced down due to bad weather and they had to land in Chicago. From here they continued the trip by automobile.

In Kansas City, Richetti would admit nothing, and contributed little but additional drama to the investigation. When he was finished with his testimony, he was put on a train with two agents and returned to Wellsville. This was in accordance with the writ of habeas corpus that had allowed them to take him to Kansas City.

In Ohio Missouri officials and highway patrolmen were waiting to request his custody for the slaying of one of their members and the slaying of a county sheriff near Columbia, Missouri.

Eventually Richetti was returned to Missouri, where he was tried and convicted of that crime. Then he was tried and convicted of participating in the Kansas City massacre. Just prior to his execution, another hoodlum confessed the killings of the highway patrolman and the county sheriff.

This turn of events did little to help Richetti, however, and on October 7, 1938, after all his appeals had been exhausted, he died in the lethal gas chamber at the Missouri State Penitentiary at Jefferson City, Missouri.

The body of Charles "Pretty Boy" Floyd was returned to Sallisaw, and buried in Akins on Saturday, October 28, 1934. He was 31 years old at the time of his death. The funeral at Sallisaw was attended by a crowd estimated to be in excess of 10,000 people. Not all were mourners, however. There were the usual number of morbid curiosity seekers, newspaper reporters, and police officials.

Before they could get the coffin into the ground, people, through devious means, managed to steal some of the nails from it. And for months it was a task for graveyard attendants to keep enough dirt on the grave to cover it. People kept stealing the dirt for souvenirs. Even a nearby tree was neatly stripped of its leaves and some of its bark.

xiii

Back in Kansas City, the echo of machine guns died slowly. The chief of police resigned his post, and was later indicted for perjury by a federal grand jury. Also indicted were the chief of detectives, and the head of the Police Motor Car Theft Bureau.

The conspiracy between politics, law enforcement, and crime was apparent to all, and the final results of the Kansas City massacre would eventually topple even the powerful Pendergast machine.

From November 1934 until January 1935, conspiracy trials would be conducted against Richard Tallman Galatas and his wife, Herbert (Deafy) Farmer and wife, Louis (Doc) Stacci, Mrs. Vivian Mathis, and Frank (Fitz) B. Mulloy.

The Farmers were arrested in Joplin on July 10, 1933 on charges of conspiracy to free a prisoner of the Attorney General of the United States. Farmer was wearing overalls, as he and his wife, Esther, were arraigned in Kansas City; their bond was set at $25,000. Bond would be posted for Mrs. Farmer, but the 42-year-old Herbert remained in custody until the conspiracy trials began in November.

Frank B. Mulloy, known as Fitz Mulloy, was taken into custody at his home, at 14 E. 56th Street. Mulloy was a former bootlegger from Chicago, and had passed on orders issued to him by Louis (Doc.) Stacci to Vernon C. Miller. The charges against him were the same as for the Farmers, and he posted a bail of $25,000.

Stacci, alias Louis Stacy, was arrested August 8, 1933, in a Maywood suburb of Chicago on the same conspiracy charges, and he also posted a $25,000 bond.

Mrs. Frances Nash, alias Frances Miller, alias Mrs. E. B. Conners, returned to Kansas City on July 11, 1933 from Wenona, Illinois, where she had been hiding since the massacre. Verne Miller had instructed her to go to his residence, at 6612 Edgevale Road, but she had panicked, and instead fled to Wenona, where she stayed with her cousin, Jake Orsen.

Vivian Mathis served her year and a day for her Chicago caper with Verne Miller, and was rearrested and returned to Kansas City for the hearing. Prior to the trial, she pleaded guilty before Judge Merril E. Otis to the charge of harboring a known criminal. She was given a sentence of another year and a day and placed on probation.

After an exhaustive and sometimes frustrating search, Richard Tallman Galatas and his wife were apprehended September 22, 1934, in New Orleans, where they were living under the name of E. Richard Lee. Galatas was doing business as the distributor for a products company. A detective fan had recognized Dick's picture in a magazine and tipped the FBI. At last the set was complete; the trials commenced in late November and would continue into January 1935.

The testimony of Mrs. Frances Nash was perhaps the most important of the trial. In return for a promise of immunity from prosecution she agreed to testify against her co-defendants.

On January 1, 1935, Mrs. Nash testified, as her friends sat in the court room and eyed her coldly. The five foot five Mrs. Nash weighed 140 pounds and had brown hair and eyes. She had been born in Minnesota as Frances Nichols in 1902. She attended State Normal at Stevens Point, Wisconsin, and had taught school there.

She met Wayne Luce in 1924, and they were married the same year. Then they moved to Melrose Park, Illinois, where they operated a dog kennel, owned by a Chicago stockbroker. The kennel was next door to the O. P. Inn, owned by Louis Stacci, and it was here that she met Frank "Jelly" Nash and Vivian Mathis— whom she knew as Vi Page—and Verne Miller, who also went under the name of Verne Moore.

In 1930 she divorced Luce and gained custody of her daughter, Darnell. She had first known Nash as Frank Harrison, and had married him 18 months before. He had told her that he owned a chain of roadhouses in Chicago.

She and Nash had moved to Cicero, and were often visited by the Millers: Vivian and Verne. In June 1933, she and Nash had moved into the Oak Park Tourist Camp at Hot Springs, Arkansas.

She told the court, presided over by Judge Merril E. Otis, of receiving, while in Joplin, a long distance telephone report from Verne Miller just seven hours before the massacre. Miller, she related, had been on a reconnoitering trip to the station, and had called to tell her not to worry, that he'd take care of everything.

She also told how Mrs. Esther Farmer had called Miller in Kansas City in the first place, to get his assistance in freeing Nash from the FBI. As she related slowly and precisely the tangled web of telephone calls that had set up the massacre, she implicated each of the defendants.

Later the defendants admitted to the series of telephone calls, which had been proven by the prosecution. The phone company had furnished the FBI with a complete list of all calls made. This was damaging evidence, because it clearly indicated the sinister web of communications it took to set up the massacre. It showed the time, date, and locations where the calls were placed, and to whom they were directed.

But, the defendants insisted, they had no idea that Nash was an escaped criminal. The calls, they explained, were merely placed to insure that Nash would be furnished sufficient bail for whatever charge he had been arrested on.

The attorneys for the defense then sought to expand the idea that Nash had actually been assassinated by people who wanted to silence him. They insisted that the massacre had absolutely nothing to do with the defendants.

Dick Galatas, trying to explain why he had fled Hot Springs and had taken up residence in New Orleans, where he hid for almost a year, said he had feared for his life.

"I read in the papers that Mr. Hoover had given orders to bring me in on a slab. I didn't think I'd have a chance and I wanted to be sure my mothers were cared for, so I sent my wife and mother-in-law to New York, and my mother to California. Then I bought a small car, assumed the name of Richard Lee, and set up business in New Orleans."

In the final summation of his personal case, Galatas claimed he had no idea Nash was an escaped convict, or even a criminal. He said he thought Nash was a doctor, because he had lots of doctors as customers.

The jury was composed of people from all walks of life, and when they removed from the courtroom to consider the guilt or innocence of the six conspirators, they did so with serious determination.

Back in the courtroom, however, at least two of the defendants seemed to be taking matters very lightly. Louis Stacci chased Herbert (Deafy) Farmer about the cortroom, pointing a camera at him, in a mock attempt to take his picture.

A sobering effect suddenly swept the courtroom, when the jury, looking solemn and pious, filed into the jury box. Rapt attention was given, as the foreman of the jury handed to the bailiff the verdict, which he in turn would hand to the judge. The judge then read the verdict to the six defendants. It was "Guilty as charged!" The jury was then polled to ascertain whether or not the verdict had been unanimous. It had.

Suddenly, among the defendants, there were sobs, curses, and the stony silence of two gamblers who had lost. Mrs. Farmer, whose devoted attention to her deaf husband had marked the four-day trial, wept uncontrollably as the verdict was read.

Her husband, Herbert, unable to hear the verdict, watched her face anxiously. "Which of us was it?" he asked, as she started to weep."

"Both," she sobbed loudly into his ear, apparently unable to write a note—their usual method of communication.

Mrs. Elizabeth Galatas gasped when she heard the verdict, but quickly regained her composure. Her friend, Louis Stacci, swore and then wept.

Fitz Mulloy, without a change of facial expression, handed his overcoat to his wife with the remark, "Here. Take this. I won't be needing it."

Richard Tallman Galatas did not change his expression, and he said nothing.

The charge they had been found guilty of was that of conspiring to liberate a prisoner in the custody of the Attorney General and carried a maximum penalty of two years in prison.

Galatas, Farmer, and Mulloy were sentenced to Alcatraz for a period not to exceed two years. Louis Stacci was sentenced to Leavenworth for a like period.

Considering the extent of their involvement, the women fared much better. Probation was given to Vivian Mathis (Mrs. Vernon C. Miller), Elizabeth Galatas, and Esther Farmer.

The government, in keeping with its agreement, didn't prosecute Frances Nash, and she walked out of the courtroom with all but her conscience free.

And so the final chapter was at last written to the short and violent life of Charles "Pretty Boy" Floyd, who had ended many lives and had touched the lives of as many more.

••3••

Mother Barker and Her Boys

i

This is a story of a mother—not a mother as we fondly think of her, but a mother who had strange beliefs, limited virtues, and four sons.

Arizona Clark was born in 1871, in the Ozark Mountain area of Missouri, some 18 miles from Springfield. Just why her Scotch-Irish parents chose to burden her with a name like Arizona is not recorded, but it was eventually abbreviated to Arrie.

In later years, she wouldn't like this name either, and would begin to call herself "Kate," and Kate it would remain.

Growing up on a poor but tidy Missouri farm, her childhood was not unusual. Her parents were hard-working, church-going people, who reared her to be a law-abiding, God-fearing Presbyterian.

In 1892, Kate Clark met and married George Barker, a poor but honest farmer-miner from Lebanon, Missouri, and they settled down in Aurora to raise a family.

Life was hard for the couple, and they lived in a tumbled-down miner's shack. George did some farming to raise a limited crop and a few vegetables for their table. He also worked in the nearby mines to supplement his meager income.

On October 30, 1893, mother Barker's first son arrived, and she named him Herman. He was followed by Lloyd in 1898, Arthur (Dock) in 1899, and finally Fred in 1901. With each arrival, George Barker had to farm just a little more and work just a little harder in the mines. But even with this he could barely scratch out enough to feed his large family.

At last George Barker decided to move his family to Webb City, a small settlement just north of Joplin. Since he was still the head of the family at this time, mother Barker dutifully packed up the family and meekly followed.

The early relationship between father and sons was very good, and Herman and Lloyd, as soon as they were old enough would go hunting with their father in the lovely Ozark woods, with its teeming wild life. Because of this, it wasn't too long before the boys had an expert knowledge of shotguns and rifles.

Kate Barker, or "Ma," as she was now called, did her part as a good wife, devoted mother, and reliable churchgoer. When the church organ played "Oh Promise Me," and the congregation sang, Ma's voice was one of the loudest to be heard. Beside her on the seat each and every Sunday, and singing loudly too, were her well scrubbed little boys.

George Barker went to work in the lead and zinc mines near Webb City, but as before, his wages were meager for the menial labors he performed. They lived in a small shack. The one good friend Ma had was a Mrs. Farmer who had a little boy named Herbert.

Herbert became one of the Barker boys pals and playmates, and in later years would play an important role in criminal history. The Farmers and the Barkers were both dirt poor, and this brought them closer together. Both Mrs. Barker and Mrs. Farmer were described by their neighbors as kind of strange, and stand-offish.

Arthur (Dock) and Fred Barker were just babies when the move to Webb City was made, but Herman and Lloyd lost no time in introducing themselves to the local police. Activities of petty theft and vandalism were usually their forte.

George Barker, a timid soul, tried half-heartedly to get the boys to behave themselves, but he soon stopped this foolishness. Without a warning, Ma turned on him, and told him to shut up. She would raise her boys, and she wouldn't need any help from him.

That seemed to handle that, and George Barker from that time on maintained a hands-off attitude. Whenever a neighbor would complain to him about some of the boys' mischief, he would merely shrug his shoulders. He would tell them, "You'll have to talk to their mother; she handles the boys."

When Herman was caught by the police and charged with a petty theft, Ma descended upon the police station with all the venom of an adder protecting its young. She raked them from pillar to post, but then, after seeing that these tactics were getting her nowhere, she immediately changed into the tearful mother and pleaded for mercy.

This worked better and she got Herman free. After Ma took him home she really gave him a tongue lashing—not for stealing, but for being stupid enough to get caught. Then she told him what he should have done. This would soon become her "motherly advice" to each of her four children, as soon as they were old enough to steal.

George Barker, who had abdicated his role as a father and the head of his own household, would later alibi, "She'd pack up them boys and take them to Sunday School every week. I don't know just why. Because when I'd try to straighten them up she'd fly into me. She never would let me do with them what I wanted to."

Because of Ma's strange belief that her boys could do no wrong, Herman and Lloyd were soon on a first name basis with the police in both Webb City, and Joplin. Carefully and skillfully, she molded them into the little beasts she wanted them to be. They were right in whatever they did, and "the whole, damn, rotten world was their enemy."

In 1910 Herman was arrested by the police in Joplin, on a charge of highway robbery, but the evidence was weak and he was released. Ma was furious. This was the last straw, she screamed. They were going to leave this town, with all its persecutions.

And so it was in 1910 that Ma packed up the family, and with George trailing behind like a pet poodle, they moved to Tulsa. Tulsa, Oklahoma, with a population of 18,182 in 1910, was in the middle of a building boom. Oil pipelines had been opened to the Gulf of Mexico, and the price of oil was climbing. The town was really growing, and so was Ma.

By now Ma was a dumpy, fat forty, and growing more evil each day. The old clapboard shack they moved into was something to behold. It had two rooms, if you could call them that, and the floor was bare boards, laid on the ground. The "bathroom" was a fly-infested shed in the backyard, and when the flies got through breeding there, they swarmed into the house through the unscreened windows.

The house was so crowded that the boys had to sleep on the floor. This would be home to the Barkers, and here Lloyd, Fred, and Arthur would grow to killing age. Herman, whose ego had been inflated by his arrest for "highway robbery," was now traveling. He was "living off the land," and Ma would keep up with him, in and out of jail, by mail.

The old shack stood at 401 North Cincinnati Avenue, near the railroad tracks, in the old Central Park District. It was here that the boys formed a gang, teaming up with other young hoodlums of the area. They soon became known to the local police as the "Central Park Gang."

This collection of juvenile delinquents went to school during the day, while during the night they turned into burglars, hijackers, muggers, and bandits. At one time the gang numbered 22 boys, and posed a real problem to the small, overworked Tulsa police department.

Headquarters for the gang was, of course, Ma's shack, which had become a teeming little underworld of its own. Here the gang held its meetings, with Ma presiding over them as chairman of the board. Here they laid their plans for future criminal activities, reviewed the past, and listened to Ma's freely given sage advice.

This criminal education was really a two-way avenue, as Ma was also learning. She absorbed the details of their criminal adventures, learned from their mistakes, and gradually became a true emissary of the Devil. Along about this time, George Barker, fearing for his life, elected to leave the family, No one attempted to stop him.

In 1918 Arthur (Dock) Barker was caught stealing a government automobile. The world war was on, but the Barkers were just getting started with their own war. A war against society. Ma rushed to the jail to demand, and then plead, but this time it didn't work, so Dock broke out. He was caught a short time later, but he escaped again, and fled to the safety of Ma's shack.

In 1920 Arthur (Dock) Barker, and Volney Davis were arrested, and charged with the killing of a night watchman at the St. John's Hospital, then under construction. Ma again rushed to the jail, but this time she offered her sage advice to Volney Davis. He had a firm alibi, as he had been in a hotel room with two young women when the killing had taken place.

Ma, with her glib tongue and persuading ways, conned him into giving his alibi to Dock. She told Davis she would get him off anyway. Volney Davis wasn't too bright so he agreed; but it didn't help, and they were both given life sentences at the Oklahoma State Penitentiary at McAlester.

While Dock was stewing in McAlester, Herman, Lloyd and

Fred staged robbery after robbery, taking most of the loot home to Ma. Then Fred got caught, and was sent to the Reformatory for five years. Ma screamed; yelled; wrote letters; and protested to anybody who would listen to her that her innocent boy was being persecuted. Eventually she got him out on parole.

Fred was so grateful that he immediately went out and robbed a bank for Ma, but they caught him again. This time Ma started her campaign while he was still being held in jail, and she got him out on a $10,000 bond. Grateful once again, Fred promptly fled the state, and Ma lost her $10,000. She didn't really care, though, for her boy was free.

Ma Barker soon gained a reputation as a woman who could furnish protection, and give out shrewd advice to the criminal types. Now ex-cons from McAlester, Jefferson City, Huntsville, and Lansing streamed into Tulsa, always dropping off at Ma's place. Here they picked up their mail, got addresses, met friends, made contacts, and got some of Ma's sage advice—all for a price.

She had graduated the Central Park Gang, and they had gone forth to flex their muscles and try her teachings upon an unsuspecting world. Now her followers were the more mature criminals.

Then the heavy hand of the law again caught up with Fred Barker while he was in the middle of a burglary in Kansas. He was sent to the Kansas State Penitentiary at Lansing.

In the meantime, Herman Barker teamed up with an Oklahoma bandit and killer named Roy Terrill. The two of them tried to pull a robbery in Missouri but were caught. Terrill was returned to McAlester Penitentiary, but he escaped within sight of the gates.

Herman was sent to Fayetteville, Arkansas, where he was wanted for further investigation. While here he also escaped, and he again joined forces with Terrill. Then they went on a robbery spree, and in between they would drop in and see Ma. She was now alone: Dock was in McAlester; Fred was in Lansing; Lloyd was "on the road," and Herman was running around with Terrill. But Ma didn't like loneliness, so she had found herself a lover, a former billboard painter by the name of Arthur "Old Man" Dunlop.

Suddenly tragedy struck the Barker clan, on August 29, 1927. Herman Barker and a hood named Charles Stalcup were caught in the act of armed robbery by the police of Wichita, Kansas. They elected to shoot it out, and Patrolman J. E. Marshall was killed by Herman. Herman took a bullet in the head, which blinded him, and Stalcup got a bullet in the arm and shoulder.

As the pair started to make a break for their car, Stalcup yelled to Herman that he wouldn't be able to drive, as he had been shot in the shoulder. Herman yelled back that he couldn't drive because he couldn't see.

Stalcup then told Herman to take the wheel, and he would use his eyes to show him which way to go. Herman rammed the car into a tree less than a half-mile away. With the police closing in on them, Herman, before the horrified Stalcup could stop him, put his pistol to his head and pulled the trigger. For him, the rat race was over.

For a brief period Ma and George Barker met at a small country cemetery just five miles out of Welch, Oklahoma, on the road to Miami. The occasion was the burial of their first son, Herman. Ma, flush with stolen money, bought him a suitable marker of grey granite. Then they parted again and went down separate paths.

The next blow to Ma's crumbling empire came when Lloyd was arrested in 1931 for mail robbery, and sentenced to 25 years at Leavenworth. Now one son was dead and the other three were in jail.

But fate smiled upon Ma Barker, for on March 30, 1931, Fred got his release from Lansing. He didn't head for Ma's place right away, however, but went to Herbert (Deafy) Farmer's place in Joplin, to await the release of a buddy he had made in Lansing.

Two months later the buddy, who called himself Alvin Karpis, was released, and joined him there. Karpis, whose real name was Francis Albin Karpaviecz, had grown up in Chicago, where he had buddied around with Lester M. Gillis. (See Chapter 4.)

When Fred took Alvin home with him to Tulsa, Ma was a mite short of sons, and she took an immediate liking to the pimply-faced young hoodlum. Soon Alvin Karpis became a member of the Barker Clan, and was introduced as "one of the boys."

With Ma's kindly guidance, Fred Barker and Alvin Karpis plotted their first big job together. It was to be a $5,000 jewelry robbery, at Henryetta, Oklahoma.

After the robbery they returned to Ma's shack in Tulsa, where they divided the loot. Ma was pleased that her decision to accept Alvin Karpis into the family fold had proved so lucrative. She had an iron clad rule, however, that no loot should be kept in her place, so Alvin and Fred left to dispose of it.

After such a long period in jail, Fred and Alvin longed for female companionship—something Ma would never allow—so they

rented an apartment in downtown Tulsa and found themselves
a couple of girls.

On June 10, 1931, Fred and Alvin were cornered in the northside apartment by the Tulsa Police. Alvin was captured, but Fred
shot his way to freedom and escaped to Ma's place. Alvin was
sentenced to four years at McAlester. Less than three months
later, he had been paroled and was back at Ma's.

Right then and there Ma decided she had had about enough
of Tulsa, so she sent Arthur Dunlop into Missouri to find them a
likely hideout. He located a nice secluded cabin near Thayer,
and the Barker-Karpis gang moved here.

On December 19, 1931, Alvin and Fred robbed a store in West
Plains, Missouri, using a De Soto sedan for their getaway. The
following day, forgetting all that Ma had taught them, Fred and
Alvin drove the car into town to a garage to get some repair work
done. Sheriff C. R. Kelly approached the car to question the two,
and they shot him dead.

They rushed back to Thayer, where they reported their latest
activities to Ma, who seeing the handwriting on the wall packed
up the gang's possessions. They all fled to St. Paul, Minnesota.
Ma had never been there, but her underworld connections had
told her it was one of the "safe" cities for criminals on the run.

ii

Shortly after the World War, a figure by the name of "Dapper
Dan" Hogan, a short heavy-set Italian, had assumed control of
St. Paul's underworld element. He had his headquarters in the
Hollyhocks speakeasy at 545½ Wabasha Street, from which he
controlled all the criminal activities in the city. He was the man
you had to see if you wanted to settled down in his town and
"cool off."

Things rocked along real well for Danny until December 4,
1928, at 11:30 A.M., when Danny stepped on the starter of his car.
The explosion that resulted shoved his head right through the top
of his car, shattered his right leg above the knee, and mangled
his right hand. Somehow, he managed to live until the next day.

Into the vacuum left by Danny Hogan stepped a Russian immigrant named Harry Sandlovich, who called himself "Harry
Sawyer." Harry wasn't the man that Danny had been, but he did
take over most of the organization. He had a couple of female

accomplices—Bessie Skinner, who was known simply as "Ruth," and a Negress known as Alma Powell. Both of these gangster "broads" would figure prominently in the Dillinger story.

Ma Barker, following the accepted custom of gangdom, promptly notified Harry Sawyer that she and her gang had arrived in town for a "cooling off period." Arrangements were made for her to rent a house at 1031 South Roberts Street in West St. Paul. The house was in a respectable neighborhood, and the landlady had no connections with the underworld. This was one of the requirements for a good hideout.

Secretly the gang used this address for the base of their new operations. Through the efforts of Harry Sawyer, they were joined in their forays throughout the northwest by such well known hoods as Harvey J. Bailey, Frank Nash, Verne C. Miller, Earl Christman, and Fred Goetz, alias "Shotgun" George Ziegler.

Although these individuals did not become permanent members of Ma's gang, they did join it on occasions to pick up a few extra bucks. Through his efforts in joining these individuals together, Harry Sawyer got his cut, and Ma grew richer and fatter.

Their operations culminated swiftly one day, when Nick Hannegraf, the son of Ma's landlady, who lived at 1035 South Roberts Street, became suspicious of them. He was an avid reader of detective stories, and was intrigued by the fact that Fred and Alvin always carried violin cases on their frequent trips to and from the residence. In these cases, unknown to Nick, were the tools of their trade—machine guns.

While reading one of his detective magazines, Nick Hannegraf suddenly found himself staring at pictures of Fred Barker and Alvin Karpis. They, the magazine said, were wanted for the murder of Sheriff C. R. Kelly, White Plains, Missouri, among other things.

Though it was 1:00 A.M., he excitedly called Chief Braun of the St. Paul Police. He was told to go to the Central Police Station, and report his suspicions to the desk sergeant there. He then rushed to the station, where he excitedly told the desk sergeant of his discovery. The sergeant, singularly unimpressed, told him he would have to see Inspector James Crumly, and advised him to come back later. At 7:30 A.M., Hannegraf returned, this time clutching the magazine in his hand.

At 8:00 A.M., April 24, 1932, the police finally raided the house, and of course found nothing. Ma, Dunlop, and the boys had received one of the Sawyer alerts, as guaranteed in their contract with him, and they had fled. They even had sufficient time to pack everything and depart in an orderly manner.

For reasons known only to themselves, Ma and the boys decided that Arthur (Old Man) Dunlop had been the one who tipped the police. Accordingly they took him out to the banks of Lake Freaster, in Wisconsin, on the night of April 25, and shot him three times. They then stripped the body of all clothing and identification.

The body was found the following day, along with a woman's blood-stained glove, on highway 35, which led to the macabre scene. Officers identified the body as that of George E. Anderson, alias George Cooper of 1031 South Roberts Street, West St. Paul, Minnesota.

A short time later, through fingerprints, his body was correctly identified as that of Arthur Dunlop, and his killers were promptly listed as Fred Barker and Alvin Karpis, with the probable assistance of Ma Barker.

With these positive identifications, the three had no recourse but to leave town, so they went to Kansas City, Missouri. This was another of the "safe" towns, and was headed by a short, thickset Italian, named Johnny Lazia. Lazia was the "Harry Sawyer" of Kansas City, and his setup was the same as the one in St. Paul.

Upon their arrival they immediately contacted Lazia, who recommended the fashionable residential district of the Country Club Plaza. Here, in a sumptuous apartment, they were soon joined by Harvey J. Bailey and his buddies Ed Davis, Jim Clark, and Bob Brady.

Ma and Fred took a trip across the state line into Kansas, and down to Fort Scott, where she paid a visit to the Citizens National Bank. Inside she noted the lovely walls, the stunning ceiling, and chatted gaily with bank officials, talking of the possibilities of opening an account. Of course they couldn't know that Ma was casing the bank, with the intent of making a rather large withdrawal.

Back in Kansas City, Ma drew up the plans for the coming bank robbery, and made the getaway charts, which showed such items as landmarks, conditions of the roads, alternate routes, and speeds to be driven. Then the Barker-Karpis gang surged out of Kansas City and struck the Citizens National Bank at Fort Scott, getting $32,000. Everything went smoothly, as Ma knew it would, and they were soon back telling her all the details.

On July 7, 1932, FBI agents, accompanied by Kansas City police, surrounded Thomas Holden, Francis Keating, and Harvey J. Bailey, who were playing golf on the Old Mission Golf Course. They missed Frank "Jelly" Nash, who was a part of the foursome, but, being a bad player, was trailing far behind them.

Keating and Holden were arrested and returned to Leavenworth, from which they had escaped on February 28, 1930. Harvey J. Bailey was held for trial, as he was found with a bond from the Fort Scott robbery in his pocket.

Now, back at Ma's place, Nash hurriedly told them what had happened, and the whole group promptly moved out. Nash headed for Chicago, while the Barkers and Karpis returned to Tulsa for awhile to await further developments.

A short time later one Charlie Harmon was killed by members of the Keating-Holden gang, of which he was a member. They had just held up a bank and were making their getaway. The gang shot Harmon and kicked the body out of the car. They had hoped the police would think they themselves had done the killing.

Harmon was reputedly a noxious individual and an ardent golfer. It had been Harmon's phone call to a golf manufacturer in Kansas City that had ultimately led to the arrest of Keating, Holden, and Bailey. The call had been traced by the FBI, and after many weeks of arduous sleuthing they had located and arrested the trio. The underworld didn't tolerate mistakes like this.

While in Tulsa, Ma Barker hired attorney J. Earl Smith to represent Bailey. When he failed to show up in the courtroom, Ma was mighty upset. She called him and they made a date to meet at the Indian Hills Country Club, located in an isolated part of Tulsa. The following day his bullet riddled body was found by the police. Another mistake had been corrected.

Harvey J. Bailey went back to Leavenworth, and the Barker-Karpis gang fled to St. Paul again. But Harry Sawyer wasn't too happy to see them for they were still wanted very badly for the Dunlop killing. So he suggested they settle down in a very nice lake resort he knew of over in Wisconsin.

Ma took the hint, and as "Mrs. Hunter," with two sons, she moved into a nice two-story house on White Bear Lake. And just down the road lived a short bald-headed man with a hooked nose, called Frank "Jelly" Nash. He had moved there from Chicago for a rest.

When the money began to get a little short, Fred and Alvin drove down to Nash's place, picked him up, and then continued into St. Paul where they were joined by a few of Sawyer's friends. Then they all drove to Concordia, Kansas, where they held up the Cloud County Bank and got the fabulous sum of $240,000.

Then, in September, 1932, Ma got another lucky break: Oklahoma's Governor William H. Murray granted Dock Barker a banishment parole. He was released from McAlester Penitentiary on the condition that he leave the state of Oklahoma and never return. Volney Davis was also given his release.

Both men returned to Tulsa. Fred didn't like the idea of being booted out of Oklahoma, so he hung around Tulsa for awhile, and even joined Pretty Boy Floyd in a couple of bank robberies. He thought Floyd's methods were pretty risky, though, so he decided to go north and join Ma.

When he and Volney Davis arrived in St. Paul, Ma Barker was ecstatic with joy. Now she had two of her sons, and Alvin Karpis, to build a real gang around. They celebrated Ma Barker style and then, when her head was turned, the boys went out, found themselves some female companionship, and really hung one on. Had Ma found out about this she would probably have had a fit. She denied her boys just two things, women and liquor; so they took these pleasures on the side.

December 16, 1932: the Barker-Karpis gang hit the Third Northwestern National Bank, in a small neighborhood community in Minneapolis, and got $20,000 in cash and $10,000 in securities.

There were six patrons and ten employees in the bank when the bandits entered. One of the tellers hit the burglar alarm button, which was connected with police headquarters, while the gang was still busily lining up the customers and employees.

From police headquarters a call was put out for the car nearest the bank to proceed there and investigate. False alarms were an almost daily occurrence.

Patrolmen Ira L. Evans and Leo R. Gorski were cruising nearby when they received the radio alert, and they sped to the scene. Just as they pulled to the curb, three of the gang came rushing out, their arms filled with loot. A fourth followed, armed with a machine gun, and seeing the officers opened fire.

At point blank range the machine gunner cut down both officers. Evans received over twenty of the machine gun bullets, and Gorski five. They were both killed. Then the gang loaded into the getaway car and sped away from the bloody scene.

At Como Park, in St. Paul, the gang was busily changing cars when they noticed another coming their way. The car was driven by Axel Erickson, 29. Together with his passenger Arthur Zachman, he was peddling Christmas wreaths.

When their car slowed down, and the driver appeared too interested in what was going on, the machine gun spoke again, and Erickson slumped over the wheel, his scalp torn away. Zachman quickly took the wheel, and jammed his foot down on the accelerator, but he was too late to help Erickson—he was already dead. These killings would force the gang to lay low for awhile.

Then the gang, which had scattered, was called together again in Chicago, where Ma was making plans for a really big bank robbery. She had visited the bank in Nebraska, and was thoroughly familiar with its security setup. She had checked thoroughly the routes to be used for the getaway, and was now busily drawing up the complete plans.

The National Bank of Fairbury, Nebraska, reeled, as it was hit for $150,000 by Alvin Karpis, Fred and Dock Barker, Frank Nash, Volney Davis, Eddie Green, Jess Doyle, and Earl Christman. However, Christman was badly wounded in the getaway.

Rather than risk taking him back to St. Paul, Eddie Green, the newest member of the gang, was instructed to take Christman down to Kansas City, to Verne Miller's place at 6612 Edgevale Road. Verne would get him a doctor.

Green did as he was told, but Christman died a short while later. Green thereupon called Ma in St. Paul, and asked her what to do. Typical of the underworld Green followed his orders, took the body into the open country, and buried Christman in an unmarked grave.

Back in St. Paul, Ma issued orders that Earl Christman's mother was not to be told about his death and strange burial. "She might get mad and talk, or do some other damn fool thing to bring suspicion down on the gang," Ma concluded.

In St. Paul, a speakeasy called the Hollyhocks was a favorite hangout of many of the visiting underworld characters. It was owned and operated by John P. "Jack" Peifer. Peifer was under the protection of Harry Sawyer, a former Omaha gangster himself.

One chilly evening toward the end of May, the Barker-Karpis gang assembled at the Hollyhocks to plan the details of a coming big caper. It was to be a kidnapping—a new venture for the Barker-Karpis gang.

The finger man (that is, the man who would actually pick the victim, the place and the time) was Jack Peifer himself. Harry

Sawyer, of course, was to handle the protection and warning systems.

The actual plans were drawn up by Shotgun George Ziegler, a college man whose real name was Fred Goetz. He was a former employee of Al Capone, and a prime suspect in the St. Valentine's Day Massacre.

In addition to the Barkers and Karpis, Volney Davis and Charles "Big Fitz" Fitzgerald attended the meeting.

iii

It was 12:20 P.M., Thursday, June 15, 1933. William Hamm, Jr. had just left his office at the Hamm Brewery, 681 E. Minnehaha Street in St. Paul. He had started out on foot for his house at 671 Cable Street. His habit was to walk up the hill to his home, and have dinner with his aged mother. Today, he wouldn't get there.

At the corner of Greenbrier and Minnehaha Streets, at approximately 12:45 P.M., two men stepped up to William Hamm. One of the men, Charles "Big Fitz" Fitzgerald, reached out and grabbed his hand, shook it, but didn't let go. "Hello, Mr. Hamm," he said, just as Alvin Karpis took Hamm's free arm, and together they guided him to the curb, where Fred Barker was waiting in a large black sedan.

The two then forced Hamm into the car, where they placed a white hood over his head and told him to lay quietly on the floor. He did as he was told. Then the car drove steadily for about 30 or 35 miles, until it made a rendezvous with a second automobile.

Hamm, still sitting, and sometimes lying on the floor of the car, now had his hood lifted so he could see the four pieces of paper placed before him. "Please sign these papers, Mr. Hamm," one of the men told him, and he did as he was told.

He was then ordered to close his eyes tightly; the hood was removed and a pair of goggles, stuffed with cotton, was substituted. After this change, Hamm was allowed to sit on the seat of the car. Then they continued into Illinois, to the small town of Bensenville.

Hamm was still blinded with the goggles and had not the slightest idea of where he was (he thought he must be in northern Minnesota) when a woman's hand took his arm; he was guided up some stairs and into a house, then up a second flight of stairs. Next he was herded into a small room; its two windows were boarded up, and a single light bulb hung from the ceiling.

Hamm was then relieved of his goggles, but was told to always face the wall whenever anyone entered the room or he would have to be killed. For hours, then days, he would stare at this wall, until the pattern of the wallpaper was firmly burned into his memory.

Back in St. Paul, about 3:00 P.M. the same day, the phone rang in the office of William W. Dunn, manager of the Hamm Brewing Company. When he answered, the conversation was terse and brief, "We have kidnapped Mr. Hamm; you will hear from us later."

Dunn, thinking the call was perhaps some kind of practical joke, nevertheless called Mr. Hamm's home, and was shocked to learn that he had never arrived. Dunn then notified the police, and went directly to the office of Michael Kinkead, the Ramsey County Attorney.

That night the Hamm and Dunn residences were both placed under surveillance by the St. Paul police department. At 2:00 A.M., this net snared a scared taxi driver, who was trying to deliver the first note from the kidnappers. He told Detectives Charles Tierney and Thomas Brown, "A man told me he would give me two dollars if I would take a note to this address. He said his name was Gordon, and that he lived in the Lowry Hotel. I took the note, and was delivering it when you arrested me."

The taxi driver was released; the address at the Lowry Hotel turned out to be completely false. The note demanded $100,000 in twenties, tens and fives, and cautioned that they should not be marked, on forfeit of Hamm's life. It further stated that the contact would be made later, and the ransom would be delivered in one of the Brewing Company's own trucks. The truck was to be open, so that the interior could be entirely visible from a passing automobile.

The second note was left on the table in a drug store owned by Clarence J. Thomas, at Prior and Grand Streets. Thomas's wife worked as secretary for Michael Kinkead. The note said, "If you value Mr. Hamm's life, and you don't want him killed, you better pay up."

L. J. Sullwold, an employee of the Brewery's Real Estate Department, received a call at his home on Saturday, telling him to go into his garage and look in the seat of his car. Before he could ask what the call was all about, the party hung up. In the seat of his car was the third ransom note.

At the Hamm Brewing Company's parking lot on Minnehaha

Street, a delivery truck sat, stripped and ready to make the payoff. Then on Saturday night Dunn received a phone call about 8:30 P.M., and drove north on Highway 1 to make the contact. When he received the prearranged signal from two automobiles which passed and repassed him switching their lights on and off, he kicked the bag containing the $100,000 out and drove on.

In Bensenville, Illinois, in the house of Edmund C. Bartholmy, soon to be appointed postmaster of the town, Hamm was still a captive. At about 3:00 A.M. Sunday morning, Fred Barker came into his room and told Hamm he had good news for him. The money had been paid, and they would take him home that night. Then he was allowed to clean up and get ready for the trip. He still hadn't seen any of his captors and had no idea who they were.

Sunday night, June 18, Hamm was bundled into a car, wearing his cotton-stuffed goggles, and driven for about eight hours. It was around 5:15 A.M. Monday morning when the kidnappers let him out in the vicinity of Wyoming, Minnesota. At 5:30 A.M., Hamm stumbled to a farmhouse, where he called home and reported that he had been released. Police Chief Thomas E. Dahill and Detective Thomas Brown drove up to Wyoming and brought him home. It was all over.

Although the taxicab driver furnished the only clue to the kidnapping, by identifying a picture of Verne Sankey as the man named "Gordon" who had given him the kidnap note, the police doubted Sankey was implicated. It just wasn't his *Modus Operandi.*

Then, on August 12, 1933, the police got what they thought was a real break. Roger Touhy, Gus Schackel (alias "Gloomy Gus" Scheafer), Eddie (Father) McFadden, and Willie Sharkey wrapped their car around a telephone pole.

The four of them had been up in northern Wisconsin on a fishing trip. They came barrelling into Elkhorn, Wisconsin, with Willie Sharkey driving, and Willie had had just one too many. Although they ruined the telephone pole and messed up the car, no one was hurt and the incident had almost passed unnoticed.

When the police arrived, the four were taken to the station, where a report was made out. Now, they wanted to know, "who was going to pay for the broken telephone pole?" The whole affair was rather pleasant and very proper, until an officer took a closer look inside the car. There, hidden among the fishing tackle, were several pistols, a rifle, and lots of ammunition.

Since the Elkhorn police thought all this weaponry rather strange equipment for a group of "fishermen," they tossed all

Left to right: George (Machine Gun) Kelly, Shannon, Bates, and Bailey in Federal Court for the trial in the Urschel Kidnapping Case. (UPI Photo)

Machine Gun Kelly and wife confer in court, October, 1933. (UPI photo)

Pretty Boy Floyd with wife and child. (UPI photo)

The scene as the participants in the Kansas City Massacre were sentenced on July 5, 1935. Those sentenced were Louis Stacci of Chicago, Herbert Farmer of Joplin, Richard Galatas of Hot Springs, Ark., and Frank Mulloy of Kansas City. The women are Mrs. Farmer, Mrs. Galatas, and Mrs. Frank Nash who pleaded guilty. In this photograph before the Bar are: Left to right: Mrs. Farmer; Herbert Farmer; Mrs. Galatas; Richard Galatas; Frank Mulloy, and Mrs. Vivian Mathis. (UPI photo)

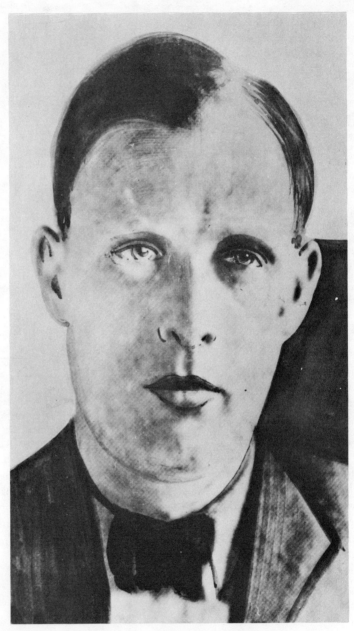

Vernon C. Miller. (UPI photo)

The scene at Kansas City, just after the massacre. (UPI photo)

Mug shots of Frank Nash. (UPI photo)

Adam Richetti (center) shown with John H. Fultz, Chief of Police of Wellesville (left), and Mayor W. H. Doherty (right) after his capture by a posse. (UPI photo)

Two views of "Ma" Barker, allegedly with her husband George. (UPI photo)

Author's note: the man with her is most likely Arthur (Old Man) Dunlap.

The Barker boys. Left to right: Herman, Arthur, Fred. (UPI photo)

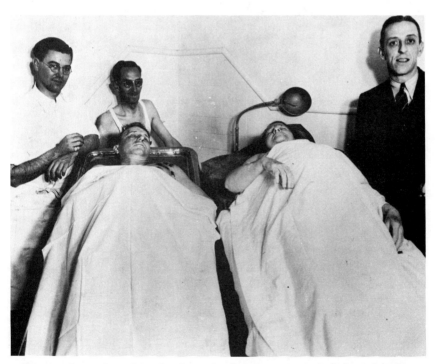

Ma and Fred Barker, dead. Federal men surrounded their bunga-low hideout in Oklawaha, Florida, and killed them in a four-hour machine gun battle. (UPI photo)

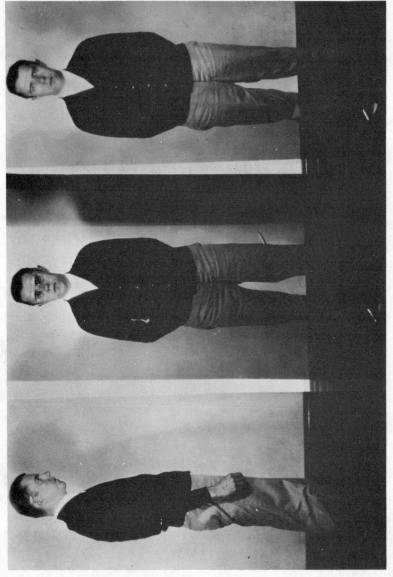

Alvin Karpis. (UPI photo)

Clyde Barrow and Bonnie Parker.

John Dillinger, 1934 (Wide World photo)

Dillinger poses with wooden gun used in his escape from the Crown Point jail. The picture was taken at his father's home near Mooresville, Indiana, while police were searching for him. (Wide World photo)

Dillinger's most famous pose: his arm is around prosecutor Robert Estill. (Wide World photo)

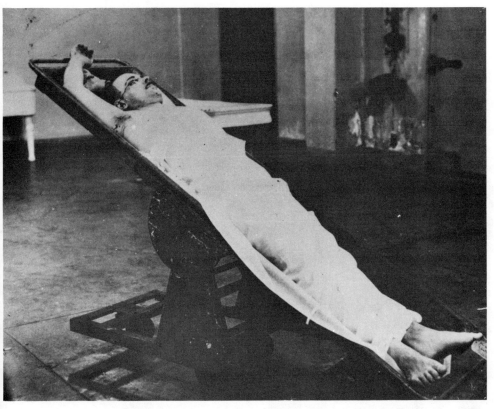

Dillinger's body after he was gunned down by FBI agents in Chicago. (Wide World photo)

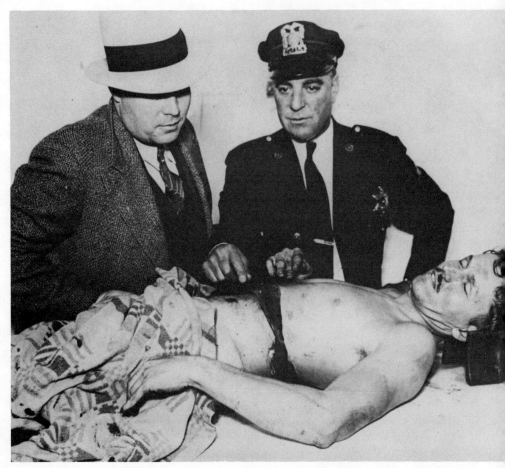

Police Chief Axel C. Stollberg of Niles Center, Illinois (left) and a policeman stand over the body of Baby Face Nelson. Brought down by 17 pieces of lead, the blanket was his covering when his body was found in a ditch. (UPI photo)

John Paul Chase (right) with two federal agents. (UPI photo)

The now-famous photograph of the cigar-puffing, pistol-packing Bonnie Parker. (UPI photo)

four of them in the pokey, and called the FBI in Chicago to find out if they were wanted for anything.

Several agents of the FBI and a detail of Chicago police went to Elkhorn at once, and brought the quartet back to Chicago. The "Terrible Touhy" mob was chief suspect in the kidnapping of William Hamm, Jr.

On August 12, 1933, all four "fishermen" were indicted for the kidnapping of Hamm—much to the amusement of the Barker-Karpis gang.

When word of the Touhy gang's arraignment hit the news-stands, the Barkers and Karpis laughed, but they didn't let their guard down. The Touhy gang wasn't laughing, though; they knew they were innocent.

As ludicrous as it sounds, the gang had, on July 1, 1933, kid-napped John ("Jake the Barber") Factor and held him for ran-som. At the moment, only they knew this, but were in the im-possible situation of being guilty of one kidnapping, and being tried for another.

It is a tribute to our jury system that all of the Touhy gang were acquitted of the Hamm kidnapping. A cry of foul went up across the nation, for everyone "knew" they were guilty. The Touhy gang was not released, however, but held for further in-vestigation regarding the kidnapping of Factor, a Chicago hood-lum. Willie Sharkey couldn't stand the suspense and hanged him-self in his cell.

The Barker-Karpis gang watched all these shenanigans with humor and interest. But business was business, and the Hamm money was too hot to spend; so on August 30, 1933, they held up two bank messengers on the steps of the South St. Paul Post Office.

Although they got a nice $30,000 payroll for their trouble they killed Patrolman Leo Paviek, 35, and seriously wounded a second patrolman, John Yeaman. While this did not especially worry any of the Barker-Karpis gang, it seemed to upset the people of St. Paul quite a bit, so the gang split up for awhile and a number of them went to Chicago.

Off and on the gang hit a few more banks, and continued to come back to St. Paul, which had become the headquarters for the Barker-Karpis mob. The gang had now grown to an enor-mous size, and had an insatiable appetite for money; and since the Hamm kidnapping had gone so well they had the effrontery to plan another, right in the same city.

The larger the gang grew, the looser Ma's control became. She still denied her boys only whiskey and women. The boys, however, were human, and as the gang took on more and more women they began to play around a bit. It was an open secret, but there seemed to be little Ma could do about it.

She tried to get rid of the women by pitting one against the other. She would confide to one certain remarks that another had made about her size, shape, or morals. Then she would go to the other women, and give out the same story. This kept them always at each other's throats, while Ma enjoyed it from the sidelines.

Bank holdups for such a large gang were becoming a problem. Only a limited number of them could participate in a holdup without it becoming a mob scene. And $30,000 divided between 25 or 30 members of a gang didn't net anyone very much. What they needed was a big job that would give everybody plenty of spending money, and that must, of necessity, be another kidnapping.

Not all the gang members agreed that this was a good idea, particularly in the same city, and this caused much dissension among them. They pointed out all the trouble Machine Gun Kelly and his gang had gotten into over a kidnapping, but Ma brushed all their arguments aside with a wave of her pudgy hand. Then the boys and Karpis settled down to plan the big hit.

iv

A little after 8:00 A.M., January 17, 1934, Edward George Bremer, 37, of 92 North Mississippi River Boulevard, St. Paul, Minnesota, drove his eight-year-old daughter, Betty, to the Summit School, at 1150 Goodrich Avenue. She was in the third grade. He then started downtown to the Commercial State Bank, where he held the position of president.

As he stopped for the light at the corner, the door of his car suddenly opened, and Alvin Karpis slipped in beside him. At the same moment Fred Barker came up on the driver's side, unseen by Bremer. Startled, Bremer opened the door on the driver's side and tried to get out, but Alvin brought a gun butt down on his head several times, and Fred shoved him over and took the wheel.

They abandoned the car in an outlying residential district, transferring the unconscious Bremer to a car, driven by Dock, who, together with Harry Campbell, had followed Bremer's car.

When Bremer came to, he was blinded by a pair of taped goggles, and his own blood. Someone, he never knew who, lifted his goggles just enough to allow him to dimly see, and ordered him to sign several kidnap notes. The voice, probably Dock's, in a stage whisper told him to name "the man who will handle the paying of your ransom. A contact man."

He signed the notes as he was ordered, and then the gang took several objects from him for identification. Among these were his gold watch and chain. He had named Walter W. Magee, a prominent contractor and close friend, as his contact man.

About two hours after the abduction, Mr. Walter W. Magee received a curt telephone message. "Well, we've got your friend Bremer, and if you're not damn careful, we'll get you too!" They also told him to look on the back doorstep of his office, where he would find a note.

The note said that Bremer's car would be found at the Highland Park Water Tower, at Snellings and Otto avenues. It also demanded $200,000 in fives, tens and twenty dollar bills—not in consecutive numbers, and not marked. He was also warned not to communicate with the authorities or the newspapers. He was, however, told to place an ad in the *Minneapolis Tribune* morning edition when the money was ready, reading, "WE ARE READY. ALICE."

Bearing Bremer's signature, the postscript read: "I have named you as payoff man. You are responsible for my safety. Pay the full amount of the money." The note was poorly typed and badly spelled. The signature of Bremer, while authentic, was decidedly shaky.

The abandoned car, a Lincoln, was not found at the corner of Snellings and Otto, but near 1910 Edgecombe Road. Fear for Bremer's safety was immediate, as the front seat and parts of the back were covered with blood.

Sawyer reported to the Barkers that Magee's house was being watched day and night, and that his phones had been tapped. It would be entirely too risky to try to communicate with him further. He suggested they deliver the next notes to Dr. H. T. Nippert, who was a family physician and a good friend of the Bremers.

Early on the morning of January 18, the phone of Doctor H. T. Nippert rang. He was told by a husky voice to go to his front door and see what he would find. He immediately got out of bed and went to the door. Someone had shattered a glass panel with a milk bottle, but since the bedroom was in the rear of the house he had heard nothing.

Lying on the floor, where it had been shoved under the door, was a large brown envelope, which contained three separate notes. Two of them were sealed in other envelopes, but the third was addressed to him, and instructed him to deliver the others to Walter Magee.

Also included in the note to Dr. Nippert were instructions for him to follow. He was warned, under penalty of death for both himself and Bremer, to follow them explicitly and tell the police nothing. He was told that Bremer had been injured, and needed medical attention. Being a doctor, he followed the instructions.

Meeting the kidnappers at a prearranged rendezvous, he was blindfolded and taken for a five-hour ride to their hideout. Here he was allowed to administer to the injuries of Bremer. These consisted of head wounds, which had bled profusely and were badly discolored. They had been doctored by both Fred Barker and Alvin Karpis, who had given him the injuries, but their efforts were amateurish.

Dr. Nippert and Bremer were not allowed to speak to each other, for fear some clue might be given out as to the hideout location. When the hurried treatment was finished, the doctor was again blindfolded and returned to St. Paul. Here he immediately reported the incident to the police, and to Walter Magee.

Walter Magee then told Bremer's mother and father. His father was Adolph Bremer, part owner of the Joseph Schmidt Brewing Company. He told them that the wounds were not too serious, but that Bremer was suffering mostly from exhaustion and depression.

On January 22, another note turned up in the office of a Coal Company official, and was immediately turned over to the police. The note was written in anger, the grammar horrible, and the spelling impossible; but it made one thing clear. They were tired of waiting, and they wanted the police and the newspapers out of the picture. It ended, "From now on you get the silent treatment until you reach us someway yourself. Better not wait too long."

Then Adolph Bremer released a statement to the press in an effort to smooth the ruffled feelings of the kidnappers and save his son's life. "I am sorry the impression has been spread that information has been given to the police. Whatever information has been passed out has been given against my will and has created, through the newspapers, a wrong impression."

January 25, another note turned up, in a coffee can placed on the front porch of a St. Paul resident whose only connection with the Bremer family was what he had read in the newspapers. He immediately contacted the police and turned over the note.

Here, at last, was something tangible. The note demanded the $200,000 be delivered that night. Walter Magee was to go to the Jefferson bus station, and use an enclosed baggage check. In a bag which had been checked there he would find a note. He was to read it at precisely 8:20 P.M.

When Magee picked up the bag and read the note, he followed it to the letter. He took the 8:40 P.M. bus to Des Moines, Iowa, where he checked into a hotel, using the name John B. Brakeeham. However, when Magee received word to deliver the money, he couldn't get at it. It was under a time lock in the bank at St. Paul. So Magee waited at the hotel for some word from the kidnappers, but no one contacted him and he returned to St. Paul.

Over a week had passed since the kidnapping, and by now the family of Edward G. Bremer feared the worst. Adolph Bremer called another hasty press conference and told the kidnappers, through the newspapers, that all police authorities, including the FBI, had been called off the case for 72 hours, to allow contact.

Days passed, then on February 4, two and one-half weeks after the kidnapping, a final note, addressed to "Honest Adolph," was left at a Catholic church. It instructed Walter Magee to bring $200,000 to 969 University Avenue, where he would find a Chevrolet with an oil company sign in each window. Before entering it, he was to take a note from the pocket in the door, stand with his back to the curb, and read it.

Magee followed the instructions, carrying the heavy package of money with him. The note was in the pocket; he read it, replaced it, then went to his own car and drove down State Highway 1, through Farmington and Northfield, and on to Faribault. From here he took a cross road out, driving at the rate of 15 miles per hour. While driving down this side road, he saw four red flashes of light. This was the signal. He was to stop here, get out, and place the money on the ground. Then he was to get out of there fast. He did as he was instructed.

Early on the morning of February 7, Edward G. Bremer was led from his place of long imprisonment to a car. A short while later, they transferred to a second car, and he was made to sit on the floor in the rear. Several hours later, he was pushed from the small sedan, and Fred and Dock Barker and Alvin Karpis drove away rapidly.

Bremer had been told to count up to fifteen before he removed his blindfold on penalty of death. He slowly counted, making certain they were a long ways from him, before he slipped the blindfold and squinted at the sudden light.

Bremer had been given a few dollars for bus fare back to St. Paul, so now he limped into Rochester, where he called a cab and went to the bus station. Here he learned that he had missed the last bus for the Twin Cities, so he went to the railroad station, where he took a train to Owatonna. Here he got a bus to St. Paul, arriving at his father's house around midnight.

Suffering from exhaustion, and still dazed from his experience, Bremer perhaps never thought of calling his home for help. He was also gripped with a fear that the kidnappers might still be watching him. One of the gang had remarked, within his hearing, that another gang had offered them $50,000 to turn him over to them when they were through with him.

When he arrived at his father's house, Bremer was unshaven, and very close to a nervous collapse. He was immediately ordered to bed by Dr. Joseph Sprafka, another family physician, while authorities sought to question him about his ordeal.

Upon the return of his son, Adolph Bremer issued a statement thanking President Roosevelt, who was a close friend of his, and who had promised all the facilities of the federal government to bring the kidnappers to justice. He also thanked Minnesota Governor Lloyd B. Olson for his help and encouragement. He prayed "that other fathers and mothers will be spared the agony of a similar ordeal. The hideous hours of suspense have been almost unbearable for us all."

With only one case lost (The Touhy acquittal) out of the 20 they had undertaken since the passing of the Lindbergh Law, the FBI pledged its help. J. Edgar Hoover said that each of his 314 agents would remain on the alert; that they would follow up the slightest clue which might lead to the arrest of any implicated person, no matter how remotely connected with the case.

During the entire period of the kidnapping, which lasted 22 long days, Ma Barker had been the adhesive that had bound the gang together. Including the hanger-ons, the gang had become an unwieldly affair of some 35 people.

She had acted as a kind of "crime computer" into which was fed the bits and pieces of information. Based upon this material, she barked forth her orders and made the important decisions. Now the ransom had been paid, and she was elated.

It must be remembered that $200,000 ($85,000 in $5.00 bills, and the rest in $10.00 bills) was a large, and unwieldly mass of money. To hide such an amount safely took some doing. Fred Goetz was given the responsibility for hiding half of it. He was fully trusted by Ma and the other gang members. Ma buried the rest of the money herself.

v

For such a perfect kidnapping, things began to fall apart with a startling suddenness. First the victim remembered that on the way back from the gang hideout they had stopped along the road to refuel. This was done from gas tins carried in the back of the car.

When a farmer found four empty gas cans, together with a gas spout, beside his fields, he notified the local police, who in turn notified the FBI. Soon agents were on the scene, but not before the helpful farmer had neatly arranged the cans for their removal. His fingerprints were all over them, but on the outside chance that he hadn't obliterated all others, they were sent to the FBI laboratory.

Luck was with them, and the laboratory turned up the print of an index finger that was not the farmer's. After an exhaustive search of FBI files, the print was matched. It was Dock's. The gang responsible for the kidnapping had been identified.

FBI agents also searched the shoulders along the route taken by Magee when he delivered the ransom money. This search also paid off, when agents found four discarded flashlights, with red lenses. They had been wiped clean of fingerprints, but, fitted with their red lenses, they were unusual.

The name of the flashlights, "Merit Product," also gave the FBI a clue. Agents visited every store in the St. Paul-Minneapolis area, trying to trace their purchase. Here again, the tiresome legwork paid off, when a girl in the F & W Grand Silver Store in St. Paul remembered selling them. From a picture, she also identified Alvin Karpis as the purchaser.

Now there was no doubt in the world that the Barker-Karpis gang had pulled off the kidnapping. And there was something else the FBI knew: They had the serial number of every bill in the 23,200 that made up the $200,000 ransom. This list was circulated throughout the country, and sent to Canada, Mexico, and Cuba.

Joseph P. Moran, an honor graduate of Tufts Medical School, Boston, Massachusetts, an officer in the A. E. F. in France during the World War, and a former physician of LaSalle, Illinois, was also a member of the large and complicated Barker-Karpis gang.

"Doc" Moran's decline as a law abiding citizen came in July 1928, when a grand jury indicted him and a woman aide in La-Salle, Illinois. They were charged with performing an illegal abortion, which had resulted in the death of the patient. They were both found guilty, and given a sentence of one to ten years in the penitentiary. Moran served his in the Illinois State Penitentiary at Joliet.

While there Moran made many friends, as he worked in the prison hospital. One of these friends was a powerful one: Ollie Berg, who was serving a ten year to life sentence; he told Moran he would soon be free, and would, for favors, take care of him.

"Doc" Moran was paroled a year and four months later, and went to Chicago, which was Berg's center of power; soon he had his medical license restored. He opened an office in Chicago, where he treated regular patients by day and hoodlums by night.

Just when things were going along real smooth, "Doc" Moran's old weakness, liquor, and his insatiable appetite for money got him in trouble again. Back he went to Joliet, for violation of parole—another abortion complaint.

The underworld needed him, though, so strings were pulled; money changed hands, and in eleven months "Doc" Moran, with his license again restored, was doing business at the same old stand. Shortly thereafter, his benefactor Ollie Berg secured his own release.

Soon business was brisk for the Good Doctor. The prohibition gang wars in Chicago gave him a lot of patients. If the patient died on the operating table, he was simply taken out on Lake Michigan and dumped. If the patient lived, the doctor collected a handsome fee. He couldn't lose—or so he thought.

In late 1933, Moran was introduced to Russell Gibson, alias Slim Gray, a member of the Barker-Karpis gang; through this introduction, "Doc" Moran was also absorbed into the gang. By now he was drinking more and more, and with each drink his abilities grew and grew, but only in his own mind.

He finally agreed to take on a few cases of plastic surgery, although he was no plastic surgeon. But with enough liquor under his belt there was nothing he wouldn't attempt. And so it was that "Doc" Moran agreed to alter the faces of Fred Barker and Alvin

Karpis. He also told them he would erase their fingerprints, with the use of acid and a mechanical pencil sharpener.

At his Irving Park Hotel address in Chicago, "Doc" Moran operated on both Fred and Karpis, and butchered them but good. The pain they suffered afterward was in a small measure some retribution for their many crimes. The operation did change the appearance of Alvin Karpis a great deal, but the attempt to erase the fingerprints was a dismal failure.

Fred Goetz, better known as Shotgun George Ziegler, became a member of Ma's gang shortly before the Hamm kidnapping. He was an enigma, to say the least. He was 37 years old when he joined the Barker-Karpis gang in 1933, and was already a classic criminal.

During the World War he had been an army pilot, holding the rank of second lieutenant. Prior to this he had been a landscape engineer, and was a graduate of the University of Illinois. He was also an excellent golfer, and a former football player. He was a handsome man, gracious, well spoken, well dressed, and the owner of a personality well-suited for a con-man.

He graduated from the University of Illinois in 1922, and a short time later was arrested on a charge of rape. He denied his guilt, and was released on bail pending trial. He wanted to jump bail, but didn't want his parents to lose the money, so he decided to raise it quickly.

With two others, Goetz tried to hold up a doctor, in front of the Edgewater Beach Hotel on Chicago's lakefront. He knew the doctor carried a large amount of money on him at all times. The doctor, however, knew of his vulnerability, and always carried a gun.

When the three jumped him, he started shooting; but Goetz, the better shot, killed the doctor. By now there were so many people pouring out of the hotel that they had to abandon the idea of robbery. This would start Fred Goetz on his career as Shotgun George Ziegler.

Later he would become a gunman in the Al Capone mob. He was also a prime suspect in the 1929 St. Valentine's Day massacre in Chicago. Here, several members of the Bugs Moran gang, and two visitors, were waiting for Moran in a garage at 2122 North Clark Street. At 10:30 A.M., a black touring sedan pulled up outside, and four men—two in police uniforms—came in and lined up everybody.

The gangsters, thinking the men were from the police, offered no resistance. Then, with a chatter of machine guns, the phony officers killed Pete Gusenberg, James Clark, John May, Adam Heyer, and the two visitors, Al Weinshank and Dr. Reinhart H. Schwimmer, an optometrist. Frank Gusenberg, fourteen bullets heavier, crawled 20 feet to the garage door, still alive. He died later.

The prime suspects for this butchery were John Scalise, Albert Anselmi, Verne Miller, Machine Gun Jack McGurn, Shotgun George Ziegler—all of the Capone mob—and Ed Fletcher and George F. Lewis of Detroit's Purple gang. From here on out the career of Shotgun George Ziegler went only one way, and that was up.

Eventually, as noted previously, he became so trusted a member of the Barker-Karpis gang that they gave him a large and generous portion of the Bremer kidnapping money to hide for them.

Ziegler had the money stashed in the garage of his wife's uncle, and the gang sat back to wait for the money to cool. Before this could happen, though, Ziegler's past began parading before him, and he slowly began to lose his mind. With the gears in his brain slipping, his tongue began to wag, and wag, and wag.

One night it was decided by the gang that Shotgun Ziegler had to go. Fred, Dock, and Alvin Karpis were elected to take care of this little chore. So, on March 22, 1934, just two months after the Bremer kidnapping, Shotgun George Ziegler stepped out of his favorite cafe, in Cicero, and into history. Four shotguns, probably belonging to Ziegler himself, barked in unison, and he fell dead, his head blasted to pulp.

In bumping off Ziegler, the Barker-Karpis gang made two dreadful mistakes. First, now only Ziegler's bereaved widow knew where their money was hidden; second, they opened a whole new vista of investigation for the FBI.

Ma Barker promptly took care of the first mistake. She rushed over to the saddened, but trusting, widow and persuaded her to turn over the Bremer money. There was nothing they could do about the second mistake, for the FBI—never ones to waste time— were already acting on it.

Interesting things were found on Ziegler's body: membership cards to the Mohawk Country Club of Bensenville, Illinois, and the Chicago Yacht Club, plus a $1,000 bill. His address was also found, and a search of his apartment gave further evidence and names of members of the Barker-Karpis gang.

Ziegler had had his mail delivered to a service station so it couldn't be traced to him. The FBI found the station, run by Frank Blohoweak. Blohoweak told them he had accepted Ziegler's mail for quite some time, as he (Ziegler) was an interior decorator and traveled a lot.

With this sudden turn of events, the Barker-Karpis gang began to break up and spread throughout the country. Some of its members included Volney Davis, Russell Gibson (alias Slim Gray), Homer "Big Homer" Wilson (also known as "Charley Potatoes"), William E. Meade (called "Christ Kid"), William "Bill" Weaver (alias Phoenix Donald), Harry "Dutch" Sawyer, Harry Campbell, Jesse Doyle, "Doc" Joseph P. Moran, and Charles "Big Fitz" Fitzgerald.

Then the FBI traced some of the Bremer kidnap money, passed in Chicago banks, to John J. McLaughlin, known as "Boss" McLaughlin. He was a prominent politician and had many influential friends, who were leading Democrats. This didn't help him, though, for he had handled over $57,000 of the kidnap money. For this he was eventually sent to Leavenworth for five years. He later died in prison.

Fear gripped members of the gang, as the FBI began chipping away at their numbers. Even Ma Barker decided it might be a good idea if she dyed her hair a different color. Everybody's nerves were frayed, and they started to quarrel among themselves.

Ma had long held a violent dislike for Volney Davis's girl friend, Edna Murray. She had been known as "The Kissing Bandit," because she would kiss her victims, after she held them up. Later the gang named her "rabbits," because she had escaped from jails three times.

Volney Davis was a Cherokee Indian, and had been with the Barkers off and on since 1920; but past loyalties were soon forgotten in the underworld, and the smoldering argument between Volney Davis and the Barkers now flared into open flame. But he fared better than most people who tried to win an argument with Ma Barker. Dock gave Davis some money, and told him, "Don't ever let me see you again." Davis took off.

Nerves were also twanging elsewhere. In Toledo, Ohio, "Doc" Joseph P. Moran got very, very drunk in the Casino Club. He began to boast of how good he was, and how dependent the gang was upon him and his skills.

Turning to Russell Gibson he said, "Slim Gray, you know what's the trouble with you. You're yellow—you're all yellow." He was yelling and waving his arms wildly. "I've got this gang in the hollow of my hand," and he banged his palm, "right here." And then he stood there, weaving unsteadily, staring down at his cupped hands.

It was then that a few of the boys persuaded the Good Doctor that what he really needed was a cooling ride in a boat on Lake Erie. Today, somewhere at the bottom of the lake, Joseph P. Moran's bones gently shift with the moving waters and the stirring of the silt.

When the big split came, Ma and Fred decided to head for Florida, while Dock elected to remain in Chicago. Alvin Karpis, Bill Weaver, and Harry Campbell voted to stay together, and just keep on the move. Still other members of the gang went down to Hot Springs to take a few of the hot baths, and cool off.

On January 8, 1935, the tailing of a few of the Barker-Karpis gun molls paid off, when they led FBI agents to a Northside Chicago Apartment on Surf Street. The agents surrounded the building, and then called for the surrender of its occupants.

Byron Bolton, Clare Gibson (wife of Russell), and Ruth Heidy surrendered without an argument. Russell Gibson, however, was not so accommodating. He was not only wanted for his part in the Bremer kidnapping, but also for murder in Oklahoma. In addition, he was a confirmed dope addict, and was now hopped up.

He tried to flee by using a rear fire escape, but an agent was posted there. They traded shots, and the agent proved to be the better marksman. Although Gibson was wearing a steel vest, he was drilled through the heart by a bullet from a .351 rifle. The steel jacket bullet plowed through the "bulletproof vest," passed through Gibson, and then smashed itself against the vest again.

Inside the apartment agents found automatic pistols, automatic rifles, police revolvers, a 20 gauge shotgun, lots of ammunition, and a map of Florida, *with the Ocala region circled.*

The apartment where Dock was thought to be staying was on Pine Grove Avenue, and it was empty when agents broke in. Dock had gone to the Surf Street apartment address. The FBI was still keeping this place under surveillance. So, when Dock Barker and Mildred Kuhlman walked out of the apartment, they stepped right into the waiting arms of the agents. All Dock had to say about the situation was, "This is a hell of a time to be caught without a gun!"

As expected Dock would tell them nothing, and nothing was found on him, or in his apartment, that would help in the search for other missing members of the gang. It was decided, however, to keep his capture a secret for awhile, until agents checked out the Florida map found in the Gibson apartment.

It was Byron Bolton who began talking, and narrowed the search just a bit more. He said he had recently met Dock Barker and Russell Gibson in Georgia, and they had returned to Chicago together. On the way back he heard talk between Gibson and Dock about an alligator named "Ole Joe," and how they had tried to shoot him.

They had put a pig in a barrel, and towed it, on a lake, behind a motorboat. When the alligator tried to get at the pig, they shot at it with machine guns. They had missed the alligator, and he had gotten the pig. They all had a great laugh over this.

A special squad of FBI agents flew from Chicago to Ocala, Florida, and were later reinforced by agents from several of the southern states. Their first order of business was to find out where there was a lake, in the Ocala region, occupied by an alligator named "Ole Joe."

A senior citizen was found who occasionally led fishing parties to various parts of the county. "Yes, I know of two such alligators," he told them, "One is in Lake Walbert, near Gainesville, Florida, and the other in Lake Weir, near Oklawaha."

Lake Walbert was out, as it was too far away to be considered in the Ocala area. Lake Weir, however, would do very nicely, as it was only 19 miles south of Ocala. So all attentions were turned to a small town with the unlikely name of Oklawaha.

It was not much of a town. If you passed through at 60 miles per hour, all you would see was a blur. Sprinkled along the highway, it consisted mostly of a small grocery store, a couple of filling stations, the summer houses for northern folk, and a few permanent homes.

The FBI began infiltrating this small village in twos, to avoid suspicion. They came dressed as tourists, complete with fishing and hunting gear. They took extra pains not to congregate, or recognize one another.

House by house, they began the process of elimination, until at last all attention was centered on a white, two-storied bungalow nestled along the banks of Lake Weir. It was almost hidden from the road by large oak trees, dressed in long tresses of Spanish moss.

One of the agents reported he was sure he had seen Ma Barker standing near a boat at the lake. The next day one of the agents packed his fishing gear, and settled himself comfortably on the pier belonging to the house under suspicion.

Before long Fred Barker walked up to him and asked how the fishing was. "Pretty bad here," the agent answered, all smiles. "Guess you people have fished this side all out." Fred laughed, shaking his head, and then went back to the house. The agent quickly reeled in his line, and then, trying not to show his excitement, left.

Other agents had been busy too. They had found out that the people in the suspected house were the T. C. Blackburns. Mrs. Blackburn was a real generous woman, the local people explained. Why, she would buy a dozen eggs from a local chicken farm, and pay for it with a dollar and not even wait for her change. This when beef roast was selling for 12½ cents per pound.

Her boys were just as generous about the town. They would buy four dollars worth of groceries, pay for it with a ten dollar bill, and leave without asking for their change. Yes sir! The Blackburns were real fine people, and well liked in the village.

"Blackie," as Fred was affectionately called in the village, often went hunting and fishing with some of the local boys. He was a good hunter, but acted just a little bit odd. But these eccentricities were put down as those you expect to find among the idle rich.

Blackie would never stray very far from his car radio. Even when hunting he would keep the car in sight, and return ever so often to listen to the news broadcasts. Most people thought he was just a sports fan, who wanted the ball scores.

There had been two other boys who came and went. They had been here just a few days ago. They were Alvin Karpis, who posed as a Mr. Wagner, and Harry Campbell, who went under the name of Summers. Both Alvin and Campbell cagily left their girl friends back in Miami. They knew how Ma was about women, and besides, Delores Delaney, Alvin's girl, was pregnant.

All the boys were fond of hunting and fishing, and had really enjoyed themselves. Once, one of them got a snootful in a local home, and the other two boys had to hide him in the woods until he sobered up. Ma Blackburn, the local people explained, would have raised holy hell if she had seen one of her boys drunk.

The group often went to Ocala for shopping sprees, as it was the nearest large town. Here, other agents got positive identification of the Barkers and Campbell, but a rather vague identification of the disguised Karpis. Little by little, and piece by piece, the FBI established beyond a shadow of a doubt that the house was occupied by Ma Barker and her son Fred.

vi

At approximately 6:45 A.M., Wednesday, January 16, 1935, an agent of the FBI, E. J. Connelley of the Cincinnati office, approached the Blackburn house in Oklawaha, and ordered those inside to come out. Ma Barker came to the door, and demanded to know who was there.

"Is your son here?" Connelley asked her.

"Who wants him?" Ma snapped.

"A Federal officer," Connelley replied.

With this Ma jumped back out of the door, and Fred stepped up with a machine gun and cut loose. Connelley jumped deftly behind a large oak tree and was not hit. But the battle was on.

Just to the west of the house was the servants' quarters. Inside were Willie Woodbury, a Negro cook for the Barkers, and his wife. They had heard strange mutterings and whispers going on outside the house for some time, but not for one minute did it occur to either of them to investigate.

Willie and his wife had worked for the "Blackburns" for about two months, and they knew she was a strange woman. They also knew better than stick their nose into any of her business. She had one room in the house (the arsenal) that they were forbidden even to enter.

Whenever Willie or his wife wanted to leave the main house, they had to ask Ma's permission. When he drove the "boys" into town for a shopping trip, she always gave him the third degree when they got back. She wanted to know if they had been drinking, or playing around with women.

No sir! Willie and his wife stayed right there in their warm bed, and let the mutterings and whisperings go on. When the chatter of machine guns started, however, their complacency vanished. Particularly when a few of Ma's answering shots splattered themselves against the bedpost. Willie and his wife hit the floor, face down, and there they would lie for over five hours.

The FBI agents had been eyeing the servants' quarters warily, but they had made no attempt to enter it. Now, however, they began to pound on the door, and demanded those inside to open up. Willie told them, "They's just two Negro servants in here, laying on the floor, and we ain't about to open that door. If you wants it opened, you do it!"

With this the agents kicked open the door, and seeing the two on the floor told them to stay there and they would be all right. Terrified and bewildered, the Woodburys lay huddled, and shaking, on the floor. Machine gun bullets were flying all around, and an occasional one would enter the small house.

Across the road was the house of Mrs. A. F. Westberry. She and her daughter were both asleep. When the commotion broke out, and bullets began to penetrate her bedroom, she yelled to her daughter, "Let's get out of here." They kicked out a window at the rear of the house, crawled out, and fled.

Almost immediately two FBI agents jumped up out of the brush, and ordered them to stop. The two terrified women, startled, only put on more steam. Then the agents fired a warning burst from their machine guns, but the women never slowed down. They fled to the safety of a neighbor's home, where they remained throughout the battle.

A later examination of Mrs. Westbury's bedroom showed three bullets, from the Barker's guns, had entered the bed, right where her head had been only moments before she had fled.

The battle between Ma, Fred, and the FBI raged with unrelenting fury. There would be a terrific barrage for about fifteen minutes, then an eerie period of silence. Suddenly someone, either in the yard, or in the house would shift positions, and the fusillade would begin, again.

This was to continue for over four hours, during which time the FBI would fire over 1,500 rounds of machine gun and rifle fire into the attractive house. Later damage estimates would range from $2,000 to $3,000. In 1935, this amount of money would represent a comfortable yearly income for millions of Americans.

A little before eleven o'clock, the shooting from the inside stopped entirely. The agents now moved in a little closer, and were able to get a few teargas shells into the upstairs windows. Prior to this, the shells had fallen short, choking the agents themselves, or had crashed harmlessly against the side of the house.

After a period of about 45 minutes with no returning fire, it became obvious that an entry would have to be made; but apparently none of the fifteen agents wanted to be first. Such was the respect they held for the fury of that old woman, Ma Barker, and the marksmanship of her son, Fred.

So Special Agent Connelley sent for Willie Woodbury, and told him to go into the house and see if the Barkers were dead. "They won't hurt you," he told Willie, "you've worked for them." This, unhappily, was not entirely true. If Willie had unexpectedly entered, either the room where a very much alive Fred and Ma Barker were crouched with smoking machine guns, he would have been stitched right up the middle.

Willie's face was ashen as he approached the front steps and slowly began to climb them. He was urged on by words and by the guns of the agents, who remained behind their large oak trees. When he reached the top of the stairs, he made a dash to the door and tried it. It was locked! Happily, he raced back, shouting, "That door's shut."

"Well, go back and cut the screen; then kick the door down," he was ordered.

Unhappily, Willie again crossed the porch, each step taken by a foot that seemed to weigh a thousand pounds. He took out his knife and slit the screen, reached in and unlatched the door, then kicked at the main door, furiously, expecting a bullet from that strange woman to hit him at any moment. The door suddenly yawned open, but no bullets came.

Putting his handkerchief over his face, he slowly entered, choking from the teargas fumes. About sixty seconds later he appeared at an upstairs window, and shouted down, "They's all daid."

Cautiously, one of the agents left the security of his oak tree, and with care entered the house. The Barkers could be holding a gun on Willie, making him say what he had. But about a minute later the agent appeared at the window, and confirmed that both Ma and Fred were indeed dead. Suddenly the place was alive with agents, searching and probing, looking for others that might be hiding inside.

At 10:30 that morning a volley had been fired by the agents into the house, and these were probably the shots that had killed them both. Ma had taken a shot through her heart, and Fred had eleven wounds, mostly in his left shoulder.

In the room where Ma lay, folded over on her back, there were empty machine gun shells all over the floor. A still-hot machine gun was in her fat, stubby hands. Near the upstairs window, where she had been crouched, were several fresh machine gun clips, ready for instant use.

On the dresser lay an envelope with ten $1,000 bills in it. There was $4,000 more found on Fred, in a money belt, and an additional $273 was turned up in Ma's purse and Fred's pockets.

There were a number of violin cases scattered throughout the house. They had been used to carry submachine guns in—certainly Fred, Ma, Karpis, or Campbell had never owned a violin. At one time, when Willie was carrying a couple of the violin cases into the house, he muttered that they were sure heavy fiddles.

With the furor over, the larger number of the agents were now busy taking the house apart board by board, looking for money— Bremer kidnapping money. What their bullets hadn't wrecked, their crowbars now would. Other agents had to devote their attention to directing traffic, for there were hundreds of cars filled with gawking curiosity seekers.

On the lower floor lay Fred, still twisted where the bullets had tossed him. He had taken a complete burst from one of the agent's machine guns in his left shoulder.

The bodies were removed to a mortuary in Ocala, while the FBI continued the systematic search of the house. Agents remained here for over a week (Willie cooked for them) and they pried up the floor boards and tore holes in the walls. When they finally left, the interior, as well as the exterior, was a shambles.

Following the agents' empty-handed departure, the morbid curiosity seekers moved in. The throng became so large, and so insistent, that the owners of the house finally gave up, and started charging admission. This would continue for some time, and the profits would pay for most of the renovations.

The house had been rented in November 1934 by Ma and Fred while in Miami, from Carson Bradford, President of the Biscayne Kennel Club. He was represented in the deal by his associate, Joe Adams.

Ma and Fred were staying at the posh El Commodore Hotel at the time, and when the deal was consummated, with rent set at $75.00 a month, Adams had flowers sent to Ma's room. He described her as being a "nice, sweet old lady."

vii

With the killing of Ma and Fred Barker, and the capture of Dock, J. Edgar Hoover was elated. "The backbone of the gang is broken," he announced. "We intend to knock off every one who ever worked with this gang. It may run to 25 or 30 people. We have always felt that the Barker-Karpis mob was the brainiest and most dangerous in the country. As long as it was at large, we felt that a kidnapping or a big bank robbery might take place at any time. It roved from the Pacific across the continent, through the middle west and the south. We never heard of any of it's activities around here, or New York."

He also had a few unkind remarks to make about Ma Barker, "She was a jealous old battle axe. She dictated who her four sons' lady friends were to be. We even heard that when they wanted to go out on a party, they would go to another town, from the one where she was. There is a legend that she taught her boys never to be taken alive; however, Arthur Barker is the second member of the family to be in federal custody."

After several days, plans were made to give the Barkers a pauper's funeral, however Sheriff S. C. M. Thomas, of Ocala, received a telegram on January 17 from Sheriff Rogers, of Jasper County, Missouri. George Barker of Carthage, Missouri, wanted to claim the bodies of his wife and son, and also their property.

George Barker was working as a handy man for a filling station in Carthage, and had read of the deaths. He wanted to bring them back and bury them beside Herman, but he just didn't have the money.

The cash found in the house at Oklawaha was confiscated as evidence by the FBI; but they knew it couldn't be Bremer kidnap money—the serial numbers didn't check. It could have been exchange money, or even money from a bank robbery, but there was no way this could be proven.

Long months would pass, and Ma and Fred would lay on slabs in the mortuary in Ocala, while George Barker waited for money so he could take them back to Oklahoma. In the meantime he forbade their burial in Florida. The situation would become almost intolerable.

Eventually, however, George Barker was to claim sufficient sums to allow him to take the bodies back to Welch, Oklahoma, for burial. He arrived in Ocala, one day with an ambulance, and the now mummified bodies were loaded aboard. Then it was overland to Tulsa, and on to the lonely cemetery, near Welch, where they were laid to rest beside Herman, in poorly marked graves.

Even today, the only Barker grave with a proper marker is Herman's, with its grey, granite stone, bought and paid for with stolen money. And even today, the nearest grave to the Barkers' is over 300 feet away. In death, they are still as unacceptable as they were in life.

On May 18, 1935, Dock Barker, Olive Berg, and others were

found guilty of complicity in the kidnapping of Edward George Bremer. Both Dock and Berg received sentences of life imprisonment.

Dock was sent to Alcatraz, where for four years he spent most of his time in one fight after another. At 3:30 A.M., Friday, the 13th of January, 1939, Dock Barker, Rufus McCain, William Martin, Henri Young, and Dale Stamphill made a break.

They sawed through the steel bars of their cell, and made their way out into a thick fog. The break was discovered a short while later, and searchlights caught up with them, with their piercing beams, and the guards immediately opened fire with machine guns.

Two of the convicts, wounded, gave up immediately, and a few minutes later, two others surrendered, unhurt. Dock chose to ignore the commands of the guards for his surrender, and plunged into the icy waters of San Francisco Bay, but the machine gun bullets caught up with him.

In the prison hospital, his skull smashed by the bullets and his left leg broken, he muttered: "I was a fool to try it. I'm all shot to hell!" He died at 5:45 P.M., the following day. His body unclaimed, he was buried in potter's field on the mainland.

Eventually the other members of the Barker-Karpis gang were brought to task for their crimes. Several died in shootouts with the FBI or police, and many others would disappear behind the grim grey walls of prison (see Chapter 4).

After finishing his term at Leavenworth, Lloyd "Red" Barker, now 51 years old, was released. He lived for a number of years in Denver, Colorado, where he became assistant manager of a bar and grill. He married, children were born, and to all intents and purposes this should have ended the Barker story.

But, on the night of March 22, 1949, Red Barker, coming home from work, put his key into the lock of his front door, and before he could turn it, his wife, Jean Barker, 37, blasted him, right through the door, with a 20 gauge shotgun. She was mentally ill, and later told the court, in her own defense, that she had feared her husband was going to kill her and the children.

Only George Barker would live the honest life, and die a natural death. And remembering his words about his family, one wonders about him: "She never would let me do with them what I wanted to," was his cry of innocence. This became his crutch, as he saw his wife and sons turned into vicious killers.

He would live the decent life, working at menial tasks, until his death. He would click his disapproval at the actions of the family he had sired. Perhaps his was the greatest crime of all, for his failure to exercise control over his family had made possible all that had come to pass.

••4••

Old Creepy

This is the narrative of a person who was a marbles champion in Topeka, Kansas; a kidnapper in St. Paul, Minnesota; a murderer in Wisconsin; and Public Enemy Number One In America.

Francis Albin Karpoviecz was born in Montreal, Canada, to Lithuanian immigrant parents, August 10, 1909. He had three sisters, was the baby of the family, and grew to be a pale, thin, and sickly boy. Because he was the youngest, and such a fragile child, his parents, John and Anna Karpoviecz, were more than indulgent with him, and he became a spoiled brat.

The Karpovieczs first immigrated to England from Lithuania and settled in London. As an unskilled laborer, John Karpoviecz found the going tough, so he and his family moved to New York. From here they moved on to Grand Rapids, Michigan, where he found work as an automobile painter. Next they moved to Montreal, where Francis was born.

After four years in Canada, the Karpovieczs again moved, this time to Topeka, where John obtained employment with the Santa Fe Railroad, and he remained here for twelve years.

Seemingly always on the go, the Karpovieczs again moved, this time to Chicago, in 1923, where they settled in the stockyard slums. This was the neighborhood of the five-points gang, and the home of Lester M. Gillis (see Chapter 7).

It was here that the frail Canadian met Lester, a Chicago hood with a baby face. They became fast friends. From him, Francis learned the art of boosting cars, and stripping them. From these humble beginnings they would later go on to bigger things.

Francis, with his sickly body, and Lester, with his small stature and his baby face, were naturals for each other. Neither of them were wanted as members by the local gangs, so they elected to go it alone. They were just getting organized when Francis suffered a sudden relapse. The doctor of a nearby charity clinic diagnosed it as a defective heart valve, and he recommended plenty of rest for Francis.

Since there is no record that Francis ever did any honest or hard work in his entire life, this made no great change in his way of living. His family, however, were worried about their dear boy, so they sent him to live with his married sister in Topeka. His brother-in-law, Andrew J. Grooms, was a hard worker, and was employed in the nearby quarries. He and Lester did not become good friends.

Coincidental with Francis's arrival in Topeka in 1927, police were suddenly plagued with complaints of petty robberies. Candy and grocery stores were broken into at night, and many small items were taken. Gas stations lost automobile accessories and had their cash registers rifled.

One night Francis broke into a jewelry store, and stole a few pieces of valuable jewelry. At a local pawn shop he tried to sell some of it, but the owner refused to consider it. When Francis left, the owner called and reported the incident to the police. They traced Francis to his sister's house, where they arrested him.

He was tried before a judge as Alvin Karpis—the name he had given—and was sentenced to ten years in the State Reformatory at Hutchinson, Kansas. There, for two years he studied the art of crime, under the guidance of some of its masters, other inmates. Here he also met Lawrence Devol, alias Harry Barton, and the two of them sawed their way to freedom. They fled to Chicago, and Alvin bunked with his parents for a while. He also made long, and unexplained trips out of town with his new buddy Devol.

Alvin's parents were well aware that their son had escaped from the reformatory, but they made no effort to notify the authorities of his presence. Possibly they thought reformatory life was bad for his weak heart.

Karpis and Devol were arrested in Kansas City, March 23, 1930, and the car they were driving was found to be loaded with safe blowing equipment. Fingerprinted, they were soon identified as fugitives, and returned to the Kansas Reformatory. Still later, authorities found two knives on Alvin, and they immediately sent him to the State Penitentiary at Lansing. He arrived there on May 19, 1930. This is where he met a fellow named Fred Barker, and they immediately took a liking to each other. On March 30, 1931, Fred got his parole; Alvin's followed in a couple of months.

They met, as planned, at the Joplin, Missouri, chicken ranch of Herbert (Deafy) Farmer. Herbert, a graduate of Leavenworth, was an old childhood friend of the Barkers and always held open house for ex-cons and their friends.

Then Fred took Alvin home to meet his mother in Tulsa. Ma Barker was short of sons at that moment, and she took Alvin under her ample wing. He was now accepted as a member of one of America's strangest families, and the Barker-Karpis gang was born.

From Ma he learned crime methods he had never dreamed of before. He was schooled in the art of charting getaways, casing a hit, and all the other details that go into the making of an arch criminal. He also became indoctrinated with Ma's own creeds, such as "Crime does pay—if you're careful," and "Cops is lousy." It was Fred Barker who gave him the nickname "Old Creepy," because of his piercing eyes and cold-bloodedness.

While in Tulsa Alvin met a young woman named Dorthy Stayman. There ensued a short courtship, followed by marriage. Ma had counseled him against it, and she proved to be right. The responsibility of marriage was just too much for him. Within a few months he had left his bride, never to return.

Under Ma's supervision, Alvin and Fred plotted their first big job together. It was the $5,000 jewelry robbery at Henryetta, Oklahoma. They carted the loot to Ma's, but she ordered them out. "No loot in this house, ever!" she spat.

June 10, 1931, the Tulsa police cornered Alvin and Fred in a northside apartment. Alvin was captured, but Fred shot his way to freedom, then took refuge in Ma's shack.

Taken to Okmulgee, Oklahoma, Alvin was tried before a judge, on September 11, 1931, and sentenced to four years at McAlester. He never reached the penitentiary, however, for three months after his arrest he was paroled by the same judge who had sentenced him. With this, the Barkers moved their operations to the state of Missouri. In West Plains, on December 19, 1931, Alvin and Fred held up the owner of a store, and fled in a DeSoto sedan. The following day, using more nerve than brains, they returned to West Plains, to a garage, to get their auto repaired.

Sheriff C. R. Kelly saw the pair, and thought he recognized the automobile, so he decided to question them. They saw him coming, and, in no mood for conversation, one of them shot him dead. It was never established just who did the shooting.

This done, they sped off to tell Ma that she had more troubles.

The gang then moved to St. Paul, Minnesota, where they rented an apartment at 1035 South Roberts Street, in West St. Paul, and commenced again their robbery operations. Then the landlady's son saw their picture in a detective magazine and reported them to the police. When the house was finally raided the following morning it was empty. Alvin and the Barkers had fled.

That same morning Ma, Fred, and Alvin took Ma's latest lover, Arthur (Old Man) Dunlop, to the lonely banks of Lake Frester, in Wisconsin, where they pumped three bullets into him. They had decided that it was he who had reported them to the police.

Now they moved into a fashionable neighborhood apartment house, in Kansas City. The gang added new members, then drove to Fort Scott, Kansas, where they raided the Citizens National Bank.

When Harvey J. Bailey, one of their temporary members, was arrested on July 7, 1932, on a Kansas City golf course, the gang was forced to hit the road again. Ma was loyal, though, so they stopped in Tulsa long enough to hire a lawyer, J. Earl Smith, to represent Bailey. When he failed to show up in the courtroom to defend his client, Ma was furious.

Early in August, she called the attorney and made a date to meet him for a confab. The rendezvous was the Indian Hills Country Club, located in an isolated part of Tulsa. Attorney J. Earl Smith kept the date, and so did Alvin Karpis and Fred Barker. The following day, his bullet-riddled body was found near the first tee.

Having taken care of this little piece of business, the Barker-Karpis gang moved to a nice little cottage on a quiet lake in Wisconsin. Then, with lightning ferocity, the gang struck again. The Cloud County Bank, in Concordia, Kansas, lost the princely sum of $240,000 in cash and securities.

December 16, 1932, they struck again, and got $30,000 from the Third Northwestern National Bank of Minneapolis. In this caper they left three men dead in the streets—two policemen, and one private citizen. Lawrence DeVol, Alvin's old reformatory buddy, helped out in this raid.

Next came the National Bank of Fairbury, Nebraska, with Karpis, Fred and Arthur Barker, Frank Nash, Volney Davis, Eddie Green, Jess Doyle, and Earl Christman taking part. They got over $150,000, but Christman was fatally wounded. Eddie Green, under orders from Ma, buried him in an unmarked grave.

While hanging around Harry Sawyer's Green Lantern Saloon,

on Wabasha Street in St. Paul, Karpis met one Dolores Delaney. Dolores was only 19 years old, but she was soon enchanted with "Old Creepy." Following in the footsteps of her two sisters, also gang girls, Dolores became Karpis's woman. It is extremely doubtful that Karpis gave even a passing thought to his wife, waiting and wondering, back in Tulsa.

Flush with so much success, Karpis decided it was time for the gang to hit the really big time. A kidnapping! It was on June 15, 1933, that the Barker-Karpis gang snatched William A. Hamm, Jr., and held him for $100,000 ransom.

They got their ransom, and then sat back and watched and laughed as the Touhy Gang of Chicago, was arrested and indicted on August 12, 1933, and charged with this crime. They were later acquitted.

August 30, 1933, two 21-year-old bank messengers, Joseph Hamilton and Herbert Cheyne, guarded by Patrolman Leo Paviek, 35, descended the post office steps in South St. Paul. They were carrying pouches containing a $30,000 payroll—a payroll intended as wages for employees of Swift and Company.

A second patrolman, John Yeaman, had just parked his car down the street and was hurrying toward them. Then, roaring into the Livestock Market Center came an automobile with a screaming siren. It raced up to the steps of the post office, emitting a large cloud of black smoke from the rear, and five armed bandits jumped out. One of the hoodlums yelled to the two messengers and the guard to "stick 'em up!" The three men promptly raised their hands, and let the money pouches fall to the steps. Three of the bandits then approached them, took Paviek's pistol, then began tossing the pouches toward their unusual car.

Another bandit stood in the middle of the street, with a machine gun, and continually pivoted, keeping all spectators at bay. The others guarded the messengers and Paviek, and loaded the sedan. Suddenly, Patrolman John Yeaman, came into range, and he began to shoot toward the car. Then everybody began firing, with the machine gunner raking the streets. One of the machine-gun-carrying bandits then turned his attention to the unarmed Paviek. Without any provocation, the gunner shot him down, killing him. Patrolman John Yeaman was also hit and fell, seriously wounded.

With the smoke again pouring from the rear of the car, the bandits then roared away as quickly as they had come. The Barker-Karpis gang had struck again, leaving behind them one dead man, one wounded man, and a pall of silence.

The robbery had been well planned, and the use of their unusual automobile with its siren and smoke screen was a recent "military" innovation of Shotgun George Ziegler's.

The accompanying furor and notoriety this spectacular robbery and killing caused convinced the gang that they should transfer their operations elsewhere for a while, so they moved to Chicago.

Alvin Karpis was still convinced that the painless and fast way to get a lot of money to satisfy their large and unwieldy gang was to pull another kidnapping. In this he had a very powerful ally. Ma Barker concurred. So the gang set about planning another kidnapping; it was the Bremer kidnapping, described in Chapter 3.

With the FBI so close, panic swept the gang. Alvin Karpis and Fred Barker decided to have "Doc" Joseph P. Moran, a drunken one-time doctor, change their identities. They eventually paid him $5,000 for an operation to erase their fingerprints. He also did a face-lifting job on Alvin Karpis. The operation on Karpis did change his appearance somewhat, but the finger-tip operation did nothing but torture them.

Karpis's nose had been broken in a gang fight back in Chicago, during the days when he had been running with Lester Gillis. Now "Doc" Moran straightened it, then tried to give him something that looked like earlobes. (Karpis had none.)

Karpis added to this by combing his hair straight back; he also bought a pair of glasses. Now "Old Creepy" took on the look of a teacher or banker; but not even the glasses could change those cold, hard eyes.

Meanwhile, the FBI was busy at work, questioning people who lived in the rooming house where Shotgun Ziegler had lived. They found he had visited "Doc" Moran frequently, at a small Chicago hotel. So they went to the hotel, where they got the descriptions of other visitors. These were later identified, from FBI files, as Oliver Berg, Russell Gibson, Harry Campbell, Alvin Karpis. There were also many others; the pieces were fitting together.

In a booze joint called the Casino Club, in Toledo, Ohio, "Doc" Moran began to spout off about his importance in the Barker-Karpis gang. He had been getting on a lot of people's nerves lately, and his loud and loose talk dangerously annoyed them. Orders were given: "Doc" was taken for a boat ride on Lake Erie, and his weighted body was dumped overboard.

By now the gang decided the safest thing to do was to scatter. Ma and Fred Barker headed for Florida, some went back to St. Paul, and still others stayed in Chicago or headed for Hot Springs.

Most had their pictures and descriptions scattered across the country in magazines and newspapers.

In September 1934, Alvin Karpis decided that Chicago was too hot for him. For that matter, he thought the entire country was too hot, so he and Dolores went to Havana, Cuba, to rest and relax.

The Barker-Karpis gang had underworld connections in the Cuban capital. These friends were changing Bremer kidnapping money for them. However some of the loot had been spent, and the FBI had secured Cuban cooperation, and arrived there to investigate. Karpis was tipped by friends, and he and Harry Campbell, with their girlfriends Dolores Delaney and Winona Burdette, fled Cuba in a small boat, landing at Key West, Florida. From here they took the bus to Miami, and checked in at a local hotel as Mr. and Mrs. E. M. Wagner (Karpis), and Mr. and Mrs. G. F. Summers (Campbell).

The confinement of a small hotel didn't suit Dolores, who was very pregnant and becoming cranky. Because of this, Alvin rented a house in a secluded neighborhood, and hired a nurse.

Occasionally, Mr. Wagner and Mr. Summer would take trips up to a small town in Central Florida. Here they visited with Mrs. T. C. Blackburn and her son Fred. These visits were all very cozy and most reassuring to all members, but the women had to stay behind. They couldn't risk riling Ma.

Here, on the banks of Lake Weir, Karpis, Campbell, and Fred Barker (known locally as Blackie), spent many leisure hours hunting and fishing. Once in a while they were joined by local sportsmen, who had no real idea who they were. Life was sweet and simple, for a few quiet weeks.

Then Alvin decided it was time to return to Miami. He was worried about Dolores. So the cheerful gang members, now smug in their anonymity, said their goodbyes to the Blackburns, and to the locals. They told everybody they were heading North, but then they headed South, back to Miami.

January 8, 1935, the busy FBI found two apartments in Chicago, where members of the Barker-Karpis gang were hiding. Out of one they flushed Byron Bolton, Clare Gibson (wife of Russell Gibson), and Ruth Heidy. Russell Gibson refused to come out, and elected to wage a gun battle with the agents. He was killed.

Then the FBI nabbed Arthur (Dock) Barker, and Mildred Kuhlman, just as they were leaving. Dock had left his gun behind, so he was taken without a fight.

Wide coverage was given by the press and radio, to the capture of some members of the gang, and the killing of Russell Gibson. No news was released regarding the capture of Dock.

January 16, 1935, the news again electrified Karpis and Campbell, who were still in Miami. The FBI had found the house, in Oklawaha, and in a five-hour gun battle they had killed Ma and Fred Barker. Now they were searching all of Florida for more members of the gang. The net was tightening.

Karpis and Campbell packed up the girls, and they all headed North, running scared. The same contact that had helped Karpis find suitable quarters in Miami now gave them the name of a safe hotel in Atlantic City, New Jersey.

Their abrupt and unexplained departure from Miami puzzled the nurse. She notified the owner of the house, who reported it to the police. Acting on a hunch, the police then called the FBI and asked if they were interested. They were. From neighbors, agents learned the make and license number of the car. Routinely, the police in Atlantic City received an alert for the car, but were not notified as to its suspected occupants.

Following this alert, Atlantic City detectives, concentrating on automobiles with Florida license plates, found the car parked in the Coast Garage at the foot of South Kentucky Avenue near the famous Boardwalk. From the manager they got the address and name of the owner.

Still ignorant of the identities of the persons they were seeking, detectives went to the fourth floor of the Dan-Mor Hotel. They were interested in questioning a Mr. Carson (Karpis), and a Mr. Cameron (Campbell). The girls had registered separately and were in an adjoining room. It was 5:00 A.M., January 20, 1935, and the door to suspects' room was ajar. One of the detectives poked his pistol through the open door, and called "Stick 'em up! We're officers."

Karpis shouted right back, "Stick 'em up, yourselves, coppers, we're coming!"

Then Karpis, who was fully clothed, and Campbell, in his underwear, started shooting. Hoping to warn the girls, Karpis had fired his first shot through the wall into the adjoining room. By a million to one chance he shot Dolores in the leg. This alerted them.

Karpis then grabbed a machine gun, while Campbell kept his .45. They came out of the room, guns ablaze. The gun fire drove the detectives around a bend in the hotel corridor, and Karpis and Campbell raced out a back door and down the fire escape. In the alley below stood three officers. Over 200 shots were fired. It was amazing, but no one was hit. The hoods then rushed to the garage, but found it filled with police; so they took the first car they found, a Pontiac sedan.

Twice they rounded the block, watching for Dolores and Winona, but soon they had 20 policemen after them, so they ran. The police were right behind them, firing as they went, but Campbell had a machine gun, and shooting from the rear seat, he out gunned them. All traffic lights in the city were now blinking red, as police called for a "general alarm," but Karpis and Campbell still eluded them and escaped.

Back at the Dan-Mor Hotel, Dolores Delaney, 21, and Winona Burdett, a 22-year-old radio singer, were arrested and held for the FBI. In their room were seven suitcases filled with women's clothing, and a trunk full of infant clothes. Additional checking revealed that the previous day Alvin Karpis had called the police surgeon, Dr. Carl Surran. Sure of his cover, Karpis had told the good doctor he wanted him to take care of Dolores when the baby arrived. He also told him, "We've got plenty of money, and we want the best for my little girl."

The women were returned to Miami, where they were tried for harboring fugitives. They both received five-year sentences at the Federal Detention Farm at Milan, Michigan.

John and Anna Karpoviecz had been located in Chicago, where they were working as janitors in an apartment house. After the Barkers had been killed, Anna Karpoviecz appealed to her son through the newspapers to give himself up before he too was killed.

When Dolores's baby was born, he was turned over to John and Anna. They would have at least five years to do a better job raising him than they had done with Alvin.

But Alvin Karpis and Harry Campbell were having problems of their own. Their car conked out as they were passing through Quakertown, Pennsylvania, so they stopped an Allentown psychiatrist named Horace W. Hunsicker and commandeered his. They also took the doctor on a wild 21-hour ride to Ohio.

Near Wadsworth, Ohio, they tied Hunsicker with his own belt and the bottom of his pajamas. Then they stowed him away in a nearby Grange Hall, and drove to a resort area near Toledo. They were met here by George "Burrhead" Keary, a local hoodlum friend of Alvin's, and he took them into town in his car. They left the stolen automobile, with its motor still running, near the banks of Lake Erie. It was discovered later by a mail carrier.

Burrhead—so-called for his unkempt, whiskbroom hair—found them suitable quarters in Toledo, and they dropped from sight for a while.

Desperation for money eventually drove them out of hiding, and the three of them held up a US Mail truck near Warren, Ohio, and took $72,000 from the mail sacks. Then Karpis and Campbell quarreled over a suitable split, and they parted.

Underworld connections in Cleveland found Karpis a hideout in a secluded cabin in Hot Springs, Arkansas. Here, with the knowledge and cooperation of Dutch Akers, chief of detectives, and his boss, Joseph Wakelin, Karpis found safety. He paid them well for his protection, and made arrangements for a warning. Now he enjoyed the fishing nearby, and when it struck his fancy, he drove into town in his pretentious Cadillac. Here he spent money lavishly in the local brothels and nightclubs.

On November 7, 1935, Alvin Karpis, Fred Hunter, Sam Coker, John Brock, and Burrhead drove to a depot at Garrettsville, Ohio. Here, they waited for the arrival of the Erie Line passenger and mail train. It was traveling from Cleveland to Pittsburgh.

When it arrived, they struck. Karpis and Hunter entered the cab of the train, and at gunpoint forced the engineer, Charles Shull and the fireman, P. O. Leuschner, to dismount. Karpis then fired a shot into the mail car, and the clerks, P. E. Christy, Orlin Workman, and Steve Warren, promptly came out. Hunter held a machine gun on the clerks, while Alvin tossed the mail pouches out of the car. Burrhead and Brock then forced Christy and Robert Rochett, local mail carriers, to carry the pouches to the automobile. With this done, the gang, all armed with machine guns, lined up the people on the back platform, and warned them to remain there.

Exactly ten minutes had passed since the robbery began, and they had collected a payroll of $34,000 consigned to the Republic Steel Corporation, and $11,500 in United States Treasury Bonds. With Fred Hunter at the wheel, the car drove away, and they all disappeared into the mist of the underworld.

Karpis, feeling sure of himself, and smarting from the pressures of constant pursuit, sent word to J. Edgar Hoover that he was coming to kill the Director. Not satisfied with this, he followed it up with threats to kill key FBI agents across the country.

Karpis was already wanted as "Public Enemy Number One,"

and Hoover now referred to him as "Public *Rat* Number One," and continued to make references to him as a dirty rat. The connotation "Dirty Rat," has little meaning now, but at that time, it was being used by George Raft, Edward G. Robinson, and James Cagney in all their gangster pictures, and was the worst thing you could call a man in printable language.

Following the robbery, the FBI redoubled its efforts to catch Karpis. Witnesses from the train gave the agents new descriptions of Karpis, and they changed their records accordingly. From informers in Cleveland, the FBI learned that three men had chartered an airplane and flown to some place in Arkansas. One of these men was believed to have been Karpis. Further investigation revealed that an airplane, license number NC 12180, had landed at Hot Springs about four days after the mail train robbery. A check with the Department of Commerce revealed that the owner of plane No. NC 12180 had registered it. He told agents he had sold it the day following the robbery. They located the new owner, a pilot named John Zetzer. He confirmed the fact that he had taken two men to Hot Springs, and another to Tulsa. He was shown several pictures of suspects, and identified pictures of Alvin Karpis, Fred Hunter, and John Brock. Brock had been his Tulsa passenger.

When FBI agents began arriving in Hot Springs, disguised as hunters and fishermen, Dutch Akers found out who they were, and he flashed the word to Alvin Karpis. Alerted, he, Fred Hunter, and Fred's girlfriend, Rose, promptly headed southward.

Dolores Delaney, while still professing undying love for Karpis, talked loud, long and freely about her paramour. She told agents Karpis had been bitten by the fishing bug while they were in Cuba. She said he had spent most of his time either fishing, or talking about fish and fishing.

When agents located the cabin Karpis had rented, they found fishing boots, mud coated shoes, and fishing catalogues. What they didn't find, however, told them even more about him. There was no fishing tackle, which probably meant Karpis had taken it with him, and that he would seek a place to use it again.

Since the month was December, and it was too cold to do any sport fishing on Lake Erie, they reasoned that Karpis and his still unknown companions had headed South. Consequently they directed their attentions in that direction, paying particular attention to those places which boasted of sport fishing.

Concentrating on all roads that led South, their search gradually narrowed to the state of Texas. In Corpus Christi, agents located a tourist camp where the fugitives had stopped. They were only a week behind him. Someone remembered Karpis, and the fact that he had mentioned going to New Orleans.

All attention shifted again, and agents in New Orleans began checking all stores dealing in fishing tackle. They showed his picture to anyone who would look at it. By this painstakingly slow method, they located the store where he had purchased some minor articles of fishing equipment. He was identified as a Mr. O'Hara, who drove a Cadillac. More questions, more checking, and more patience, and soon they had the license number! Encouraged by this, the FBI now began a series of street patrols.

Then, suddenly, there it was. Parked, in broad daylight, right in front of 3343 Canal Street, a most pretentious apartment house, stood the white Cadillac.

For personal reasons, Director Hoover had reserved this capture for himself. Word flashed to Washington, while the place was put under heavy surveillance. The next morning, an all-night flight arrived at the New Orleans airport, bringing Director Hoover and additional FBI agents.

Then, with 20 FBI agents backing him, Hoover approached the building. Karpis, Fred Hunter, and his girlfriend were located in apartment No. 1, and it was the plan to enter and arrest them. But before they could even get to the building, out came the hoodlums, and they entered Karpis's Cadillac.

Before Alvin Karpis could get his key into the ignition, Director Hoover snatched the door open and told Karpis he was under arrest. With 20 FBI agents swarming all over the automobile, neither Karpis nor Hunter made any objections.

When the call came for handcuffs, the embarrassed agents found that no one had brought a pair. One agent took off his necktie and Karpis's hands were bound with this.

At 3:30 P.M., May 2, 1936, Alvin Karpis was bundled onto a plane and flown back to Washington. From there, he was taken to St. Paul, Minnesota, where he pleaded guilty to the charge of kidnapping William Hamm, Jr. He was tried, and quickly found guilty. His sentence was imprisonment for the rest of his natural life. This sentence officially ended the short but violent life of the Barker-Karpis gang.

At Alcatraz, Karpis became a most pitiful example of a former Public Enemy Number One. His title of "Old Creepy," soon was changed to "The Creep." He started off wrong by calling another

prisoner, Allie Anderson, a "fink." Anderson answered that charge
by flooring Karpis with one blow. Then he waited until Karpis
had revived before cooling him again.

Meanwhile, Volney Davis had been captured by the FBI in
Kansas City, had escaped, and was recaptured. He also went to
"The Rock," for a life sentence. Somehow, he blamed all his
troubles on Alvin Karpis.He got the unshakeable idea that Karpis
had "ratted" on him, and on the entire gang, by cooperating with
the FBI. The first time he saw Alvin in the recreation yard, he
added to Karpis's humiliation, by pounding the taller and heavier
Karpis into the ground.

From here on out Karpis's standing in the criminal community
dropped below zero. Dock Barker, once a buddy of his, wouldn't
even speak to him. Eventually the outside world would also forget
Karpis, and when he was transferred to McNeil Island, at the age
of 53, few people took note.

During his life, Karpis had managed to bring almost total
humiliation upon his hard-working parents, had abandoned a
wife, as well as his paramour and their unborn child. He had
also killed an undetermined number of men, robbed many banks,
and assisted in the kidnapping of two men. And now, Francis
Alvin Karpoviecz, alias Alvin Karpis, would waste another 32
years of his miserable life in federal penitentiaries.

On January 15, 1969, Karpis was paroled and promptly de-
ported to his native Canada. Almost 60 years old, and suffering
from arthritis, the nearly bald and bespectacled "Old Creepy"
was described by his former jailers, at McNeil Island, as being
"mild-mannered and friendly." A private social welfare agency in
Montreal, promised to find this "mild-mannered and friendly"
hoodlum his first honest employment.

As far as this country is concerned, the shame of Alvin Karpis
has been removed from its borders. Behind him he leaves almost
60 years of life utterly wasted. Ahead of him may be a few years
of productivity. Who knows? *Who even cares?*

••5••

The Thrill Seekers

You've read the story of Jesse James—
Of how he lived and died;
If you're still in need of something to read.
Here's the story of Bonnie and Clyde.

So reads the opening lines of Bonnie Parker's long and dreary poem that she called "The Story of Bonnie and Clyde." It is a depressing verse, which will be quoted in its entirety at the end of this chapter, for those who collect the morbid.

i

Hubert Parker was only two years old, but he knew something was happening, because of all the fuss being made over his mother, and the lack of attention he was suffering.

There wasn't much to do in Rowena, Texas, a small village about 21 miles northeast of San Angelo, but today, October 1, 1910, was a busy one at the Parker house. Then suddenly it was all over and the house was pierced by the thin, reedy cry of a new-born baby. The proud parents would call her Bonnie.

The arrival of a second child didn't trouble the Parkers, for Mr. J. T. Parker was a bricklayer, and managed to provide his family with moderate prosperity. There was always plenty to eat, nice clothes to wear, and the entire family packed off to church each and every Sunday. The Parkers were both devout Baptists.

Three years later, Bonnie would sit beside Hubert, as they awaited the arrival of the third and last child born to the Parkers. They named her Billie, and being the youngest she became the pet of the family.

Tragedy struck the Parker family a hard blow when, in 1914, Mr. J. T. Parker suddenly died. Bonnie's mother was then forced to pack up her little brood of three children and move in with her mother, who lived in Cement City, a suburb of Dallas. Then Mrs. Parker found employment and became the wage earner of the family.

Since their mother was away all day earning a living, the children were raised by their indulgent grandmother. They attended school in Cement City, and here Bonnie was rated as an average student. She had little trouble with her grades, and her deportment was satisfactory.

When Bonnie was only 15 she met a boy named Roy Thornton. He was also a student at Cement City High, and they fell madly in love with each other. In fact, Bonnie took the affair so to heart that she went out and had a large one tattoed on her thigh. Right across the middle of it was the name "Roy." He was highly flattered, and the following year they were married.

This marriage, while not a perfect one, did manage to hold together until August, 1927. By then Roy, unable to stand the responsibility of marriage, started taking trips. These became progressively longer, and when he returned he offered no excuses. Each time, however, Bonnie would take him back, with no questions.

On December 5, 1927, Roy took off on an extended journey. Bonnie, unable to stand the loneliness, moved in with her mother. During this period she brooded about her Roy, and then began a search for a job to occupy her time and bring in some money.

It was New Year's Eve when Bonnie decided to tell all her troubles to her diary. It was a new one, and keeping it was a passing fad that lasted only 16 days. From its pages one gets a peek into the secret thoughts of a lonely young girl—a girl who in a very few years would become a vicious killer.

Dear Diary:

Before opening this year's diary, I wish to tell you that I have a roaming husband with a roaming mind. We are separated again for the third and last time. The first time, August 9–19, 1927, the second time, October 1–9, 1927, and the third time, December 5, 1927. I love him very much and miss him terribly. But I intend doing my duty. I am not going to take him back. I am running around with Rosa Mary Judy and she is somwhat a consulation (sic) to me. We have resolved this New Year's to take no men or nothing seriously. Let all men go to hell! But we are not going to sit back and let the world sweep us by.

January 1, 1928. New Years nite. 12:00

The bells are ringing, the old year has gone, and my heart has gone
with it. I have been the happiest and most miserable woman this
year. I wish the old year would have taken my "past" with it. I mean
all my memories, but I can't forget Roy. I am very blue tonight. No
word from him. I feel he has gone for good. This is New Year's Day,
Jan. 1. I went to a show. Saw Ken Maynard in the Overland Stage.
Am very blue. Well, I must confess this New Year's nite I got drunk.
Trying to forget. Drowning my sorrows in bottled hell!

January 2, 1928.

Met Rosa Mary today and we went to a show. Saw Ronald Cole-
man and Vilma Banky in A Night of Love. Sure was a good show.
Saw Scottie and gave him the air. He's a pain in the neck to me.
Came home at 5:30. Went to bed at 10:30. Sure am lonesome.

January 3, 1928.

Searched this damn town over for a job today. I guess luck is against
me. Havn't heard a word from Roy. I wonder where he can be.
Diary, every night I look at his dear little pictures. That's all I have
of him. I don't suppose he wants me to know where he is. He doesn't
love me any more. "Where is my wandering boy tonight?" I am
fully discouraged, for I know I can never live with him again. I
hunted up Reba Griffin today, just to know that she is not with him.
She has taken my place in his heart but she will never take my place
by his side. I am going to bed as it is 10:30. I wonder what tomorrow
will bring.

January 4, 1928. Wednesday

Stayed home all day and slept. Went to the Pantages tonight with
L. T. Haven't heard from Roy yet. Lewis called me.

January 5, 1928.

Got a telegram from Harlingen. Little Roy is dead. Oh, wont our
luck ever change? It is sure a lonesome old place tonight. I went
with Lewis and Fred but I can't have a good time. I love my husband. I always think of him. If God would only let me find where
he is.

January 6, 1928.

Well, there's nothing to do all day. Just sit around. I went with
Lewis tonight. Had a nice time, but I can't get Roy off my mind.
We went out to Mac's awhile and went driving. Sure am blue tonite.

January 7, 1928.

Well, I went down town today and saw a picture. Milton Sills in
"Framed." Sure was a good picture. Rosa Mary has been ill but is
o. k. now. Tonight I went with Lewis again. Not a darn thing
to do. I met Johnnie Baker tonite for the first time in a long

time. Still the same old Johnnie. But I don't care anything about him. Roy is always in my mind. I come home early tonite. I didn't feel like going anywhere much. Johnnie came out with Lew. Oh, God, how I wish I could see Roy! But I try my best to brush all thought of him aside and have a good time. If I knew for sure he didn't care for me, I'd cut my throat and say here goes nothing. Maybe he does though. I still have hopes. Raymond called me. I have a date with him for tomorrow. But to hell with all men. He is very nice—a perfect gentleman. But how can I enjoy life? Raymond is a decetive [detective]. I think I'll have him look Roy up. Gracie wants me to come down there but I can't bear to look at his sisters. They remind me of him. I love them because they are his. I took the blues when I went to see Mae. Well, maybe tomorrow will make things a little clearer.

January 8, 1928. Sunday

It's just another day to me. Plenty to do but no heart to do it. Got up at 11. Raymond called and wanted a date with me, but shucks, I don't feel like going. I went to the Old Mill tonight. Was a very good show but I was bored to death. Had dinner after the show. Got home at 11:30. Lewis called me three times.

January 9, 1928. Monday

We have been torn up all day. Went to hunt a job but never found it. Got a letter from Gracie, but haven't heard from Roy. I guess I am a fool to look for any word from him but I don't want to lose hopes any worse.

January 10, 1928. Tuesday

Blue as usual. Not a darn thing to do. Don't know a darn thing.

January 11, 1928. Wednesday

Haven't been anywhere this week. Why don't something happen?

January 12, 1928. Thursday

Went to a show. Saw Florence Vidor and Clive Brook in "Afraid to Love." Sure was good. Blue as hell tonight. Went to hunt a job at 903 South Harwood.

January 13, 1928. Friday

Went to a show. Saw Virginia Vallie in "Marriage." Not a thing helps out though. Sure am blue. Everything has gone wrong today. Why don't something happen? What a life!

January 14, 1928. Saturday

Went to town, saw a show, Wallace McDonald and Clara Bow in "The Primrose Path." It was good. Not doing anything tonite.

January 15, 1928. Sunday

Went to grannie's today. Stayed home tonight. Nothing particular happened.

January 16, 1928. Monday
Went to Chocolate Shop today. Got a letter from Gracie. Sure am
blue tonight. Have been crying. I wish I could see Roy.
January 17, 1928. Tuesday

Thus the diary ends, with a date, a dash, and a plaintive wail
for Roy, who was not to return until the following year.

About this time Bonnie got the job she had long been looking
for. At a cafe called Marco's, on Main Street, near the courthouse,
she found employment as a waitress. It was here, also, that she
would meet and become friends with many of the officials and
officers who would later spend two years tracking her down to her
death.

When "Roaming Roy" finally came back in the early part of
1929, he returned to a changed wife. Bonnie, her affection for
Roy now cool, refused to have anything to do with him. Re-
buffed, he left again, but soon his activities caught up with him.
He was arrested in Red Oak, on a charge of robbery, and sent
to the Penitentiary for five years.

In November 1929, Marco's Cafe went out of business, and
Bonnie now was without a husband or a job. With plenty of time
on her hands, and nothing to do, she decided to visit with a girlfriend who lived in West Dallas. While staying here, a fellow by
the name of Clyde Barrow dropped around to call on the friend,
and then stayed to visit with Bonnie.

ii

The birth of Clyde Chestnut Barrow, in Teleco, Texas, on
March 24, 1909, brought no great feeling of emotion to the Barrow
family—except perhaps a little sadness to Mr. Henry B. Barrow.
Clyde's arrival as the sixth child added another mouth to feed.
There would be two more later on.

The Barrows were poor tenant farmers, and the family rarely
had enough to eat, were clad with scanty clothing, and enjoyed
very few of the pleasures of life.

Clyde's father was a quiet, unassuming man, who could neither
read nor write. He was, however, a hard worker, and each day
toiled long and hard in the fields. Clyde's mother, with so many
children to care for had little time for anything but housework
and trying to scrape together enough food to prepare each meal.

Neither parent ever spanked the children, and they grew up
practically undisciplined. Perhaps a little spanking now and then

would have produced a better pair than Clyde and his brother Buck grew to be. Here was parental indifference, as opposed to parental overindulgence. Both are deadly, and both are discouragingly the same in their final results.

Clyde's love of guns was evident even in his early days; and being dirt poor, toy guns were a commodity the Barrows couldn't afford. This didn't deter him, however, for he used sticks for his guns, and his imagination turned them into real .45's.

The Barrow house was a ramshackled, unpainted, clapboard structure, with three or four rooms and an outhouse in the rear. Because there were so many children in the family, a number of them were required to sleep on the floor. When they were old enough to walk, they were old enough to work; so they were sent into the fields.

Life wasn't all work, of course, and the kids, particularly Clyde, took a great delight in riding anything they could find on the farm. Clyde rode the milk cows, and even the large hogs. Then of course there were the long, dusty walks to school, with all kinds of adventure on the way, and the cool dips in the swimming hole.

Clyde never went to school—he was sent. He thought it a great waste of time, and every chance he got he would play hooky. His absences were never reported, however, for the teachers, overworked and underpaid, were thankful to have one less child to bedevil them.

Times for the Barrow family were hard indeed, so in 1915 Clyde and his sister Nellie May, were sent to live with their uncle on his farm in Corsicana, Texas. He was only the first of a long line of uncles they would live with during their childhood.

When Clyde was nine, he and Nellie were living with another uncle on his ranch at Mabank, Texas. This particular uncle had a wife who knew the value of a nickel, and saved every one she got her hands on. As Nellie told it, "When a hog was butchered, she would carefully store the hams, shoulders, and bacon away for the future, and then make sausage out of all the rest."

Except for special occasions, the Barrow children never saw any of the choice pieces, but at every meal they ate sausage. They had sausage for breakfast, lunch, and dinner—until Clyde at last decided he just couldn't eat another one.

The ranch was alive with hunting dogs, hound dogs, watch dogs, and just plain dogs. So Clyde and Nellie lured all of them out to the smoke house, and fed them sausages until they puffed up like balloons and waddled like ducks.

Unfortunately there was a limit to the capacity of the dogs, and seemingly no limit to the sausages. They finally got away from the monotony of this diet when they moved on to another uncle at Kerens, a few months later.

With this constant shifting of the children from relative to relative, the Barrows sought to lessen the financial burden they were laboring under. While this did help them in a monetary way, it did little for the molding of the characters of their children.

By 1922, the Barrow family decided it had had enough of farming, and they moved to West Dallas. The children, of their own volition, began to drift into the new family home from the various farms, and by 1923 most of the family were back together again.

Those who were old enough to work got jobs, and those who were too young went to school. Clyde was entered in the Cedar Valley School, starting in the fifth grade, but four years later he quit and went to work for the Exline-Exline Company. After this he worked with various firms, including the Nu-Grape Company, Western Union, and Proctor and Gamble.

With his first real earnings, Clyde paid $50 for a stripped-down sportster, and this extravagance led to an argument with his father. In a huff, Clyde moved out of the house and in with his sister Nellie, who had married an orchestra leader.

With her husband on the road a great deal of the time, Nellie was lonely. She was more than happy to have her little brother around. She had learned to play the ukulele, a popular instrument at the time, and when Clyde discovered this, he insisted they buy one. A fairly good model could be had for $1.98.

Like a couple of kids, they searched the house from top to bottom, and with the few cents Clyde had, they got together the required amount. Then, having no money for carfare, Clyde had to hike the four miles into town.

When he returned, proudly sporting the new uke, it was discovered that neither of them could tune it. Again using their ingenuity, they searched the house and found another dime. Borrowing a few extra cents from a neighbor, they ordered two ice cream cones from a drugstore, and settled back to wait.

The instant the delivery boy arrived, Clyde pounced on him, with "Ike, can you tune a ukulele?"

"Sho kin, Mistah Clyde," was the wanted answer. For over an hour the three of them sat on the steps of the house, having a grand time. The drug store eventually called to find out what had become of their delivery boy.

Love came to Clyde Barrow, not in the spring, but in the fall of 1925. He fell "madly" in love with a pretty little girl, who was attending the Forest Avenue High School. He also changed jobs again, this time going to work for the A & K Auto Top Works. Apparently Clyde was searching for a position, and not a job.

The first real trouble entered Clyde's life on December 23, 1926, when he and his brother were arrested with a car filled with unexplainable turkeys. Marvin Ivy (Buck) Barrow, Clyde's older brother, took the full responsibility for this little adventure, and received seven days in jail. Clyde was released.

Still jumping from job to job, Clyde took one with the Palace Theater as an usher. He soon quit, when he discovered his salary was only $12 a week. Then in January 1927, he found the position he was looking for: He went to work for the United Glass and Mirror Company. He would stay with them for two years.

During the period of his first love, Clyde went out and had her name tattooed on his right arm. Their love would fade, but the tattoo wouldn't, so when he found himself involved with another girl, he had to have her name tattooed on the other arm.

This second romance happened while Clyde was in Wichita Falls, and he brought her back to Dallas with him. They were never married, but lived together for almost a year. During this period she nagged Clyde continually, for she wanted pretty things, expensive things, and he couldn't buy them on his small pay from the Glass Company.

Badgered by her, he caught a ride into Oklahoma, where he stole a car and returned to Dallas with it. To prevent its identification, he filed off the motor number, and then with the help of a friend repainted it.

Selling the car, Clyde tried to satisfy his "wife" with the extra money, but to her he was small potatoes. She packed up and went back to Wichita Falls, leaving behind a very disconsolate Clyde.

When Clyde met another young hoodlum named Frank Clause, they went on a spree, pilfering small items from stores in the area. Once, trying for the big money, they stole a safe, took it into the country, and then spent the long night trying to open it. All this hard work availed them nothing but a sleepless night.

Then Clyde, Frank Clause, and Buck were arrested on suspicion for hanging around the front of the Buell Lumber Company. They were accused of conspiracy to rob the company, which was true. But suspicion was not enough to hold them, so they were released.

A few days later the police again came to the Barrow house, but this time the boys saw them first, and started running. Buck

stumbled over something, and fell with a sprained ankle. Clyde
and Clause kept running, but stopped when the officers fired two
warning shots.

Clyde was crying as he came back, and ran to his mother,
"Gosh, mama," he sniffled, "I've just got out of that awful place—
I can't go back there—honest, I can't!" This was all very dramatic,
but the officers were unimpressed.

For one thing they wanted to know where Clyde got the yellow
Buick roadster, which was parked in the yard. Actually they
weren't concerned with the possibility that it was stolen. What
did concern them was the fact that an identical car, or perhaps
this same one, had been seen in Lufkin and Hillsboro on certain
dates. On these same dates, both towns had suffered a number
of safe burglaries.

Again, it was only suspicion that motivated the officers, and
after taking them in for questioning, they had to release them.
Driving back to the Barrow house, they laughed all the way. Only
Frank Clause failed to see the humor in it.

In October 1929, Clyde, Buck, and a new member of their gang,
Sidney Albert Moore, went to Henryetta, Oklahoma, where they
stole a car. Driving it to Denton, Texas, they broke into a garage,
and stole the safe, putting it in the back of the automobile.

Clyde was at the wheel, and driving like mad to put distance
between themselves and Denton, when police officers spotted
them. The officers were on foot, and only noticed the excessive
speed of the car, but when they blew their whistles this so unnerved Clyde, that he lost control of the car, crashing it into a
curb. The crash broke the front axle, and threw Clyde out. When
he hit the ground, he hit it running, and he never stopped, even
when he heard pistol shots behind him.

Through the long, long night, Clyde crept down one dark alley
after another, until at last he managed to sneak out of town. Then
he made his way back to Dallas. He had no idea what had happened, and it wasn't until he bought a paper that he found out.

Buck had been slightly wounded, and was being held in jail
along with Moore. Officers were looking for a third man, the
paper related, but they had no idea who he might be. Reading
this part, Clyde breathed a sigh of relief.

Buck and Moore received a 10-year sentence at the Texas
State Penitentiary at Huntsville for their part in the robbery, and
Buck began serving his sentence in January 1930.

Lonesome, Clyde went to visit one of his girlfriends in West

Dallas. While here he became enamored with a tiny blonde named Bonnie Parker. She was only four feet, ten inches tall, and weighed about 90 pounds. She had natural blonde curly hair, blue eyes, and an almost doll-like appearance.

Clyde himself, was only five feet four inches tall and his weight was 130 pounds. He had dark brown hair and eyes, and wore his hair slicked down, with the part in the middle. His elf-like ears pointed toward the rear, and he had a lopsided grin, not unlike that of John Dillinger's.

iii

When Clyde Barrow and Bonnie Parker met, it was love at first sight. A few weeks later Bonnie returned to her mother's, and the very first night Clyde came calling. He met Bonnie's mother, then he stayed so long he was invited to spend the night on the livingroom couch. He accepted.

The following morning, after Mrs. Parker had gotten her son off to work, Clyde was still sleeping. Then the police came calling, and asked to see him. Clyde was still peacefully at rest when one of the officers prodded him with a stick. He told Clyde, "If you've got any rabbit in you, Clyde, you'll run like a Buck."

Clyde grinned sleepily at him, "Buddy, I'd sure run if I could."

He was taken to Denton, Texas, for the investigation of the safe robbery. But the only evidence the police had was the fact that Buck had been one of the robbers. This was insufficient evidence to hold Clyde on, so the officers put out a call to see if he was wanted elsewhere. He was.

Bonnie was inconsolable for days, but at last began to accept the situation. Then she started writing him long, rambling letters. This is a part of one, written on February 22, 1930:

> 1406 Cockrell Street,
> Wednesday night

Mr. Clyde Barrow,
Care Denton County jail,
Denton, Texas.
Dearest Little Darling:
******* I know you're going to be good and sweet when you get out. Aren't you, honey? They only think you are mean. I know you are not, and I'm going to be the very one to show you that this outside world is a swell place, and we are young and should be happy like other boys and girls instead of like we are. Sugar, please don't

consider this advice as from one who is not capable of lending it, for you know I'm very interested and I've already had my day, and we're both going to be good now—both of us. Oh, I'm so lonesome for you tonight and I'm hoping I'll be with you in a few days. Dear, I'm going to close and try and get this all in one envelope. Forgive this awful writing, but just thank goodness that I still have sense enough to write a sentence. Answer real soon, dear, and think often of

Your lonesome Baby.

P. S. I am coming up tomorrow, even if they don't let me see you, you'll know I came and tried. I love you. Be real sweet, honey, and think of the girl who loves you best. Every one is o. k. and mother says hello, and she is hoping you can come home soon. I love you, darling, with all my heart, and maybe it won't be long till we can be together again. Think of me, darling, and what a wonderful time we will have when you come home—how happy we will be. I love you, honey.

Bonnie.

Bonnie Parker and Clyde Barrow had known each other a little less than a month when this letter was written. (The rest of this letter, and several others, will be found at the end of this chapter.)

In answer to the query issued by the Denton police, Clyde was identified as a suspect in several robberies in Waco. On March 2, 1930, he was turned over to the Waco authorities. Later he confessed to two burglaries and five motor car thefts. He was tried for these and given two years in prison on one charge, and a suspended sentence of 12 years for the others.

Bonnie, now hopelessly in love with Clyde, immediately left for Waco, so she could be near him until his transfer to Huntsville. There she stayed with a cousin and visited him each day.

In Clyde's cell was a felon named William Turner, whose home town was Waco. He had previously hidden a gun in his parents' home, and now he wanted it in the worst way. Bonnie's visits gave him an idea, and he talked it over with Clyde, who immediately agreed.

The following day, while Turner's parents were away, Bonnie broke into their house, and after much searching found the gun. To smuggle it to Clyde, she put on two belts—one under, and one over her dress. In the pocket formed by the belts, between her breasts, she carried the gun into the jail. Then she slipped it to Clyde when the guard's head was turned.

Meanwhile, down in the Texas State Penitentiary at Huntsville, Buck Barrow decided he had been in prison long enough. On

March 8, 1930, he made a successful escape from the nearby prison farm (a part of the penitentiary) and disappeared into the woods.

March 11, 1930, Clyde Barrow, William Turner, and Emory Abernathy broke out of the Waco jail, using the gun Bonnie had smuggled in. They didn't stop running until they reached No-komis, Illinois, where Clyde sent Bonnie a wire. He told of his undying love for her, and his admiration for her cool nerve. She was thrilled.

March 18, 1930, the three, broke and in strange country, robbed the offices of the Baltimore and Ohio Railroad, then a dry clean-ing shop. They were caught by alert police, and later identified by their fingerprints as escapees from Waco, Texas.

Waiving extradition, the trio were returned to Waco, where they stood trial for unlawful escape. Then Clyde's entire sentence was invoked against him, and he was faced with a fourteen year term in the penitentiary. April 21, 1930, he was transferred to "The Walls," as the Huntsville Penitentiary was called, to begin his long term.

Bonnie wrote to Clyde for a while, and he to her, but fourteen years is a long, long time. So in the summer of 1931, the letters, which had at first been a torrent, became a trickle, and then stopped altogether. With a husband and a lover in the peniten-tiary, Bonnie had found herself another boyfriend to keep her warm on cold nights.

Buck Barrow, having escaped from Huntsville, was now living in Oklahoma, where he met Blanche Caldwell of McCurtain. Buck was only five feet four, with brown eyes and hair, but he wasn't bad to look at, and had a fairly pleasant personality. He caught Blanche's eye, and after a fast courtship they were mar-ried in McCurtain, Oklahoma on July 1, 1931. A few weeks later he confessed to her that he was an escaped convict.

Blanche, thinking this over, started to work on him to give himself up. Her constant pleadings were rewarded with positive results about six months later. One can imagine the shock the Huntsville authorities felt, on December 27, 1931, when Buck drove up to the prison gates, and asked them to let him in.

Clyde, already at Huntsville, found the going tough. He never liked hard work, or any work for that matter. Now he was forced to work from daybreak to sunset, and he was despondent. He wrote pleading letters to his mother, and she was untiring in her efforts to get his sentence reduced.

Finally in January 1932, Clyde decided he couldn't stand the hard work any longer, so he took an axe and chopped off two of his toes. His philosophy seemed to be—better an idle cripple, than a healthy worker.

One can only imagine his chagrin, when a few days later, on February 2, 1932, he received a full pardon from Governor Ross S. Sterling, and had to leave the penitentiary on crutches.

The very first thing Clyde did, when he got out, was to look up his girl friend, Bonnie. Bonnie immediately told her new boy-friend to take a nice long walk, and welcomed Clyde back with open arms. Before long their relationship was even deeper than before. On March 25, 1932, she helped him rob the Sims Oil Company, in Dallas.

April 27, 1932, Clyde Barrow, Bonnie Parker, and Raymond Hamilton held up a grocery store in Hillsboro, Texas, getting $2,500. Mr. John N. Bucher, who owned the store, and who worked hard to make his money, was loath to give it up without a fight. Clyde Barrow shot him to death, and this became his first recorded murder. After this, the rest of them would be easy for him.

On May 5, 1932, Clyde and Frank Clause again joined forces, and committed a few robberies. First they held up the Magnolia Service Station, at Lufkin, kidnapping the manager. Then they drove a few blocks down the road and held up a Gulf station, also taking its manager prisoner. Driving to the edge of town, they released both men, unharmed. The managers later identified them from rogues' gallery photographs.

Now Clyde and Raymond Hamilton began to lay their plans for robbing the Neuhoff Packing Company in Dallas. They had already gone over the grounds and had mapped out the route for their getaway. Bonnie, not needed, was left at home, but Clyde told her, "Listen over the radio, honey, and see if we make our getaway."

On July 31, 1932, they hit the Neuhoff Packing Company, and escaped, taking the road through Dallas, out Industrial Boulevard and on to the West Dallas road. Then they picked up Bonnie, and drove to Grand Prairie, where they hid out for four days.

August 5, 1932, Clyde Barrow, Raymond Hamilton, and two other men, unidentified, drove up into Oklahoma. Near Atoka, Oklahoma, Hamilton, who fancied himself somewhat of a dancer, spotted a place where a country dance was being held. All of them had been drinking rather heavily and were feeling good, so Hamilton persuaded Clyde to stop.

For a while they just sat in the car, watching the dance, and arguing the rationality of horning in. Then they got out of their car and moved to another, closer to the door, still arguing. This move attracted the attention of Sheriff C. G. Maxwell, and his undersheriff, Eugene Moore.

The officers started toward the car, and Sheriff Maxwell called out, "What's going on here?" The reply was a burst of gunfire from the car, and Maxwell fell, mortally wounded. A half dozen bullets had struck him down. Undersheriff Moore, just to the rear of Maxwell, was killed instantly with a bullet in his heart, and another one in his head. Four days later, Sheriff Maxwell died.

The four leaped from the car and piled into their own, starting off down the road, firing as they went. Sheriff Maxwell raised himself up on his elbow and fired after them. Then several boys from the dance snatched up one of the fallen officers' guns and fired, but it was too late; the gang was gone.

Clyde, with a snootful of whiskey, was not driving too well, and a short distance down the road he crashed into a ditch. Mr. Cleve Brady, of Stringtown, Oklahoma, happened to be passing and saw the accident. Like any good citizen he stopped to see if he could be of any assistance. He could.

Clyde rammed a gun into his ribs, and hustled him back to his own car. Then the others climbed in, and they were off again. Fifteen miles out of Stringtown, Brady's car lost a wheel, and spun off the road, thanks to Clyde's crazy driving.

The four hoodlums then jumped out, and headed toward a farmhouse owned by John Redden. Brady, ignored for the moment, fled down the road as fast as he could run. At the farmhouse they told Redden: "We've had a wreck. A fellow down there is badly hurt, and we've got to get him to a doctor, quick. Have you got a car?"

Haskell Owens, a nephew of Redden's, said he had one, and backed it out at once, heading for the wreck. Before he got there Clyde stuck his gun into his ribs, and told him to turn the other way.

At Clayton, Oklahoma, they gave Owens his car back, and let him go. Then, a short while later, they stole a car belonging to Frank Smith of Seminole, Oklahoma, and disappeared back into Texas. Smith's car was found the following Sunday, at Grandview.

Here Bonnie joined Clyde and Raymond Hamilton, and from then on out robbery followed robbery. With Clyde driving, they would sometimes cover a thousand miles a day. In a short time he would come to know all the roads in Texas, Oklahoma, Louisiana, Arkansas, New Mexico, Missouri, Iowa, and other states. He would know all the side roads, the country lanes, and could slip into a hiding place, and elude pursuit with all the cunning of a fox.

During this time Bonnie dyed Clyde's hair a flaming red, to make him less conspicuous. The startling results were that he became even more conspicuous. Because of this he bought a blonde woman's wig and wore it. This brought so many whistles from men, that he had to dye it black.

August 9th, Clyde and Bonnie drove to Dallas and visited with their families. They seemed to be able to drive into town and pay visits whenever it pleased them. After nearly every big killing, they would always come home and give the folks all the gory details.

When they got ready to leave this time, Clyde's little sister Nellie asked him, "Where are you going now, Clyde?"

He made a sweeping gesture with his arm. "Driving," he said, "Just driving from now till they get us. Kansas, Missouri, Oklahoma, New Mexico, Texas—always Texas—where we were born. Don't look so glum, Sis. You'll be hearing from us. We'll be seeing you." Then, with one arm around Bonnie's shoulder, they drove away.

iv

Clyde decided it would be a smart idea to lay low for a while, so they drove to Carlsbad, New Mexico, where Bonnie had an aunt, Millie. Raymond Hamilton was with them, and the three tried to appear as unobtrusive as possible driving through the streets of Carlsbad.

Sheriff Joseph Johns saw the car as it threaded its way through town; he noted the Texas license and its three occupants. On a hunch, he jotted down the license number, and later checked it in his file of stolen cars.

Clyde and Bonnie decided to leave all guns in the car, to avoid unduly alarming Bonnie's aunt. They were still in the trunk, when the sheriff came calling, to question them about the car. Bonnie answered the door, and told the sheriff the boys were just dressing, and would be out in a minute.

In desperation, Clyde discovered an old shotgun in the house; grabbed it up, and then he and Hamilton went out the back door. They stole around the house, to the front where the sheriff was. The sheriff, in the meantime, was trying his best to get the trunk of the car open. This was where all the weapons were hidden.

Pressing the shotgun into the exposed rear of the busy sheriff, Hamilton grabbed his gun. Then Clyde yelled to Bonnie, "Honey, get in the car. Quick!" And the three of them roared off, taking the sheriff with them, and without even saying goodbye to Millie.

Later the same afternoon, Sheriff Johns telephoned his office from San Antonio, Texas, to report that he was safe and sound. The following day the car was found abandoned in Victoria, Texas, and someone reported that their Ford V-8 had been stolen.

The description and license number of the stolen car was immediately broadcast to all points in Texas. The police, however, were sure they knew the direction the thieves had taken, so they laid an ambush at a bridge across the Colorado River, at Wharton.

By now the trio had stolen a second car, a Ford coupe, and Clyde and Bonnie drove it, while Hamilton followed in the sedan. As the convoy neared the bridge, Clyde suddenly saw something that sounded an alarm to him. Without a moment's hesitation, he swung the speeding coupe around in the road, and in seconds he was headed in the other direction, passing Hamilton in the sedan.

The posse jumped from their hiding places, and the bullets began to fly. Hamilton continued on until he saw the officers and heard the whine of bullets. Then he too did a rapid about face, and took off after Clyde. A short while later, they abandoned the coupe, and all loaded into the sedan, with Clyde driving.

September 1, 1932, Clyde and Bonnie drove Raymond Hamilton to Michigan, so he could visit his father. Once there, Hamilton decided to remain for a while. So Clyde and Bonnie then drove through Michigan, Indiana, Illinois, Missouri, and into Kansas, robbing small grocery stores and filling stations along the way to pay expenses.

Back in Michigan, Hamilton's love of dancing again got him into trouble. He started going out every night with a different girl, and drinking a lot. The drinking loosened his tongue, and he started bragging about his escapades to the wrong girl, and she reported him to the police.

The police picked him up on suspicion, and based upon his boastings, sent a query to the Dallas police, to see if he was wanted by them. They sent word that they would be delighted to talk to Hamilton about a number of things. Among these were the Neuhoff Packing job and the Hillsboro murder. He was subsequently returned to Dallas. Here he would be tried and sentenced to a total of 263 years in the Huntsville penitentiary. This is just a sample of what was awaiting Clyde and Bonnie.

When Clyde read of Hamilton's sentence, he sent word to him, in prison, that he'd have him out of there within a year.

Various robberies followed, with Bonnie Parker now taking a more active part in all of them. October 1932, they staged a holdup of a grocery store at Sherman, Texas. The store, owned by 67-year-old Howard Hall, was all he had in the world, and he had no intentions of giving up all his money without a fight.

As the police later pieced the story together, Hall tried to fight with Clyde, and Bonnie stepped up and slugged him on the head, repeatedly. He then grabbed her arm, and wouldn't let go, so she shot him. Still, he clung to her arm, so she fired four more shots into him, and cursed him as he fell dead. Then feeling homesick, they decided to go back to Dallas and tell of their adventures.

Back home they visited with their families, and told them all the thrilling details. As usual no one had the Barrow or the Parker home under surveillance, and the visit came off without a hitch. While here, Clyde recruited a couple of new helpers. They were Hollis Hale and Frank Hardy, who were thrilled to be chosen to help such famous people in a few holdups.

Driving up to Missouri, the four of them pulled a series of small robberies, but, the new recruits grumbled, this would never make them rich. What they wanted to do was rob a bank. Now Clyde had never given bank robbery much thought, for he wasn't after a lot of money—only enough to pay expenses, while he and Bonnie experienced the thrills, which seemed to give them sexual satisfaction. But suddenly he had a gang, and to keep them happy he agreed to hold up a bank.

He selected the bank in Oronogo, Missouri, as their target, and Bonnie was sent into the town to case it. She was quite conspicuous in her appearance, and was about as subtle in her "bank casing" as a bum in a jewelry store. When she left, the bank notified the sheriff that they had just been "looked over" by Bonnie Parker.

When they hit the bank on November 30, 1932, they were expected. Leaving Bonnie in the car, the three men entered the bank with drawn guns. The second they went through the door, guns started shooting, but the marksmanship was horrible. The question remains, who was afraid of whom?

Only their desperate need of money kept the gang in the bank, and shooting in every direction, they scooped up what money they could find, and retreated in a hail of bullets.

Surprisingly, with all the bullets flying around, no one was even hurt. But when it came time to count the loot, Hardy and Hale were appalled. They had almost gotten themselves killed for $115. If they had held any visions of getting rich following this pair, it now disappeared, and so did they.

Early in December, Clyde and Bonnie were back in Dallas again, and waiting for them was a former schoolmate of Clyde's. His name was William Daniel Jones, a 17-year-old car thief, who was all fired up with the idea of joining Clyde and Bonnie on some of their adventures. For days both Clyde and Bonnie basked in the radiance of his open admiration for them.

With Jones in tow, they drove to Temple, Texas, December 5, 1932, and searched for a likely looking car to steal. Then they found it, parked right in front of the owner's house, with the keys in the ignition. What better invitation could they have asked for?

Bonnie remained in their own car, as Clyde and Jones entered the one they were going to steal. Jones, in the driver's seat, was having trouble getting it started, and the commotion alerted Doyle Johnson, the owner. He dashed out of the house, and just as they were pulling away from the curb, jumped up on the running board, and tore at the door handle.

Clyde pulled out his pistol, and calmly placing the barrel against Johnson's neck, he fired. The dead Johnson slowly slipped to the street, all threats now silenced. Then they roared away in their new car, with Bonnie trailing along behind. "This kid will do fine," he later told Bonnie. "He never batted an eyelash."

In Dallas, during the early thirties, Lillie McBride, the local Ma Barker, ran a kind of open house for hoodlums. Here they could find temporary safety, for a price. They could pick up their mail, make contacts, and meet with old friends. The police knew about the house, but had been unable to get enough evidence to close it.

Then, on December 31, 1932, an ex-convict named Odell Chandless robbed a bank in Grapevine, Texas, and the police believed he was heading for Lillie's house to hide out for a while. Lillie was away, visiting Raymond Hamilton at Huntsville, so the house was empty.

Accordingly Deputy Sheriff Malcolm Davis secured a search warrant, and he and four other officers staked out inside to await the arrival of Chandless.

A few hours later a car pulled up in front of the house. The driver was a blonde-headed woman, and there were two men in the car with her. One of the men, a short fellow, then got out of the car, and approached the front door of the house.

Instantly, Deputy Sheriff Davis threw open the front door, and commanded, "Throw up your hands!" The startled Clyde Barrow fired his pistol point blank at Davis, killing him. The other officers started firing, but by this time they were receiving fire from the car, and Clyde slipped away into the brush.

Bonnie stepped on the gas, and drove away from the house, but she circled back, looking for Clyde. Suddenly she saw him, coming on a dead run, and she slid over, letting him take the wheel. They didn't stop until they were across the Oklahoma border.

In eastern Oklahoma the three of them rented a cabin in a quiet tourist camp, and stayed here into late January, 1933. To pay expenses, they robbed a number of small businesses, but always a long distance from the cabin. The heat generated by the killing of Deputy Sheriff Malcolm Davis made returning to Texas impossible.

It was during one of their forays for expense money that they were seen exceeding the speed limit by a motorcycle patrolman. It was January 31, and he started out after them, his siren blaring, and after a short run, pulled them over.

Stopping his cycle in front of Clyde's car, he propped it up, and started back, taking out his summons book. "Where's the fire, buddy?" he asked Clyde, as he fished out his pencil.

"Down the block a piece," Clyde grinned at him, then glancing at Jones, he said, "Let's take him, W. D."

Before the surprised Thomas Persell could make a move, Jones had a gun pointed at him, and they disarmed him. Then they forced him into the car, made him lie on the floor, and Clyde covered him with a blanket. Then with a gun held at his head by Jones, they took him on a 200 mile ride.

They passed through such towns as Buffalo, Fairplay, Golden City, Carthage, and on to Oronogo, where they had to stop and steal a new battery. Then on to Poundstone Corner they went, where they let Officer Persell out, unharmed, and sped away laughing.

On March 22, 1933, Buck Barrow was pardoned from the Huntsville Penitentiary by Governor Miriam A. Ferguson—in consideration of his surrender and subsequent good behavior. A few days later, he and Blanche drove to Fort Smith, Arkansas, where they joined up with Bonnie and Clyde.

v

Clyde, posing as a Mr. Callahan, a civil engineer from Minnesota, rented a garage apartment in the rear of a house at 34th Street and Oakridge Road, in the Freeman Grove Residential District of Joplin.

A short time later Mr. Callahan was joined by Bonnie Parker, Buck, Blanche, and W. D. Jones. In the garage, under the apartment, they parked a Ford V-8, with Oklahoma license plates 78-872, and a newly stolen Ford coupe. At another garage, rented at 3339 Oakridge Drive, they parked a Ford sedan, with Kansas license plates.

Here, for nearly two weeks, the Barrow gang enjoyed themselves. They swapped news, badly wanted since Clyde and Bonnie hadn't been home in three months, and occasionally went out at night to replenish their resources with small robberies.

By April 13, they were pretty well settled; the apartment was just like home. Bonnie was cooking red beans and cabbage, her favorite dish; Blanche, her little white dog at her feet, played a game of solitaire; Buck was sacked out on the couch.

After checking the food, Bonnie, dressed in house slippers and negligee, sat down at the table, and put the finishing touches to her latest poem, "Suicide Sal." Since the gang's finances were down to $8.00, Clyde and Jones were out in the car scouting a likely place to rob.

Suddenly Clyde was hit with a hunch, and told Jones they were going back. "I can smell it. It's in the air. Something's going to happen. We're not scouting this evening." With this, he wheeled the car around, and went back to the house. He was just closing the garage doors when the police arrived.

The Joplin police had kept the apartment under investigation for several days. A police informer had told them the place was full of bandits. They weren't sure who was living there, but their investigation had turned up some interesting facts.

One of the men had used one name for purchasing a license plate, then switched to another to make a deposit on the gas and lights. Neighbors could offer little informaton about them, except that they kept to themselves and kept the shades drawn.

Certain the occupants of the apartment were either bootleggers or the bandits responsible for a recent series of local burglaries, they decided on action. So, at about 5:00 P.M., April 13, armed with a liquor search warrant, they drove to the apartment.

In one car, driven by Detective Tom DeGraff, was Constable J. Wes Harryman and Highway Patrolman W. E. Grammer. In another were Detective Harry McGinnis and Highway Patrolman George B. Kahler.

Just as Detective Tom DeGraff arrived at the scene he saw a man at the partially open garage doors. He told Harryman and Grammer, "I'll just head right in," and with that he drove the car right up to the garage doors. Then DeGraff yelled to Harryman, "Get in there as quickly as you can, before they close the door!"

Harryman was out of the car in a flash, and leaped toward the partially opened door. As he did, Clyde fired point blank at him with a shotgun, loaded with #1 buckshot, and it nearly blew him in half. Then Clyde shouted up to the apartment, "It's the law, Bonnie."

Bonnie snatched up a rifle and began shooting at the officers from the upstairs window. They returned her fire, shattering a window, splattering glass all over Blanche. Terrified, Blanche threw open the door, and fled down the stairs. The little dog was at her heels, and she still gripped the deck of cards in her hand.

So startled were the officers that no one fired at her, and in a matter of seconds, with Clyde yelling at her to come back, she was over a half block away. She was still running, still screaming, and a little white dog was still yapping at her heels.

Seeing Harryman fall, Detective McGinnis leaped from the second car, which was still on the street, and sprinted up the driveway. As he scrambled toward the garage doors, Clyde fired at him with the shotgun and he fell, his right arm almost severed at the elbow.

Detective DeGraff yelled to Patrolman Grammer, "For God's sake, run to that house and phone the station to send more men out here." Grammer ran to the house of Harold N. Hill, and phoned the station.

DeGraff then moved toward the east side of the house, and shot out the glass windows in the garage doors. Then he worked his way to the rear of the house, hoping to find another entrance.

Patrolman Kahler had fired his gun until he had only one bullet left, so he retreated to reload. Backing up, he tripped and fell; seeing this, Clyde came out of the garage, thinking he had hit him. A moment later he was joined by Jones, who asked, "Where did that other fellow go?" Just as Jones turned and started back into the garage, Kahler fired his last shot, and Jones staggered forward.

Bonnie and Buck had gotten into the car, where they were joined by Clyde, who suddenly discovered blood on his shirt. He asked Bonnie, "Can you find it?" She probed the hole with her fingers, and located the bullet. It had done little damage, so she pulled it out with a hairpin.

Then Clyde swore, and got out of the car. Bonnie called after him, "For God's sake, come back and get in the car."

"Not until I get the dirty rat that shot me," he barked. "Get the car out and get going." About this time DeGraff stuck his head around the corner, and Clyde let loose with his shotgun, blowing a big hole in the wall, but he missed his victim, who retreated.

Bonnie ran back to the car, and Clyde opened the garage doors, but the drive was blocked by the officer's car, so Jones ran out, released the brakes, and gave it a shove. It ran down the drive, across the street, and careened into a tree. Constable Harryman and Detective McGinnis were also blocking the drive with their bodies, so Clyde rolled them to the side.

Then, bleeding from his chest wound, Clyde took the wheel, and Jones, spouting blood from his head wound, crawled in the back, and they rolled down the drive. When they reached the road Bonnie tugged at Clyde's arm and pointed. "Blanche went that way." Clyde nodded, and turned down the street, with everyone looking for Blanche.

About two blocks away they found her. She was still running, and sobbing, her face white as chalk, and her eyes popping with fright. The little dog was in her arms, and she was in a daze as they pulled her into the car and sped away. She still clutched the deck of cards in her hand, and Bonnie couldn't get it away from her.

Behind them they left J. Wes Harryman, 41, dead, and Harry McGinnis, 53, dying. Inside the apartment they had abandoned a money sack from the McDaniel National Bank of Springfield, a badge of the Police and Sheriff's Association of North America, Bonnie's poem "Suicide Sal" (which is quoted at the end of this chapter), five diamonds taken from the Neosho Milling Company, and Blanche's purse containing her marriage license, Buck's pardon from prison, and several rolls of film.

When the film was developed there were four snapshots of the fugitives. In this group was one of Bonnie Parker with a cigar in her mouth, and a gun on her hip. From here on out, she would be known far and wide as Clyde Barrow's cigar-smoking gun moll.

Driving the car as fast as it would go, Clyde pulled into Amarillo, less than eight hours later. Here they purchased drugs and bandages for Jones' and Clyde's wounds.

The gang avoided tourist camps for a while, living, eating, and sleeping in the woods. They often drove at 60 miles an hour, traveling over hundreds of miles of highways in a day. They camped along little used country lanes, in dense underbrush, sleeping always in relays. At all times someone was on guard to call out and awaken the others, if the occasion should arise. To pay expenses, they robbed small stores and filling stations.

Getting a bandit's family wash done was a ticklish job. They would usually leave the clothes in some small, sleepy-eyed town, then drive on for a couple of days, circling back to get it. This was the dangerous part, for they never knew if they had been recognized and a trap set for their return.

Baths were taken in wayside streams of cold water, as was the morning shave. To get a haircut, they went to a small town barber shop, while someone stood guard in the car in front, ready to blow a signal on the horn if danger threatened.

Usually one of the men would enter the barber shop, while it was crowded. He would then check all the reading material to see if there were any detective magazines with their pictures in it. If not, he would then signal the other two, and they would enter and take their turns.

Food was bought in small, isolated places, and the choice was usually limited to pork and beans, canned soups, cheese and crackers, and canned meats. They didn't dare enter and enjoy a meal in a restaurant, except upon rare occasions. When they did it was a little like playing Russian roulette.

By April 27, 1933, the car Clyde was driving was ready for the junkyard. He had driven it long hours, at furious speeds, and with little or no maintenance. This was a problem, of course, that bothered the Barrow gang very little. They simply stole another.

In Rushton, Louisiana, they saw an unattended car with the ignition keys in it, so the gang piled in and took off. It had been unattended all right, but it wasn't unwatched. D. D. Darby, an undertaker, and his girlfriend, a Miss Stone, came charging out of the house, yelling, but they were too late. Not ones to give up easily, however, they loaded into Miss Stone's car, and gave pursuit.

Darby was not in the habit of driving the heart out of a car, as Clyde was, so he gradually fell behind. At last they lost interest in the seemingly useless chase, and turned around, to seek out the police.

Clyde and Bonnie had been watching their futile efforts in the rear view mirror. When they saw Darby turn around, Bonnie smiled at Clyde and said, "Let's go take 'em, just for a lark." They had been chased so much, she thought it would be great fun to chase someone else for a change.

Without giving it a second thought, Clyde swung the car around, and the horrified Darby found himself being chased by his own automobile. He did the best he could to outrun Clyde, but Miss Stone's car just couldn't make the grade. Clyde forced them off the road, and the Barrow gang tumbled out, guns bristling.

Brutally they forced the young couple into the back of Darby's car, and drove the terrorized pair to Magnolia, Arkansas. Here they graciously gave them $5.00 and let them loose. The Barrow gang laughed about this for days, and could hardly wait to get back to Dallas and tell their families about the fun they'd had.

A short while later they were credited with the robbery and brutal beating of a filling station attendant at Broken Bow, Oklahoma. Then on May 16, the Barrow gang pulled one of their rare bank robberies.

About 17 miles north of the Iowa State line sits the small village of Okabena, Minnesota. It's one of those friendly, dusty, little towns, that sits off the main roads, and exists primarily to serve the farmers in the area. One of its most imposing buildings was the First State Bank, which dominated the main street.

The Barrow gang, keeping to the backroads, stumbled across the town, and its bank, by accident. After holding a hasty meeting, they decided to rob it. There was no planning, or "casing" of the bank, or any of the delicate activities that normally go into a really big job. They just walked in, leaving the two women in the car, and held it up. Then they walked out with $2,500. This was a fortune to them.

As Clyde Barrow later described it to his family and friends in Dallas—"The three of us went in and held the place up. We locked the people in the vault, and got away with twenty-five hundred dollars. But everybody in town seemed to know about the holdup before we did, and there was a regular reception committee waiting for us when we came out. Everybody shooting right and left. I was driving with Bonnie beside me, ready to hand me freshly loaded guns; Buck was in the back seat, and I couldn't depend on him to do any shooting.

"When I saw this old man running out toward us carrying a great big log—he was on Bonnie's side of the car—I said, 'Honey, shoot him before he wrecks us.' Bonnie just sat there, and when I saw she wasn't going to do anything, I had to jerk the car away over to one side to keep from hitting the log, which he tried to throw under our front wheels. I almost turned the car over.

"'Why in the name of God didn't you shoot him?' I asked Bonnie, 'It's a wonder we weren't all killed.' 'Why, Honey, I wasn't going to kill that nice old man,' Bonnie told me, 'He was white headed.'"

Speeding toward Erick, Oklahoma, for a rendezvous with Buck and Blanche, on June 10, 1933, Clyde piled the car into a ditch. He was thrown clear, so he pulled Jones out, and then unloaded the weapons. Suddenly the car burst into flames, and he discovered Bonnie was still trapped in it.

A couple of farmers witnessed the wreck, and hearing Bonnie's screams came running. Between the four of them, they managed to get Bonnie free of the wreck, but not before she received first and second degree burns on her arms, her leg, and her face.

To show his gratitude to the two farmers who had helped him, Clyde drew his gun quietly, and ordered them to carry Bonnie to the farmhouse. Without a doubt they would have done this anyway, but kindness was a human emotion Clyde had no understanding of.

She was carried up to the Prichard farmhouse, and Mrs. Prichard did what she could to ease Bonnie's pain, but she insisted that they should get her to a doctor at once. When Clyde found out the Prichard's didn't own an automobile, it put him in a dark mood.

Clyde then ran back to the burning automobile and gathered up his precious guns. Each and everyone of them had its own name, and he tenderly cleaned them every day. By the time he and Jones had their arsenal in a safe place, they discovered that one of the farmers was missing.

Clyde was in an almost-maniacal mood. First he had no car, and now one of his prisoners had escaped. He stood in the kitchen, looking at Bonnie, burned and aching, when he suddenly saw the door to an adjoining room open. In a flash he fired, and Mrs. Jack Prichard staggered into the room, with her hand shot away.

Just at that moment a car started up the country road, leading to the farmhouse, and Clyde knew at once it must be the police. "That damn farmhand probably brought them," he told Jones, and then he had an idea. He motioned to Jones, and they ran out the back door, and hid in the nearby shrubs.

When the officers arrived, they decided to make their entrance through the back door, so they drew their guns, and crept around the house. But just as they reached for the back door, Clyde and Jones stood up and ordered them to throw down their guns.

The officers were handcuffed and forced into their own car. Then Clyde, forcing Mr. Jack Prichard to help him and Jones, loaded Bonnie in back, and they drove away. In the kitchen sat Mrs. Prichard, badly bleeding from her severed hand, in shock, and alone.

After a three-hour drive at high speeds, they reached the outskirts of Erick, Oklahoma, where they joined up with Buck and Blanche. Now the two officers, Sheriff Corry and Marshal Paul Hardy, were excess baggage, so they were tied to a tree with some wire taken from a nearby barbed wire fence.

It was here that Clyde showed the world how kind he could really be if he wanted to. Blanche and Buck had watched the proceedings with a kind of detached interest. When Clyde had finished tying them, Buck asked, "Aren't you going to kill them?"

"Nope," Clyde replied, "They've been with me so long I'm beginning to take a shine to them." Then with gales of laughter from all but Bonnie, who had troubles of her own, the five of them drove off.

Clyde explained to the manager of the tourist court, in Fort Smith, Arkansas, that his wife had been badly burned by an oil stove explosion. He rented two cabins, and asked if the manager could recommend a good doctor. He could and did, and the doctor arrived a short time later. He bandaged Bonnie's burns, but insisted that the best place for her was a hospital.

Of course this was impossible, so Clyde explained that it was a matter of finances, and the understanding doctor left some medical supplies so they could continue the treatments. Clyde decided Bonnie needed a nurse more than anything, so he jumped into the car at noon Sunday, June 19, and drove to Dallas. He reached there at 8:00 P.M., where he picked up Bonnie's baby sister, Billie, and leaving at 12:00 P.M., he was back in Fort Smith at dawn.

With their money running low, Buck and Jones went to nearby Fayetteville, where they held up two Piggly-Wiggly stores, and picked up a few hundred dollars. Their descriptions, the description of their car, and the license number were immediately flashed to all police officers in the area. The report also theorized that the two bandits were probably heading in the direction of Alma.

Marshal H. D. Humphrey of Alma and his deputy Saylars picked up the report on their radio, and began patroling the highway between Alma and Fayetteville. Before long they saw a car coming their way. It proved to be an acquaintance of theirs, and they stopped to chat. Since the road was not a heavily traveled one, they stopped, adjacent to one another, with little thought about blocking the traffic, and visited.

Just at this moment Buck Barrow and Jones came barreling along, and a rear end collision was inevitable. No one was injured, but automobile parts were scattered all over the highway. The old man they had smashed into got out of his demolished car, cussing and mad. He picked up a rock, intending to throw it at those idiots. Then he took a good, long look at the two of them, and flinging the rock aside, he galloped off down the road.

Marshal Humphrey drew his gun, but Buck Barrow and Jones piled out of their wrecked car, shooting, and he fell, mortally wounded, with a bullet in his chest. Deputy Sayers took up the fight, but facing two of them, he had to retreat and reload.

This was the moment Buck Barrow and Jones had been waiting for. They jumped into the officer's car, the only one that would operate, and sped away. They had gone only seven miles when the front tire blew, so they piled out and flagged down a local farmer. Commandeering his car, they drove off into the hills near Winslow.

When the second car also broke down, they abandoned it and took to the woods on foot. Posses were formed, spurred on by the news of Marshal Humphrey's fatal gun battle. They were sure they had the pair trapped in the hills, so they started combing them, in all directions.

Later in the afternoon, Buck Barrow and Jones stumbled across the farmhouse of Mrs. John Rogers. They forced their way in and demanded her keys, but she refused to give them up. Jones, angered by this, lashed at her with a chain he had found in a corner of her kitchen. She started to scream so loudly a neighbor heard her, and called the sheriff's office. Quickly he put together a posse.

Buck heard the sounds of the approaching posse, and called

Jones, who had taken Mrs. Rogers into the bedroom. And they
fled on foot, leaving behind a hysterical woman, who was bruised
but otherwise unhurt. She still had the keys to her car.

Several miles away, the two came out of the woods, and on to
another road. Here they managed to hitch a ride into Fort Smith
with an unsuspecting farmer. From there they made their way
back to the tourist court on foot. They told Bonnie, Clyde and
Billie of their adventures, and showed them the money that they
had gotten for their pains.

They decided to leave the motel at once, so they packed up,
and made the night's camp in the woods, many miles away. For
the next three weeks they would make the woods and fields their
home, entering towns only at night. Billie, who was not used to
this kind of existence, was put on a train back to Dallas.

June 26, 1933, the Barrows stole the car of Dr. Julian Field,
of Enid, Oklahoma. They didn't want his automobile, but they did
want his medical kit. The abandoned automobile was found the
next day, on the west side of town.

They finally tired of living in the woods, and everybody longed
for a soft bed and a shower, so on July 18, 1933, they hit three
filling stations in a row, at Fort Dodge, Iowa. With this capital
they then drove to within six miles of Platte City, Missouri, and
rented a double cabin. By 10:00 P.M., they had bedded down for
the night at the Red Crown Tourist Camp.

vi

Blanche was the least known of the Barrow gang so she was
elected to go to the nearest restaurant, and buy some beer and
five suppers. She paid for her purchases in nickles and dimes, and
this aroused the curiosity and suspicions of the manager of the
restaurant.

When Sheriff Holt Coffey of Platte County dropped in for
supper later that night, he told the Sheriff of his suspicions.
Coffey agreed with him that the matter could stand some looking
into. He then dropped by the office of the motel and questioned
the owner.

Here his suspicions deepened, as the motel owner told of the
strange people who stayed in their rooms all day with the blinds
drawn, and wouldn't let the maid in to clean up.

As the news of the triple robbery at Fort Dodge, Iowa, arrived,
the Sheriff and the Platte City police were certain the people in

the cabin were the Barrow gang. They called the Sheriff of Jackson County, at Kansas City, and requested reinforcements, as they were shorthanded, and poorly equipped for a siege.

When the Sheriff and the posse arrived at the cabins at 9:50 P.M., July 19, 1933, they brought with them an armored car and several machine gunners, equipped with curved steel shields. Most of the others in the posse were armed with shotguns, rifles, and pistols.

Sheriff Coffey went up to the cabin where Blanche and Buck were staying and pounded on the door. Then he retreated to a discreet distance to await developments. Blanche was awake; she knew it was the police and she was scared to death. She blurted out, "They are not here—they are in the other cabin." Buck jumped up and put his hand across her mouth, but it was too late.

Clyde heard what Blanche had said, and he leaped up, fully clothed. He opened the door to the garage, and flung the guns into the car. Then he yelled to Jones, "I'll bring Bonnie—you take the wheel, kid." But again they were trapped by a police car in the driveway.

Clyde aimed through the garage doors, and let loose a burst from his machine gun, bouncing shots off the armored car. Surprisingly a few of them penetrated its armor, and one shot hit Officer Ben Thorpe in the knee. This caught the officers off guard, so they withdrew the armored car to a safer distance. Then its horn, which had been shorted out by a bullet, began to wail.

Withdrawal of the car was precisely what Clyde wanted, so Jones ran and pushed open the doors, and Clyde drove through them. Jones jumped on the running board as the car went by, and they came out into a hail of bullets. Both Clyde and Jones were shooting machine guns, and the confusion was terrific.

Just then Blanche staggered out of their cabin, half-carrying Buck Barrow. He had been shot twice in the head, and she screamed at Clyde, "I can't do it alone, he's dying!" Clyde leaped from the car and got Buck into the back, next to Bonnie. Then jumping into the front seat, he shoved the throttle to the floor, and with a screech of tires they were away again.

Behind them the barrage continued; bullets crashed through the windows, and Blanche screamed as glass from a shattered pane flew into her eyes. Avoiding Platte City, Clyde turned the other way, and taking the country roads he soon lost his pursuers.

Behind them Sheriff Coffey sat on the grass, dabbing at a wound in his neck. Near by lay his son, Clarence, 19, shot in the left arm. Jackson County Deputy George Highfill had been shot in the right leg, and officer Ben Thorpe, in the armored car, hit in the knee. Miraculously no one had been killed on either side.

In the cabins the officers found a machine gun, three pistols, and many surgical bandages. Over in a corner was Doctor Julian Field's surgical kit. The one stolen from his car in Enid, June 26th.

By dawn Clyde had put hundreds of miles between them and the bloody scene at Platte City, but they were in a real mess. Bonnie was still suffering with her burns, Buck was bleeding badly from his head wounds, and Blanche was moaning with both eyes cut up.

Blanche kept insisting that Clyde take Buck to a hospital before he died, but Buck told her, "We won't give up, honey, we keep on driving."

"But you're going to die," Blanche sobbed. "I'd rather we'd spend the rest of our lives in prison than to have you die, darling."

Buck managed a weak grin, "I wouldn't," he said. "I've been in jail, you haven't. Besides, jail isn't what they'd give me if I got well. No, we keep on driving."

By mid-afternoon Clyde knew he would have to stop, so he pulled into Dexfield Park, a plot of ground covering some twenty acres, lying between Dexter and Reddings, Iowa. Here they drove until they located a secluded place, hemmed in on all sides by dense woods and underbrush. There was a river nearby, where they could get water, so Clyde decided it would be the ideal spot.

Unloading the wounded, Clyde and Jones drove to Perry, where they stole another car. Then they drove to another small town and bought five chicken dinners, some alcohol and aspirin, and returned to the park.

Talk began to buzz in the nearby communities. Someone had seen a car full of bullet holes drive through town. Another farmer had found some bloody bandages. A nearby restaurant had sold five chicken dinners to a strange acting young fellow, and a man in Perry had his car stolen. As the evidence began to pile up someone reported he had seen a campfire burning over in Dexfield Park.

When the news of the big gun battle down in Platte City broke in the newspapers it didn't take a mastermind to figure out that their interlopers were the Barrow gang.

Soon a posse was formed with everyone who could fire a gun joining in. By dawn they were creeping through the woods, Indian style, moving from tree to tree, to keep out of sight.

Jones was roasting weiners over the campfire, and Buck Barrow, in his underwear, was lying on the ground, with his head in Blanche's lap. Bonnie was sitting nearby, watching Clyde, as he cleaned his precious guns.

Suddenly she saw a movement. It was just one of those fleeting motions, but she turned her head and saw a fellow darting from one tree to another. She shouted the alarm.

All at once the woods was alive with possemen and officers, who started firing at them. Clyde snatched up a machine gun and began to shoot. Jones dropped his weiners and grabbed another gun and joined Clyde. Before the combined fire of the two machine guns, the posse retreated just a little.

"Get in the car," Clyde yelled. "Quick—get in the car, everybody." Bonnie made the car in one leap, but Blanche kept trying to put shoes on Buck's naked feet so he could walk on the thorns, completely oblivious of the whistling bullets.

"Let his shoes alone," Bonnie screamed at her, "come on."

Blanche, who could hardly see anyway, kept fumbling with Buck's shoes. At last she got them on his feet, and started dragging him toward the car. Bonnie jumped out and helped her. Clyde and Jones were too busy with their machine guns to help anyone.

The instant everybody was inside the car, Clyde and Jones jumped in, and they started off. Then a bullet crashed into Clyde's arm, and he lost control, crashing into a stump. With bullets zipping around their ears, he and Jones got out, and tried to pry the front end off the stump with the machine guns; but it was useless.

"The other car," Clyde yelled. "Pile out—for God's sake, pile out!" Bonnie helped Blanche again with Buck, and they ran to the other car, with Buck falling, twice. He was hit in the back, and buckshot spattered Bonnie all over her body, but she hardly felt a thing in all the excitement. Then Jones got another head wound, while Clyde had one arm that was bloody and useless; but they all reached the second automobile.

The possemen immediately turned their attention to the car, and they raked it from stem to stern. In five seconds there wasn't a window left in it; two tires had been shot away, and gas poured from a dozen holes in the gas tank. Buck was hit again. Once more Clyde barked orders, "Out of the car. Take to the woods, everybody!"

Buck, now bleeding from two head wounds, and shot in the

back, screamed at Clyde, "Take Blanche and run for it. I'm done for anyway. Run for it."

"I'll go and get another car," Clyde promised, "hide—they can't find you in these thickets. I'll get back."

Again Buck begged, "Take Blanche," but Blanche was down beside him with no intention of leaving.

Clyde yelled to Jones, "Take care of Bonnie," then he dived into the underbrush. Bonnie and Jones ran into the woods, but the posse kept up a steady fire.

Blanche yelled at them, "Stop. For God's sake, stop. Don't shoot anymore—you're already killed him."

"Make him throw up his hands then," someone called.

Blanche yelled, "He can't throw up his hands—he's dying."

As the posse closed in on the two of them, Blanche sat there with Buck's head in her lap, begging him, "Daddy, don't die—don't die—don't die." In the camp they found 2 machine guns, 5 revolvers, and 34 automatic pistols. The pistols had been stolen from the National Guard Armory at Enid, Oklahoma, July 8th.

When the firing stopped, Bonnie and Jones knew that Blanche and Buck were either dead or taken captive. The air was again filled with noise, shouting, pistols popping, and the rattle of machine gun fire—then silence.

Suddenly there was Clyde crawling through the bushes toward them. "I got a car all right," he whispered, "but they were waiting for me at the bridge. They wrecked it so I couldn't cross, and they almost got me. But we'll get over the river and get one. Can you make the river, kid?"

Jones said he could, so they crawled down to the river bank, and waded into the water. Halfway across the river, the posse sighted them and the bullets began plopping into the water all around them.

Their amazing luck held, and they got to the other side safely. The posse, not knowing that Clyde's pistol, waterlogged, was useless, never once entertained the idea of following them across.

Again Clyde left Bonnie and Jones in the fields, and went up to a house on a hill. There three men stood on a porch, watching the fight. Using his useless gun, Clyde held up Mr. Valley Fellers, his son Marvel, and an employee. He lined them up against the barn, and took the keys to Mr. Fellers's car. Then he drove off across the cornfield, picking up Bonnie and Jones, and they fled.

They raced 38 miles to a point near Des Moines, where Clyde held up a filling station, also taking the attendant's car.

Then they doubled back 40 miles to Guthrie Center, where they ran into another posse of about 200 people. They managed to slip by the posse, and the next report had them 100 miles north, in Kosseuth County.

Heading for Denver, they stopped just outside Colorado City, where Jones stole a newspaper from a rural mailbox. A story in the paper said the Barrows had been seen near Denver, so they turned and headed south. For several weeks they would live in little ravines, secluded woods, and down side roads. Eventually their wounds healed, and they were just as mean as ever.

Buck Barrow was taken to the King's Daughters Hospital in Perry, Iowa, and Blanche Barrow went to jail. Clyde's mother, his youngest brother (L. C. Barrow, 19), Billie Mace (Bonnie's baby sister), and Bonnie's mother, Mrs. Emma Parker, all drove to Perry.

At 2:00 A.M., July 29, 1933, Buck died. He was brought back to Dallas for burial a short time later. Blanche was arraigned July 20, 1933, and held under a $15,000 bond. She would eventually be sent to the Women's Prison Farm at Jefferson City, Missouri.

Around the middle of August, Jones, now able to travel on his own, decided he had had about all the excitement he could take. So, saying goodbye to Clyde and Bonnie, he headed back toward Dallas. They also headed toward the Texas border.

William Daniel Jones was arrested a few weeks later and returned to Dallas. Here he dictated page after page of confessions, protesting his innocence and damning Bonnie and Clyde. He claimed that he had been a prisoner of the couple. He told harrowing stories of being chained to trees, and said that they released him only when they needed his help in a killing, or in a robbery.

Clyde and Bonnie arrived in Dallas on September 7, 1933. Here, they thrilled their families and friends by telling all the intimate details of their killings, robberies and kidnappings. These people sat around for hours, and listened with rapt attention, as this pair of sadists told of their exciting adventures.

On November 21 everyone drove up to Wise County, Texas, near the farm of Robert K. G. (Boss) Shannon. There they visited, sang, and celebrated the birthday of Mrs. Henry B. Barrow, Clyde's mother. It was all very cozy—these little killers and their adoring families getting together for a little fun and celebration.

Returning to Dallas, they all made a date to meet the next

day on the Eagle Ford Road. There was one force, however, which was singularly unimpressed with these touching family scenes. He had heard news of them, and laid his plans accordingly. He was the Sheriff of Dallas County, a man with the cumbersome name of Smoot Schmid.

How he found out about the rendezvous point he would never reveal; but find out he did. And he laid an ambush for Clyde and Bonnie. He picked a ravine that was traversed by a small bridge.

While the family waited for the pair, at a point about 75 feet off the main highway, they were unaware that the Sheriff and his posse also awaited—in the ravine, not 30 feet away.

As Clyde and Bonnie neared the meeting place, the officers stood up and started firing with machine guns and rifles. Clyde shoved the throttle to the floor, and they whisked over the bridge. The bullets followed, and the left tire was shot away. Then both of them were hit in the knee, but Clyde kept the car going, bumping along on the rim.

Unfortunately the posse, in order to keep their ambush a secret, had been forced to park their cars a great distance away. They could not give immediate chase. About four miles from the scene, Clyde saw another car coming at them, and he forced it off the road.

When Clyde told the men to get out of the car, they refused. He then shot off the driver's hat, and this did a lot to make them change their minds. The car was old, and unfamiliar to Bonnie, who was trying to get it started. She couldn't find the switch, so she asked the owner where it was. He told her to go to hell. Then she looked at Clyde, and told him, "I guess you'll have to really shoot him." With this attitude, he had no choice, so he showed her where the ignition switch was.

At this moment, two nice, neighborly people happened by in their automobile, and stopped to ask Clyde if they could help him. He waved his gun in their face, and told them he was doing quite nicely. He then suggested that they would be better off if they got the hell out of there. Then, laughing at the two terrified men, standing there in the cold, they drove off to Oklahoma, where they abandoned this car and stole a better one.

In the following weeks they robbed a Piggly-Wiggly store in San Angelo, a refinery in Arp, Texas, and numerous filling stations. Then they decided to take a trip down to the Eastham Prison Farm near the Huntsville Penitentiary. They had received word from Raymond Hamilton that he would like to get out.

Monday, January 16, 1934, was a cold, foggy day. As Bonnie parked the car about a half-mile from the Eastham Prison Farm, Clyde and Jimmie Mullens, a pal of Hamilton's, got out and again made their way through the woods and brush.

The previous night they had been over this same ground, and had hidden three pistols in a brush pile, near a place where prisoners were clearing some timber. Now the two of them waited.

Eventually, coming through the fog, they saw a work party of 17 prisoners and their guards. As soon as they got near the brush pile, Raymond Hamilton and Joe Palmer made a dive for the cache. They grabbed the guns, and whirled on the guards.

Palmer fired as he rolled over, and Olan Bozeman, a guard, fell with a bullet in his hip. Then Palmer swung on another guard, Joseph Crowson, and killed him. At this moment Clyde and Mullens stood up and fired their machine guns, more for the effect than at targets. In the distance came the monotonous sounding of a horn, Bonnie's signal, to help them find the car in the thick fog.

Rather than the two prisoners Clyde had planned, five men made the break. In addition to Hamilton, they were Joe Palmer, serving 25 years; Henry Methvyn, 10 years; W. H. Bybee, life; and J. B. French, 12 years. The other twelve prisoners made no attempt to join in the break, but some of them would later identify Clyde as one of the machine gunners.

Clyde had only two sets of civilian clothes in the car. The three other men had to ride in the trunk to keep their prison uniforms out of sight. In Houston, J. B. French left them, as he had contacts there. Then they drove on to Louisiana, where Palmer and Bybee departed.

Clyde, Hamilton and Methvin waited for about a month until things cooled down a bit. Then in February they robbed the bank in Lancaster, getting $2,400. March 3, 1934, they hit the bank in Mesquite, one in Grand Prairie, and one in West.

Then they robbed the Exchange National and Exchange State banks in Atchinson, Texas, at approximately the same time. The banks, associate institutions, were located in the same building. When Ed Iverson, cashier of the Exchange State bank, told them he couldn't open the bank safe, Hamilton pounded him on the head with his pistol butt, fracturing his skull. Clyde slugged George Wolf, the assistant cashier, after he also refused to open the safe.

When it came time to go Clyde, Hamilton and Methvin rounded

up Ed Iverson (in spite of his fractured skull), Addie Mattock, Mary Low, Gertrude Weinmann, Hugh Cavanagh, Ed Mattock, John Baker, and George Wolf (not seriously hurt), as hostages, and herded them out of the bank.

As they came out of the building with their hostages, Willard Linville, Chief of Police, appeared on the scene. He was unable to shoot because of the hostages, but Clyde was not hampered. He cut the sheriff down with a short burst from his machine gun. Linville fell with six bullets in him.

They lined the outside of the car with hostages, and Miss Addie Mattock, who was an extra, was forced into the back, where she sat on Hamilton's lap. Just as they started out Ed Iverson, suffering from his fractured skull, fell from the car, and they left him.

Bonnie drove the car, and stopped about five miles west of Atchinson, where they changed to another. They left their shaken, and injured hostages behind them, and were $21,000 richer.

Clyde and Bonnie now had enough money to suit them for a while. They wanted to stop and lay low. Hamilton argued that they should keep going. He wanted money—big money, not just the peanuts they were used to living on from grocery store and filling station robberies. He had promised Jimmie Mullens a lot of money for delivering his message to Clyde from Huntsville, and for helping to free him. He also wanted to get enough money to go to Mexico, where he could cool off for a while.

They finally split up, with Raymond Hamilton going his own way. Henry Methvin, fascinated with Clyde and Bonnie, and their records, elected to stay on for a while. He wasn't too interested in money, but he was anxious to share in their adventures.

Feeling it was time to bring their families up-to-date on the latest news, Clyde and Bonnie sent word into Dallas that they would meet them near Grapevine, Texas, on April 1, 1934. They arrived several hours early, so the two of them, with Henry Methvin, lolled around in the shade and ate a leisurely lunch.

Into this serene picture rode E. B. Wheeler and H. D. Murphy, two motorcycle patrolmen who had just happened upon the scene. They saw the car and the three hoodlums, apparently picnicking nearby. So they decided to stop and check them out. Just why they stopped, no one would ever know.

Suspecting nothing, the officers didn't draw their guns, but were just putting the kick stands up on their motorcycles, when Clyde yelled to Bonnie: "Let's take them, honey," and without a warning, and certainly with no provocation, they opened with machine gun fire.

Both officers crumpled to the ground, and then, according to later testimony from Henry Methvin, Bonnie went and turned one of the officers over with her foot. He was still alive, so she gave him another burst from her gun. They then drove away from the bloody spot, laughing. A while later their families drove to the vicinity of the shooting, but couldn't get close enough to find out what had happened.

It was Saturday, April 6, 1934, and the Barrow gang had pulled off beside a country lane, near Commerce, Oklahoma, to get some sleep. Clyde and Methvin were napping in the rear of the car, while Bonnie kept watch from the front. Just then a farmer drove by in a truck, taking his cow to market. He and Bonnie looked each other over as he passed, but Bonnie didn't think it important enough to wake Clyde, who had been driving all night.

The farmer, however, thought it important enough to look up Constable Cal Campbell and tell him about the two drunks, sleeping it off, with a blonde in a car. He thought they were drunks, but Campbell wasn't so sure. He found Police Chief Perry Boyd, having a shave in the local barber shop, and told him.

Since the Barrow gang had often worked in this vicinity, Chief Boyd agreed the matter could bear looking into. They piled into the police car and drove out to investigate. Bonnie saw the car coming, and alerted Clyde, who jumped into the front seat, in his stocking feet, and tried to turn the car around.

In his haste, and still half asleep, he backed the car into a ditch, and there it stuck. By now the officers were certain their suspicions had been correct. They jumped out of their car, guns drawn, and approached cautiously. Clyde, Bonnie and Methvin all started shooting, and the 63-year-old Campbell fell, mortally wounded. Chief Boyd, himself in his sixties, and wounded, raised his hands and was disarmed.

At that moment, unaware of the gun battle that had just been fought, two good citizens happened upon the scene. They stopped and asked if they could help. Clyde, pointing his machine gun at them, said he thought they could. Under his direction, they managed to get his car out of the ditch.

Then the gang loaded Chief Boyd into their car, and sped away, leaving the two good samaritans and the dying constable in the middle of the road. They carried Perry Boyd on a 14-hour trip, finally letting him out at Fort Scott, Kansas. Just before they pulled away, Bonnie, who had become real friendly with the old man, told him to tell the world that she didn't smoke cigars. "That's the bunk," she protested.

They drove to Topeka, Kansas, then circled back to Wichita Falls, where a very shaky Henry Methvin got out and took a train home. This couple was too damn much for him. Then Clyde and Bonnie drove to Dallas, arriving on April 17th, where they told rapt members of their families the intimate details of their latest depredations.

Of course the family kept a scrap book, and the "kids" looked over their latest press clippings. They got a big laugh out of some of the cartoons. One depicted the Sheriff of Dallas County, sound asleep, and peeking out from under the bed were Clyde and Bonnie. Another had Pretty Boy Floyd, surrounded by newspaper stories about Clyde and Bonnie. He was jumping up and down, and yelling, "I haven't had any publicity for weeks."

These and other unkind cuts were chiefly directed at Sheriff Smoot Schmid. There were comic headlines which read, "Clyde and Bonnie give Sheriff Smoot Schmid twenty-four hours to get out of town," and "Clyde and Bonnie let Smoot Schmid get away again."

April 26, 1934, Raymond Hamilton held up the First National Bank at Lewisville, Texas. He then jumped into a car, driven by a companion, and they fled. Two hours later, Hamilton was captured, at a roadblock set up near the little farming community of Howe, about seven miles from Sherman. He would return to Huntsville Penitentiary, to finish his sentence of 263 years.

By now authorities knew there was a third member of the Barrow gang named Henry Methvin. They knew Henry's record, and the location of his father's home in Louisiana, so it was placed under surveillance. Then Ivan Methvin suddenly sold his home, and moved into the Arcadia area. This alerted Sheriff Henderson Jordan, of Arcadia.

Deciding on positive action, Sheriff Jordan went to Ivan Methvin, and asked him what he was doing there. The old man, almost with relief, broke down and confessed that Clyde and Bonnie had forced him to sell his house and move. It was all part of a plan they had for hiding out during the summer in Louisiana.

His son, Henry, had broken off with Clyde and Bonnie, he told him. He would help them trap the two, if they would promise not to prosecute his son in Texas. Sheriff Jordan immediately contacted the Texas authorities, and an arrangement was made. They were quite anxious to get their hands on these killers.

Then came six weeks of patient waiting, before Ivan Methvin had anything definite to tell them. He telephoned Sheriff Jordan one day, to say that the couple were on their way to see him and his son Henry, who had just arrived home. "They should be here in a couple of days," he told the sheriff.

Sheriff Jordan immediately called the Texas authorities, and they sent Bob Alcorn and Ted Hinton, deputies of the Dallas County Sheriff's office. With them was Fred Hamer, a former Captain of the Texas Rangers. Hamer had resigned after 27 years with the Rangers when the state elected a woman as Governor. He was on special assignment from the Huntsville Penitentiary, to track down Clyde and Bonnie.

Word was flashed that Clyde and Bonnie had driven up from Benton, Louisiana, and passed through Gibsland about 4:00 p.m., May 22, on their way to see Mr. Ivan Methvin. They were coming back again the following morning.

Early on the morning of May 23, 1934, the officers selected a deeply wooded section, near Black Lake, on the Jamestown-Sailes road. This lane, not far from Gibsland, was not a main route, so they expected very little traffic. Along a selected shoulder, near a cut in the road, Arcadia Sheriff Henderson Jordan, and his deputy Paul M. Oakley, Fred Hamer, and the two Texas deputies, Bob Alcorn and Ted Hinton, with Highway Patrolman B. M. Gault, took up positions and waited.

Across the road sat Ivan Methvin with a wheel removed from his truck; he was pretending to fix a flat. At 9:15 a.m., a brand-new Ford sedan bearing Arkansas license plates (stolen from Merle Cruse of Fayetteville, Arkansas, April 17, 1934) topped the rise, and then slowed as the driver, Clyde Barrow, recognized Methvin.

Clyde swung his car around Methvin's truck, and parked it in front. Just as he was about to get out of the car, a heavy truck, loaded with watermelons and driven by two Negroes, topped the rise; it was certain to come between the officers and the killers.

A decision had to be made, and Sheriff Jordan made it. He called to Clyde to surrender, that he was surrounded. Clyde had other ideas, however, and put the car in gear, slamming the throttle to the floor. Then someone fired, and the fusillade started.

The truck stopped, with a screech of brakes, and the two Negroes fled into the woods. The posse continued to pour a merciless fire into the sedan. The car crashed into the embankment of the cut, its wheels spinning crazily and uselessly, as the posse blasted it with machine gun, shotgun and rifle fire.

Then it stopped. Clyde Barrow, a Browning automatic rifle in his lap, lay across the steering wheel, his head hanging out of the window. His entire left side and head were a mass of blood and torn flesh. He had been hit over 45 times, and his left hand had been blasted away.

Beside him, with a machine gun in her lap, sat Bonnie Parker, her head between her knees. It had been almost severed from her body by the terrific fire. A little white hat she had been wearing had been blasted out the window, and her red dress, shoes, and silk stockings were getting a darker shade of red by the minute.

The car was a complete wreck, chewed to pieces by the intense fire. It was later towed into Arcadia, with its occupants still in it. Clyde's head hung out the window, gently swaying with the motion of the car. Bonnie's head, barely attached to the body, rested between her knees, as if she were ducking. In the trunk of the car were three army rifles, two sawed-off shotguns, twelve pistols, and thousands of rounds of ammunition.

Nearly two thousand morbid curiosity seekers would flock into Arcadia from all over. They swarmed across the car; cutting locks of Bonnie's hair, tearing at their clothing, and prying off hubcaps. There were insufficient officers available to keep such a mob under adequate control.

They snatched up bits of broken glass, and the more resourceful drove to the area of the ambush, where they chopped down trees to remove the bullets in them. Some of this potpourri has probably been handed down to a new generation as souvenirs. Such was the adolation of many misguided souls of that day, who looked upon bandits and banditry as something romantic.

When the bodies of Clyde Barrow and Bonnie Parker were returned to Dallas, it was Arcadia all over again. The huge, uncontrollable crowds of people were swarming all over the place. Small businessmen set up stands and sold lemonade and hotdogs. In front of the funeral parlor there were thousands upon thousands of people just milling around.

In the final verses of Bonnie Parker's poem, "The Story of Bonnie and Clyde," she wrote:

> They don't think they're too smart or desperate,
> They know that the law always wins;
> They've been shot at before,
> But they do not ignore
> That death is the wages of sin.
> Some day they'll go down together;

They'll bury them side by side;
To few it'll be grief—
To the law a relief—
But it's death for Bonnie and Clyde.

In spite of Bonnie's prophetic poem, Clyde Chestnut Barrow, age 25, and Bonnie Parker, age 23, were not buried side by side. Mrs. Emma Parker bitterly remarked that Clyde had had Bonnie for over two years and had brought her to this. Now he was not going to have her any longer.

She was buried in the family plot on the south side of Dallas. Bonnie's baby sister, Billie, was released from a Forth Worth jail just in time for the funeral. Clyde was buried in a west Dallas cemetery near his brother Buck.

The Clyde Barrow–Bonnie Parker Papers

1406 Cockrell Street
February 14, 1930

Mr. Clyde Barrow,
Care The Bar Hotel,
Dallas, Texas
Sugar:

Just a line tonight. How is my baby by now? Today has been just another day to me and a hard one. Sure wish I could have seen you today. I think I could have made it. Maybe I can see you tomorrow. I went out to your mother's today. Marie is staying all night with me tonight.

Honey, I don't know any news. Nothing ever happens any more. At least nothing interesting. I have had the blues so bad all day that I could lie right down and die. I am so disgusted honey. I don't know what to do. I wish you were here to tell me what to do. Everything has turned out wrong. I even sprained my wrist today.

Sugar, when you do get out, I want you to go to work, and for God's sake, don't get into any more trouble. I am almost worried to death about this. Sugar, when you get clear and don't have to run, we can have some fun.

I sure hate to write when I feel as blue as I do tonight. I just called Nell and she said she saw you today. I sure do like her. She is so sweet. Darling, today is the first day I've cried in a long time but I sure did cry today all day. One of the boys brought me a box of candy for a Valentine today. I was alone with the baby (Billie, her sister's baby) and the idiot tried to spend the day. I never was so irritated in all my life. Talk about a sick woman but I was the sickest. I did everything but tell him to leave, and he stayed and stayed and stayed. Finally Billie came back and I walked out. Now, it's bad enough to be sick and discouraged as I was without having an idiot to put up with. I felt like throwing the candy in his face. I didn't appreciate the old candy at all, and I thought about my darling in that mean old jail, and started to bring the candy to you. Then I knew you wouldn't want the candy that that old fool brought to me.

Baby, how is Frank? [Frank Clause] He sure holds up well. He seems to be always smiling, and I guess he figures, it's best to keep smiling. Darling, I hope you will always smile, because it kills me to see that awful look on your face when I start to leave you. It's bad enough to have to leave you, anyhow. Honey, I write books to you and only get little notes from you, but gee, how I love to get them. I wish I had a million because I have worn the ones I have completely out.

Honey, I sure wish I was with you tonight. I'm so lonesome for you, dearest. Don't you wish we could be together? Sugar, I never knew I really cared for you until you got in jail. And honey, if you get out o. k., please don't ever do anything to get locked up again. If you ever do, I'll get me a railroad ticket fifty miles long and let them tear off an inch every thousand miles, because I never did want to love you and I didn't even try. You just made me. Now, I don't know what to do.

And listen, honeyboy, you started this and somebody is sure going to finish it. Baby,—no, I didn't intend to call you that because you're not a baby. Well, darling, I'm going to have to close, as I can't seem to make this letter at all interesting. I have read it over and I can't seem to see any percentage in it at all. I'm so sorry, but I can't think of anything to say, only that I love you more than anything on earth, and I don't know if that is of any interest to you. When I find out for sure maybe I can write a sensible letter.

Tell Frank hello and not to be discouraged, because someday he'll be all right again. I hope you won't consider this letter preaching. Please pardon the mistakes, honey, but Marie has asked me ten jillion questions since I started writing. Tell Raymond [Hamilton] hell-no, I mean hello for me. I sure feel sorry for him. Just think: He has to spend two of the best years of his life in jail. Wouldn't that be awful, honey, if you had to? I'd just have to go down to the grave yard and wait. As it is, I can hardly wait. If you don't hurry and get out, I'm going to be hard to get along with. I would just simply die if you were convicted.

Honey, when I started to close this letter, Glynn said, "Don't stop. Write him a long letter, because he will have something to pass those lonely hours away." But I must stop, honey, as it is twelve o'clock, and Marie wont go to bed until I do. She's about to fall out now. Everyone says hello and they all wish you good luck. We think of you all the time. At least, you're on my mind all the time, and I keep the rest of them thinking about you by always talking about you.

Well, honey, I have to go to bed. I hate these long sleepless nights, but then time goes by as it always does, and maybe I can make it. Be sure to write me a long letter, honey, and think of me down here, thinking of you. I love you.

Just your baby,
Bonnie.

1406 Cockrell Street
Wednesday night.

Mr. Clyde Barrow
Care Denton County jail,
Denton, Texas

Dearest Little Darling:

Just a few lines tonight. How's my honeyboy? I guess you are surely lonsome. I didn't even know you'd gone till I borrowed the car and went down town and they told me you went away last night. I was so blue and mad and discouraged. I just had to cry. I had maybelline on my eyes and it began to stream down my face and I had to stop on Lamar street. I laid my head down on the steering wheel and sure did boohoo. A couple of city policemen came up and wanted to know my trouble. I imagine I sure looked funny with maybelline streaming down my face.

Well, anyhow, I told them I merely felt bad and they offered to drive me home, but I thanked them and dried my eyes and went on out to your mother's. They weren't at home. I came back to town and couldn't find mother, so I went out to Bess's and couldn't find her. By that time I was on the verge of hanging myself, so I tried to wreck the darn car but didn't succeed, and came on home and walked the floor till now.

Your mother and dad came out a few minutes ago. So tomorrow I'm going to make an effort to see you. If I drive all the way to Denton and still don't get to see you, it's going to be "jam up" for somebody, because I'm sure going to be hard to get along with. Darling, do you think of me? I never was so unhappy in my whole life before. Dear, I don't know what to do. I thought I would get a letter from you today, but I don't suppose you have any stamps and paper, do you?

Sugar, I don't know a thing that is interesting, only I love you more than my own life and I am almost crazy. Honey, if you stay in jail two more weeks, I'll be as crazy as a bughouse rat. I dreamed last night that you got "out" and I got "in." I wish I could serve those long days for you, dear. But if I were in, you'd probably forget me. This letter is like all the rest. It is sort of melancholy, but sweetheart, I am so moody, so discouraged and blue. You couldn't expect me to be happy or even to write cheerful letters, for this is more a strain on me, dear, than it is on you.

I promise you when you get out I will be happy and "never cry 'no mo'." I wish I could cry on your manly shoulder. If I even had some one who understans to tell me what to do. I don't eat or sleep. You are driving me insane. Dear, promise me you wont go away when you get out. Honey, if you should leave me, I wouldn't know what to do. Frank says you are going far away. I'm sure you wouldn't leave me for him, would you? Of course, he says if you care to have me go along, it'll be o.k. with him, but he says it in rather a disinterested manner. I know you can't ever live in Dallas, honey, because you can't live down the awful name you've got here. But sugar, you could go somewhere else and get you a job and work. I want you to be a man, honey, and not a thug. I know you are good and I know you can make good. I hope Frank will be a good boy when he gets out, for he is too young to start on that downward road.

Just think, honey, if you and he were to get twenty-five years in the pen! You would be a broken old man, friendless and tired of living when you get out. Everyone would have forgotten you but me—and I never will—but I should more than likely be dead by then. And think, dear, all your best years spent in solitary confinement away from the outside world. Wouldn't that be terrible? Dear, I know you're going to be good and sweet when you get out. Aren't you, honey? They only think you are mean. I know you are not, and I'm going to be the very one to show you that this outside world is a swell place, and we are young and should be happy like other boys and girls instead of being like we are. Sugar, please don't consider this advice as from one who is not capable of lending it, for you know I'm very interested and I've already had my day, and we're both going to be good now—both of us. Oh, I'm so lonesome for you tonight and I'm hoping I'll be with you in a few days. Dear, I'm going to close and try to get this all in one envelope. Forgive this awful writing, but just thank goodness that I still have enough sense to write a sentence. Answer real soon, dear, and think often of
Your lonesome Baby

P. S. I am coming up tomorrow, even if they don't let me see you, you'll know I came and tried. I love you. Be real sweet, honey, and think of the girl who loves you best. Try not to worry, for I do enough of that for us both. Everyone is o.k. and mother says hello, and she is hoping you can come home soon. I love you, darling, with all my heart, and maybe it wont be long till we can be together again. Think of me, darling, and what a wonderful time we will have when you come home—how happy we will be. I love you honey.
Bonnie.

1406 Cockrell St
February 23, '30

Honey Boy:—

Just a line today as I have made another unsuccessful attempt. Sugar I am so blue I could die. I haven't gotten a letter from you this week. Dear, I went to Ft. Worth today to get some money and when I got up there nobody was home. I have become so discouraged I wish I was dead. I got the car the other day and your mother and I were coming up so I didn't meet her on time and she went on the bus. I started and the muffler come off and the durn car sounded like a thresher. I was going to take a chance on getting arrested anyhow but I ran out of gasoline and had to walk about 2 miles, and Honey it was sure raining. I got so wet I was terrible looking so I came back home. But listen, dear, I'm coming to see you tomorrow even if I have to walk every step 'cause honey, I can't wait any longer. I know I can get the car and if the darn thing breaks down I'll start walking and talking 'cause I must see my daddy.

I saw Mr. and Mrs. Barrow yesterday. They came over to tell me about you. I was supposed to go out there this A.M. but I coasted over to "Cowtown" and your Sis from Denison is out there today and I have never met her. So I didn't want to go on that account. But I'm going out there tonight.

Darling do you still love your baby? Say, honey, I have written you a letter every night but, dear, I didn't think you would be there long enough to get them. Sugar, maybe you won't be there long enough to answer. I love to get those sweet letters from you but I had lots rather you would answer in person. Every night I go to bed with hopes that to morrow night will be brighter but it's always just another day. Maybe it won't be this way always. At least if I thought it would I would go down to the grave yard and wait. For I've already found out life's not worth living without you.

I've got a Majestic Radiola and they nearly drive me crazy with the music, I love music but it always makes me melancholy—and all I've heard today is "Lonesome Railroad Blues" and "I sing all my love songs to you." It nearly drives me mad. Dear, I had lots rather hear you sing than Gene Austin. He's wonderful but he doesn't mean anything to me. I know you think I have forgotten you because I haven't written you or come to see you since you went away but honey, if I could you know I would go to jail for you and more than gladly with you. I only wish I could serve those long old lonesome days for you. It hurts me lots more to have you in there than it would be to be in there myself.

Dear, someone told Bud I got my divorce on the 18th and he came out begging me not to get married the 25th of February. He had been drinking as usual. I got so irritated I almost screamed.

If he hadn't left when he did I know I would have "passed out." I hate him. I told him, No I didn't suppose I was going to get married; at least I hadn't had any late propositions. He says he thinks I should consider his feelings before I do anything "rash," but I reminded him that he wasn't in the "racket" any more. He said "Now what would you do if I should tell you I was gonna get married?" and I told him I would like to congratulate the young idiot he married for taking a "pest" off my hands. He didn't see how Bonnie could talk that way—Anyhow as bad as he feels he would like to meet the "Lucky Dog" that made me care.

Honey, I don't know any news as nothing ever happens around here. Glynn is fine; he says tell you hello. Mother was coming up to see you today and we almost knew we couldn't get in so we are hoping we can see you tomorrow. Pat sure wants you to come to work. He needs you bad. Now I want you to go back and stay with Pat 'cause you must help your Mother. She is sick and she needs you and I need you and I want you to stay here and be sweet.

Well I'll be a dirty name here it is tomorrow—what a silly re-mark—what I mean is I didn't finish my letter yesterday for I went back over to Ft. Worth and now it's 5:30 in the morning. I guess my sugar is sleeping by now. I had to get up early this A.M. as usual. But I have to get ready to go to Denton early. It looks as if it will rain today but just let it rain. I'll go anyway.

I'm sure tired this morning after driving so much yesterday. Honey, I don't know any news and it's too early in the morning to learn any, for no one is up but me. I'll have to close, baby, and here's hoping they let me see you today—Be sweet and write to me. I love you.

Just your baby,
Bonnie.

Waco, Texas
March 3, 1930

Hello Sugar:

Just a line tonight, as I'm so lonesome. Just think, honey, today is the first time I have seen you in two weeks, and just a very few minutes today. But it sure was sweet just to get to see you. Those laws are all so nice, dear. They aren't like those Denton laws.

Your mother is spending the night with me tonight. I wanted her to stay so she could see you again tomorrow. Dearest, I'm going to get me a job and stay up here; I couldn't make it in Dallas any-more without you. Sugar, how I wish you were out of all this awful trouble. I don't see how I can get along if you go away. You didn't act like you were very glad to see me today. What's wrong? Don't you love me any more? I know how you feel, honey. I guess you are awfully worried.

Listen, dear, I wont write much today, because I'll see you to-morrow, we hope, and for a long old time. And honey, just remember I love you more than anything on earth, and be real sweet and think of me, down here thinking of you.

Your lonesome baby,

Bonnie.

P. S. Don't worry, darling, because I'm going to do everything possible and if you do have to go down, I'll be good while you're gone, and be waiting—waiting—waiting—for you. I love you.

April 19, 1930
Waco, Texas

Dear Baby:

I just read your sweet letter, and I sure was glad to get it for I am awfully lonesome and blue. Why did you say you didn't know whether I would accept it or not? Now, honey, you known darn well I didn't mean what I said in my last letter. I'm just jealous of you and can't help it. And why shouldn't I be? If I was as sweet to you as you are to me, you would be jealous too.

Say, sugar, these loco guys are making so much noise I can't write, so I will finish this tomorrow.

After a long lonesome night, I will try and finish. It's Easter Sunday and I sure wish I was outside with you. Gosh, honey, I bet we could have a good time today. Where were you last Easter, honey, and who was with you? Last Easter Frank Clause and I were together, as near as I can remember. Mrs. Vaughn sent me an Easter card yesterday but it wasn't near as pretty as the one you sent me last week.

Well, dear, I sure hope you don't have to work on Sunday. Well, you ask me if I wanted Bob to come up. You got my last letter, didn't you? That is all I am depending on now. I don't think I can get my time cut any. If Bob hasn't already left, send him as soon as you get this. I think maybe he can do me some good.

Sugar, I don't see why I didn't leave you a car so you could come down to see me on Sunday. This is such a pretty day, and it is sure going to be a long lonesome one for me.

Well, baby, how are you liking your job by now? And have any of those hop-heads got smart with you? If they do, just remember the name, because I wont be in this joint all my life.

Just a minute honey, and let me see what has happened up here. It's all right, baby, everything is o. k. I thought for awhile all of them were dead, for it was so quiet, but Frank is reading, and Pat is sick; two of them are asleep and Lee is sitting by the window looking out and wishing he was outside. This is the first time this place has been quiet since I've been here and I'm hoping they wont wake up till I get through writing.

Honey, you said you would do anything I wanted you to do. Well, I'll tell you what I want you to do. Just be a good little girl and always love me. If you'll do those two things, that is all that is necessary, except coming to see me and that is the main thing right now.

Say, Sugar, you ought to see me. I've got on Frank's suspenders, and I'm sure a darb of the season, no fooling. Honey, if I could just spend one week with you, I'd be ready to die, for I love you and I don't see how I can live without you. Say, honey, when I get down yonder and get to thinking of you, I'll jump right up and start towards Big D. I may not get very far, but I'll sure get caught trying.

Well, old dear, here's Bud Russell. I don't know whether he's going to take us up or not, but I guess he will. If he does, be sure and come down as soon as you can. Honey, I don't know whether they're going to take me or not, but if they do, do what I told you. Come when you can . . . .

No, honey, they aren't going to take me this time and I am sure glad, for maybe I can get a chance to get my time cut again. Honey, Uncle Bud may come back tomorrow, but if he doesn't, I'll write to you. And if he does, I'll write to you as soon as I get to the Walls [Huntsville Penitentiary]. But I hope he doesn't come back for awhile.

Well, old sugar, I don't know any news so I guess I will close. Send Bob as soon as you can. I love you,

Clyde.

P. S. When mama comes back up here, if she comes before I go down, tell her to bring me some old kind of shirt, so I can send this one home. It's too good to throw away. I love you.

December 11, 1930

Dearest little wife:

Just received your sweet and welcome letter, and believe me, it really gave me a great surprise to hear from you. Why, honey, I couldn't hardly believe my eyes when I glanced at your handwriting on the envelope. So I took it and looked it over carefully and finally decided it was from you.

Listen, Bonnie, who the hell told you all those lies on me? Sugar, you know I didn't say anything like that about my little blue-eyed girl. Honey, I love you more than I love my own self and just because I have fourteen years is no sign I will be here always. Mother went to Waco to talk to the judge, and he said he would help her get my sentence cut back to two years. If everything works out like I hope it will, I wont have to stay away from my baby much longer.

Say, honey, I know your mother thinks I didn't want to answer her letter, but you see, Sugar, I am not at the same camp I was when she wrote me, and at this camp you can't write to anyone except your family. Be sure and tell her how it is. I am on Eastham Farm No. 2 and I get my mail at the same address, Weldon, Texas, Box 16, Camp No. 2, so be sure and answer this as soon as you get it, for honey, I sure do need your letters to pass away these long, lonesome days.

I would give anything on earth if I could get one more good look at my little blue-eyed baby. Honey, I havn't even got a picture of you, for when I left Camp No. 1 it was unexpected, and I didn't have time to get your picture, so please send me another if you have any. Well, baby, I am going to close for this time, and if you answer this, I will write more next time. I sent all my love to you from your daddy that loves you.

Clyde Barrow.

December 21, 1930

To my darling little wife:

Hello, honey, I received your most sweet and welcome letter last night and honey, you'll never know how glad I was to get it, for now I can enjoy Christmas. Sugar, what made you think I wouldn't answer your letters? Why, darling, you know I love you more than anything, and you haven't done anything to me. Listen, Sugar, mother is not mad at you. She was down here last week and asked me about you. Said she would like to see you, and I told her she didn't want to see you half as much as I did, which is really true for I am just crazy to see my little blue-eyed girl.

You asked me if I heard from Frank or Gladys. No, dear, I haven't and I don't care to, for they don't care anything about me and I am not mad about them. All I ever want for is you, Sugar, and I would give my right eye to see you. And if you can come I want you to come and see me. I can get L. C. to bring you, for I know you haven't the money to come down here with. But it wont be like that always darling. Some day I will be out there with you and then we can be happy again.

Sugar, mother just about got my time cut to two years, and I have been down here eight months already. If she does get it cut, it wont take long for me to shake it off. So you just make it the best you can till I do, and then let me do the rest.

Well, old dear, I don't know any news as usual, so be a sweet little girl and write your daddy real often, because I really enjoy your sweet little letters. Tell everyone hello for me, and I wish you a mery, merry Christmas. Answer real soon. I send all my love to you.

Your loving husband,

Clyde Barrow.

P. S. Please send me one of your pictures.

THE STORY OF SUICIDE SAL

We each of us have a good "alibi"
For being down here in the "joint";
But few of them really are justified
If you get right down to the point.

You've heard of a woman's glory
Being spent on a "downright cur,"
Still you can't always judge the story
As true, being told by her.

As long as I've stayed on this "island,"
And heard "confidence tales" from each "gal,"
Only one seemed interesting and truthful—
The Story of "Suicide Sal."

Now "Sal" was a gal of rare beauty,
Though her features were coarse and tough;
She never once faltered from duty
To play on the "up and up."

"Sal" told me this tale on the evening
Before she was turned out "free,"
And I'll do my best to relate it
Just as she told it to me:

I was born on a ranch in Wyoming;
Not treated like Helen of Troy;
I was taught that "rods were rulers"
And "ranked" as a greasy cowboy.

Then I left my old home for the city
To play in its mad dizzy whirl,
Not knowing how little of pity
It holds for a country girl.

There I fell for "the line" of a "henchman,"
A "professional killer" from Chi;
I couldn't help loving him madly;
For him even now I would die.

One year we were desperately happy;
Our "ill gotten gains" we spent free;
I was taught the ways of the "underworld,"
Jack was just like a "god" to me.

I got on the "F. B. A." payroll
To get the "inside lay" of the "job";

The bank was "turning big money!"
It looked like a "cinch" for the "mob."

Eighty grand without even a "rumble"—
Jack was last with the "loot" in the door,
When the "teller" dead-aimed a revolver
From where they forced him to lie on the floor.

I knew I had only a moment—
He would surely get Jack as he ran;
So I "staged" a "big fade out" beside him
And knocked the forty-five out of his hand.

They "rapped me down big" at the station,
And informed me that I'd get the blame
For the "dramatic stunt" pulled on the "teller"
Looked to them too much like a "game."

The "police" called it a "frame-up,"
Said it was an "inside job,"
But I steadily denied any knowledge
Or dealings with "underworld mobs."

The "gang" hired a couple of lawyers,
The best "fixers" in any man's town,
But it takes more than lawyers and money
When Uncle Sam starts "shaking you down."

I was charged as a "scion of gangland"
And tried for my wages of sin;
The "dirty dozen" found me guilty—
From five to fifty years in the pen.

I took the "rap" like good people,
And never one "squawk" did I make.
Jack "dropped himself" on the promise
That we make a "sensational break."

Well, to shorten a sad lengthy story,
Five years have gone over my head
Without even so much as a letter—
At first I thought he was dead.

But not long ago I discovered
From a gal in the joint named Lyle,
That Jack and his "moll" had "got over"
And were living in true "gangster style."

If he had returned to me sometime,
Though he hadn't a cent to give,

I'd forget all this hell that he's caused me,
And love him as long as I live.

But there's no chance of his ever coming,
For he and his moll have no fears
But that I will die in this prison,
Or "flatten" this fifty years.

Tomorrow I'll be on the "outside"
And I'll "drop myself" on it today:
I'll "bump'em" if they give me the "hotsquat"
On this island out here in the bay . . .

The iron doors swung wide next morning
For a gruesome woman of waste,
Who at last had a chance to "fix it."
Murder showed in her cynical face.

Not long ago I read in the paper
That a gal on the East Side got "hot,"
And when the smoke finally retreated,
Two of gangdom were found "on the spot."

It related the colorful story
Of a "jilted gangster gal."
Two days later, a "sub-gun" ended
The story of "Suicide Sal."

BONNIE PARKER.

THE STORY OF BONNIE AND CLYDE

You've read the story of Jesse James—
Of how he lived and died;
If you're still in need
Of something to read
Here's the story of Bonnie and Clyde.

Now Bonnie and Clyde are the Barrow gang.
I'm sure you all have read
How they rob and steal
And those who squeal
Are usually found dying or dead.

There's lots of untruths to these write-ups;
They're not so ruthless as that;
Their nature is raw;
They hate all the law—
The stool pigeons, spotters and rats.

They call them cold-blooded killers;
They say they are heartless and mean;
But I say this with pride
That I once knew Clyde
When he was honest and upright and clean.

But the laws fooled around,
Kept taking him down
And locking him up in a cell,
Till he said to me
"I'll never be free,
So I'll meet a few of them in hell."

The road was so dimly lighted;
There were no highway signs to guide;
But they made up their minds
If all roads were blind,
They wouldn't give up till they died.

The road gets dimmer and dimmer;
Sometimes you can hardly see;
But it's fight, man to man,
And do all you can,
For they know they can never be free.

From heart-break some people have suffered;
From weariness some people have died;
But take it all in all,
Our troubles are small
Till we get like Bonnie and Clyde.

If a policeman is killed in Dallas
And they have no clew or guide;
If they can't find a fiend,
They just wipe their slate clean
And hang it on Bonnie and Clyde.

There's two crimes committed in America
Not accredited to the Barrow mob;
They had no hand
In the kidnap demand,
Nor the Kansas City Depot job.

A newsboy once said to his buddy:
"I wish old Clyde would get jumped;
In these awful hard times
We'd make a few dimes
If five or six cops would get bumped."

The police haven't got the report yet,
But Clyde called me up today;
He said, "Don't start any fights—
We aren't working nights—
We're joining the NRA."

From Irving to West Dallas viaduct
Is known as the Great Divide,
Where the women are kin,
And the men are men,
And they won't "stool" on Bonnie and Clyde.

If they try to act like citizens
And rent them a nice little flat,
About the third night
They're invited to fight
By a sub-gun's rat-tat-tat.

They don't think they're too smart or desperate,
They know that the law always wins;
They've been shot at before,
But they do not ignore
That death is the wages of sin.

Some day they'll go down together;
They'll bury them side by side;
To few it'll be grief—
To the law a relief—
But it's death for Bonnie and Clyde.

BONNIE PARKER.

••6••

See Johnny Run

i

Perhaps the most overrated bank robber, and the most exaggerated killer in American criminal history, was the swaggering, boastful son of a German immigrant, with the catchy name of John Dillinger.

John Dillinger was essentially and fundamentally a product of the American press, which took this obscure, two-bit hoodlum, and built him into the personification of all American gangsters. The press got carried away, and before anyone realized what had happened, John Dillinger was being hailed as the bravest, boldest, devil-may-care bandit in American history. The Kurdish tribesmen of Iran had never heard of Jessie James, but they certainly knew who John Dillinger was. Such was, and is, the power of the press.

The first Dillinger gang consisted of Harry Pierpont, John (Red) Hamilton, Charles Makley, and Russell Clark; it had no acknowledged leader. Harry Pierpont was clearly the brains of the gang, and Makley, Hamilton and Clark had infinitely more experience at their chosen trade than Dillinger. It is extremely doubtful that they would have depended upon the questionable wisdom of Dillinger for leadership.

The second Dillinger gang, which was formed in March 1934, consisted of Baby Face Nelson, John (Red) Hamilton, Homer Van Meter, Tommy Carroll, and Eddie Green. Dillinger formed this gang, and it did take its orders from him. Because of this it lasted only a little over four months.

The brainiest member, by far, of the Dillinger gang was Eddie Green, and when he was killed in April 1934, the gang lost its steerage. Eddie Green wasn't really the moving force of the gang, but he was the planner of the getaway routes, the disposer of hot money, and the procurer of hideouts, guns, ammunition, and steel vests.

Most of the Dillinger-led bank robberies were turned into disasters or near disasters; and they usually produced a lot less money than they should have. He got shot, they got shot, and innocent people got shot. Dillinger's leadership led them into their near annihilation at the Little Bohemia Lodge fiasco, and following in the wake of his infinite wisdom, they got picked off one by one.

The following is the Dillinger Story, where the reader can decide for himself about the greatness of the "Great John Dillinger."

ii

John Herman Dillinger was born on June 22, 1903, at 2053 Cooper Street, in the Oak Hill Subdivision of Indianapolis, Indiana. His father was John Wilson Dillinger, an Alsace-Lorraine German immigrant; his mother was Mollie Lancaster Dillinger. The Dillingers had one other child, Audrey, who was born in 1889. She would take over the duties as John Dillinger's mother after Mollie died following an operation in 1906.

Dillinger's father owned a grocery store at 2210 Boyd Avenue, and was able not only to support his family adequately, but to purchase four rental houses. These brought him additional money.

Even so John Dillinger seems to have had an unhappy childhood, interlaced by battles with his domineering father. While there was undoubtedly love between the two, it was rarely if ever spoken or emotionally shown.

When Dillinger was nine his father married Elizabeth Fields, of Mooresville, but John felt only a deep resentment against this stranger intruding into his life.

During this time he attended Public School Number 38, at Winter Street and Boyd Avenue. Here he made no lasting impressions upon any of his teachers, either as a scholar or by his behavior. At the end of the fourth grade he transferred to the George Washington School, located at 17th Street and Sheldon.

Then, when John was 16 he quit school, satisfied that he had absorbed all the knowledge he would require in this life. The following year the family all moved to Mooresville, where his father had purchased a farm.

By this time the family had grown to four children. Hubert was born in 1914 and Doris in 1916. This large family settled down on a 60-acre farm, about one-half mile north of Mooresville proper. John didn't take to farming, however, so his father had to do the work, while he hung around the one poolroom in town.

Then, for want of something better to do, in 1923 John enlisted in the Navy. He immediately rebelled against the routine and regulated life of the service. He went AWOL, and began to commit other little infractions, which kept him constantly in hot water with the authorities.

Finally, when his berth, the Battleship *Utah*, made port in Boston on December 4, 1923, he deserted. He explained his sudden appearance back in Mooresville by telling family and friends that the Navy had given him a disability discharge.

A short while later he met a pert, pretty little farm girl, named Berl Hovious. She was only 16, but Dillinger wooed her, and they were married April 12, 1924. Having no visible means of support, they went to live with her parents, then with his; finally they rented a small apartment in downtown Mooresville.

This marriage wouldn't last, though, for it was one based strictly upon physical attraction. The only one John Dillinger loved, or would ever really love, was John Dillinger.

The turning point in Dillinger's life came when he met Edgar Singleton, a 31-year-old ex-convict, who had big ideas of making easy money, fast. Every Saturday night, Frank Morgan, 65, the owner of the West End Grocery Store would take his weekly receipts home with him in his pockets. Everybody in this small town of 1,000 people knew this.

On the evening of September 6, 1924, Dillinger approached Morgan from the rear and pounded him on the head with a large bolt, wrapped in a handkerchief. In his other hand he held a .32 revolver. Both Dillinger and Singleton had underestimated the strength of the old man. He put up a pretty good fight, and grabbed the barrel of Dillinger's gun. When he did so, the gun went off, and made a frightful noise that woke up half the town.

With this Dillinger forgot the purpose of his assault and ran for all he was worth. When he got to the spot where Singleton was to be parked with the getaway car, Edgar had long since departed. He too, had heard the shot, and thought Dillinger had killed the old man. Johnny then ran again and didn't stop until he got to his father's farm. Two days later the police dropped by and arrested him.

The judge John Dillinger faced was known as a hard man throughout the county, and Dillinger's surly attitude did little to soften him. He gave him a sentence of two to fourteen years, and a concurrent sentence of ten to twenty. The charges were assault and battery, with intent to rob, and conspiracy to commit a felony.

He was received at the Pendleton Reformatory, as Number 14395, on September 16, 1934. When Dillinger arrived he was a very bitter young man. He had identified his "buddy" to the police on the promise of consideration by the authorities. Of course this wasn't binding upon the judge, and he acted according to his own conscience. Then Edgar Singleton was arrested, and tried before a different judge, and for the same offense, he received only two to fourteen years.

Dillinger stood five feet, seven inches tall, with brown hair and eyes, and weighed about 160 pounds. Like Clyde Barrow he didn't like hard work, so he too decided it would be better to cripple himself than labor. While working in the prison foundry, he poured hot steel into the heel of his shoe. When it started to heal too rapidly, he managed to get some acid, and poured this on it to keep it irritated. His idea worked and he was transferred to less arduous labor in the prison yards.

While in Pendleton he met Harry ("Pete") Pierpont, a slender ladies man with large eyes and a large mouth. He had the look of toughness about him, yet when dressed up he could pose as a respectable citizen. At 19 he had tried to steal a car in Indianapolis, and when the owner objected had shot at him four times, but luckily only wounded him.

Dillinger also met Homer Van Meter, a character who looked and acted like a clown. At 17 he had been convicted of being drunk and disorderly. A little later he had stolen a car and was sent to the Southern State Prison at Menard. A year later he was paroled, but after two months he and a buddy were arrested for a train robbery.

In June 1929, Berl Hovious Dillinger, tired of waiting, divorced her husband. Then his two new buddies, Pierpont and Van Meter, were both transferred to Michigan City Penitentiary. This made Dillinger even more defiant of prison authority, and he made several aborted attempts to escape. While they were amateurish, these failures nevertheless endeared him somewhat to the other inmates.

In July 1929, John Dillinger automatically came up for parole, but with his record it was refused. When he learned of this he made a most unorthodox request. He asked to be transferred to the state penitentiary at Michigan City. The reason he gave was their ball team. He said he wanted to learn how to play ball. What he really wanted was to be near his pals, Pierpont and Van Meter.

The authorities, thinking they might pacify this restless soul, agreed to the transfer, and on July 16, he became Number 13225 at Michigan City. While here he, of course, never played baseball, but he did study, and his teachers were old pros in the business they were teaching. For let there be no mistake, crime was and is a business, and it requires a great deal of study and training. There is no such thing as a born criminal.

iii

On May 1, 1933, John Herman Dillinger was paroled from Michigan City Penitentiary, but his final release was delayed until May 22. He had served eight years, eight months and six days learning a trade that would become his life's work.

The reason for his parole was the persistent petitions his father had made to the Governor for clemency, and the fact that his step-mother was dying. Actually Dillinger couldn't have cared less that she was dying, but he played the part of the tearful son until he got his release.

The world Dillinger was released into was indeed a strange one. When he had entered the reformatory, the world had been enjoying unprecedented prosperity. But now, millions of men were out of work; thousands of businesses had gone bankrupt; hundreds of banks had folded.

When Dillinger walked out of the penitentiary a free man the world wasn't ready for him, and he certainly wasn't ready for it. With his poor education, a poorer attitude, no legitimate trade, and an extreme distaste for hard work, he took the predictable path.

In 1932 the nation had suffered 631 bank robberies, with a total loss of $3,562,371. Prohibition was the law of the country, and nearly everybody broke this law. Gangs and gangsters were ruling the land, with Pretty Boy Floyd, the Barker-Karpis gang, Machine Gun Kelly, and others kidnapping and robbing banks.

John Dillinger went back to Mooresville for awhile, and hung around the pool hall, trying to make up his mind. He had left all his buddies and friends behind him in the Michigan City Penitentiary, but he had left them with hope. He promised that he would spring them, somehow, and now he had to make plans.

He soon saw that hanging around Mooresville wouldn't help him or his friends, so he hitched a ride to Indianapolis. Here he looked up a man, whose name he had been given while in prison. In his pocket he had a list of places to rob. Harry Pierpont had given them to him to speed up his accumulation of money, so he could then make arrangements for the "big break."

Through this contact Dillinger was accepted into a gang, known locally as the "White Caps." This was a really small-time collection of hoodlums, who preyed on gas stations and chain stores. They got their name from their habit of wearing white caps on their various forays. This was a little silly, for the caps announced their identities before they could announce their intentions.

One of these small-time robberies was the holdup of a roadhouse called the Bide-A-Wee. With Dillinger at the time were William Shaw and Noble Claycomb, both members of the "White Caps." During this holdup, Dillinger slugged a customer just as they were leaving. It was a completely unnecessary bit of hooliganism.

On June 24, 1933, in an aborted attempt to rob a thread factory at Monticello, Dillinger shot his first man, Manager Fred Fisher, in the leg. He found the whole incident quite amusing, and the only regret he had was they got no money for their efforts.

Then on June 10, 1933, Dillinger, with William Shaw and Paul "Lefty" Parker, hit the big time by holding up the New Carlisle National Bank, in New Carlisle, Ohio. They got the princely sum of $10,500—Dillinger hadn't seen so much money in all his life.

On July 16, 1933, in a police trap, William Shaw, his wife, and Paul "Lefty" Parker were arrested. Dillinger and Harry Copeland, in another car, made good their escape. Shaw's wife was later freed, but Shaw admitted to over 20 holdups, including the ones at Monticello and the Bide-A-Wee.

July 17, Dillinger, Harry Copeland and one other hoodlum held up the Commercial Bank in Daleville, Indiana, but only got $3,500. It was on the list that Van Meter had given him, but things had changed since Van Meter had made it up. Many of the recommended banks had been closed, and others were barely struggling to stay open. More and more it became apparent that the list was almost obsolete.

It was in Daleville that Dillinger, with his sailor straw hat, vaulted deftly over a high divider in the bank, and became known

to the newspapers as the "athletic bandit." Shortly after this Noble
Claycomb, caught by the police, confessed his part in the holdup
of the Bide-A-Wee, and implicated his partners, including Dillinger.

Then, on August 4, 1933, Dillinger and Copeland hit the First
National Bank of Montpelier, Indiana, and fled with $10,110 and
a .45 automatic, belonging to the bank. By this time the activities
of the "athletic bandit" had come to the attention of Matt Leach,
head of the Indiana State Police. In time to come, Leach would
become almost obsessed with the idea of catching Dillinger, and
would devote a great deal of time and money toward this end.

The entire Indiana State Police Department numbered slightly
over 40 men, and this included the office help. With this "huge"
force, Matt Leach undertook to bring Dillinger to justice.

Due to the rash of bank robberies throughout the country, the
cashier of the Citizens National Bank of Bluffton, Ohio, had given
orders to keep the bank's big safe under time lock all day long.

August 14, 1933, a green Ford V-8 with Indiana license plates
drove up beside the bank and five men got out. The big day for
the Citizens National Bank had arrived. John Dillinger and Harry
Copeland entered the building, while the other three men loitered
outside, trying to remain inconspicuous. When the alarm bell
on the side of the building began clanging wildly, they began
shooting at anything that moved. The gang then fled the scene
with only $2,000. According to witnesses they escaped in a Pon-
tiac, Essex, Buick, Chrysler, or Ford sedan, which was green,
blue, black, grey, or brown.

September 6, 1933, Dillinger, Hilton Crough, and one other
hoodlum robbed the Massachusetts Avenue State Bank, in Indianapolis, of $24,000. Here again, Dillinger fingered himself by
doing his famous rail vaulting bit. Now he had the money he
needed to help his buddies still stewing in the Michigan City
Penitentiary.

Having completed his plans for the smuggling of guns into the
prison, he made arrangements with Mary Kinder, who had two
brothers and a sweetheart in Michigan City. She was to receive
the boys, and furnish them with the necessary clothing. She had
already purchased the clothing, and was ready to do her part.

Dillinger had arranged to have several pistols hidden in a
box of thread, destined for delivery to the penitentiary. The box
was marked on the outside, for quick identification, and Walter
Dietrich, who was the prison store keeper, was watching for it.

Back in July Dillinger had also looked up the sister of James

Jenkins, another cell mate at Michigan City, for purely personal reasons. She was a married woman, but was now suing for divorce, and was very happy to meet him.

Mary Longnaker lived in a rooming house at 325 West 1st Street, in Dayton, and unknown to her or Dillinger, it was now under constant police surveillance.

On the evening of September 22, 1933, the Dayton police had their usual two men posted outside the rooming house watching for Dillinger. He paid Mary a visit, but managed to enter unseen by a rear door. He wasn't smart enough to get in without the landlady knowing, however, and she signaled the detectives.

They burst into the room and caught Dillinger standing in the middle of the floor with his shirt off, and a bunch of photographs in his hand. His pistol was on a nearby table, but he made no attempt to grab it.

He was taken to the Montgomery County jail, and booked as Number 10587. Here he was given a second search, and police found a diagram that looked like a prison floor plan, but positive identification was impossible, so it wasn't considered too important.

Although Mary Longnaker's brother was a convict, she had no desire to become involved with gangsters. She was not prosecuted, so she broke off all contact with Dillinger and his friends, and later married an honest man.

Tuesday, September 26, 1933, ten desperate criminals escaped from the Michigan City Penitentiary. They were:

RUSSELL CLARK: Sentenced to 20 years at Fort Wayne, December 12, 1927, for bank robbery.

HARRY PIERPONT: Sentenced to 10 to 21 years at Kokomo, May 6, 1925, for bank robbery.

JOHN HAMILTON: Sentenced to 25 years at South Bend, March 16, 1927, for auto banditry.

CHARLES MAKLEY: Sentenced to 10 to 20 years at Hammond, June, 1928, for bank robbery.

JAMES JENKINS: Sentenced to life imprisonment at Bloomfield, April 13, 1929, for murder.

EDWARD SHOUSE: Sentenced to 25 years at South Bend, 1930, for auto banditry.

JOSEPH FOX: Sentenced to life imprisonment in Franklin County, for bank robbery.

JOSEPH BURNS: Sentenced to life imprisonment at Warsaw for murder.

WALTER DIETRICH: Sentenced to life imprisonment at Clinton, December 21, 1930, for bank robbery.

JAMES CLARK: Sentenced to life imprisonment at Clinton, December 21, 1930, for bank robbery. (No kin to Russell Clark. James Clark was one of two survivors of a gang that raided the Denver Mint, in 1922, getting $200,000. The other survivor was Harvey Bailey, driver of the getaway car.)

A later investigation would reveal that the escape was planned and engineered by John Dillinger. The guns rode in, under the noses of the guards, in a 200-pound box of thread. It was shipped by the Gordon Shirt Company, which had a contract with the penitentiary. Another contributing factor in the mass escape was manpower. Out of the 120 guards assigned to keep 2,500 prisoners under lock and key, 69 were totally inexperienced.

Walter Dietrich, the storekeeper in the prison, and a lifer, got the shipment, and retrieved the guns. He later passed them out to the chosen parties on the escape list. Paradoxically, while his buddies were breaking out of the penitentiary, John Dillinger was himself stewing in the Montgomery County jail.

James Clark was caught the following day, in Hammond, Indiana, without a fight. Russell Clark, Harry Pierpont, Charles Makley, Edward Shouse, and Walter Dietrich made their way to Mary Kinder's place, where she outfitted and hid them. Later they moved on to Hamilton, Ohio, where they had arranged another hideout, and were joined there by Harry Copeland.

Jim Jenkins, through devious means, made his way to Bean Blossom, Indiana. Here he was ordered to surrender by members of a posse, and when he reached for his gun, they shot him to death.

The gang, having been behind bars so long with no female companionship, lost no time in finding themselves girlfriends. They paired off with Mary Kinder sharing her apartment with Pierpont; Patricia Long, alias Pat Cherrington, was Makley's girl, and her sister took up with Russell Clark. John Hamilton came up with a girl who had the longest name a gun moll ever had. She was Elaine Sullivan Dent Burton DeKant.

John Dillinger had hopes that the buddies he had just helped escape from Michigan City would return the favor. But he knew that the Montgomery County jail was a tough nut to crack. His hopes lay in getting to a smaller jail. Accordingly, he surprised everyone and confessed to the robbery of the Bluffton bank.

September 28, 1933, the delighted officials sent him to the Allen County jail, at Lima, for the purposes of identification and arraignment. The Lima jail was an old one, and the police force considerably smaller. The chances for a jail delivery from here were far better.

The Michigan City gang, consisting of Pierpont, Makley, Hamilton, Clark and Shouse, needed money desperately so they drove to St. Mary's, Ohio, John "Red" Hamilton's home town. The date was October 3, and the bank was in receivership; but its doors were open. The gang hit it hard and suddenly. They managed to take over $14,000 of its money, and made a clean getaway.

October 12, 1933, Pierpont, Clark, Makley, Copeland, Hamilton and Shouse drove into Lima, Ohio. They tried to be as inconspicuous as possible, as they drove slowly down its streets in a Chrysler and a Terraplane. One block from the county jail, they parked the Chrysler, and continued on to the front of the jail, in the Terraplane.

Inside were Sheriff Jess Saber, his wife Lucy, and Deputy Wilbur Sharp. Neither the Sheriff nor his deputy were armed, but weapons were available if they needed them. In the back were about a dozen prisoners, including Dillinger.

Pierpont, Makley and Clark went into the jail, and walked right up to the Sheriff, who was sitting at his desk. They told him they were officers from the Michigan City Penitentiary. They said they would like to question a prisoner of his, named John Dillinger.

Sheriff Sarber, suspecting nothing, asked to see their credentials. With this Pierpont pulled a gun, and barked, "Here's our credentials!" The Sheriff, who had placed his gun in his desk drawer, now clawed for it, remarking, "Oh. You can't do that."

Harry Pierpont fired twice, one bullet lodging in the wall of the jail and the other entering Sarber's side, passing through his abdomen and severing the femoral artery in his thigh. Though he was dying, the sheriff tried to rise, and Makley hit him across the head with the barrel of his gun. Still not out, he again tried to rise, and this time Pierpont brought his gun down on the Sheriff's head, knocking him to the floor.

Mrs. Sarber cried, "Please don't kill him!"

"Well," Pierpont barked, "then get us the keys to the cells." All this time Clark had kept his gun trained on the unarmed deputy, Wilbur Sharp, who could do nothing but watch.

Mrs. Sarber got the keys, and Pierpont tossed them to Sharp, and told him to open the door to the cells. When Dillinger came out, Mrs. Sarber and Sharp were herded back into the cell block with the prisoners, and the door locked. When one of the prisoners came forward, as if he would like to join them, Pierpont fired a warning shot into the ceiling, "Get back, you son-of-a-bitch, all we want is Johnny!"

Then they fled out the door, piling into the car, and sped down the street to where the Chrysler was parked. Here they split up, and disappeared into the night.

Sheriff Sarber was rushed to the Memorial Hospital, when Deputy Sheriff Sharp managed to get the attention of a passerby who called the police. Just before he lapsed into a deep coma, Sarber told doctors and police that he had recognized one of the men as *Harry Copeland*. The Sheriff died at 8:05 P.M., without again gaining consciousness.

Feeling ran high in Lima over this ruthless murder. Many posses were formed, and they fanned out across the countryside. One of them raided the Pierpont farm, near Leipsic, where they found a new car, filled with gas, and no license plates.

Fred Pierpont claimed his brother "Pete" had given him the car. While they were questioning Fred, back in Lima Mrs. Sarber and Deputy Sharp were identifying the picture of Harry "Pete" Pierpont as the killer of the Sheriff.

Faced with this evidence, Fred, two days later, admitted that his brother, "Red" Hamilton, Russell Clark, Ed Shouse, Charlie Makley, and Harry Copeland had been at the farm on October 3. From this confession the jail-breakers were identified.

Needing weapons, the Michigan City gang robbed a police station, in Auburn, Indiana, on October 14, 1933. This netted them a submachine gun, two sawed-off shotguns, four .38 police specials, and two Winchester rifles. They also removed the police badges of Patrolmen Eldon Chittum, Eddie Roberts and Ambrose Clark, and took them with them, for souvenirs.

The Central National Bank at Green Castle, Indiana, lost $18,-428 in cash and $56,300 in bonds to the Michigan City gang, on October 23rd, a Monday. The gang consisted of four men, Harry Pierpont, John Dillinger, Charles Makley, and Harry Copeland. Once again John Dillinger brought attention upon himself by leaping deftly over the guard railing in the bank. Matt Leach took notice.

November 17, 1933, Harry Copeland, giving the name of John Santon, was arrested as a result of an argument with his girlfriend, at Harlem Street and North Avenue, in Chicago. He pulled a gun on her, and a bystander called the police.

The next member of the gang to leave was Edward Shouse, whose big mouth made certain members of the gang unhappy. He was lucky they didn't kill him. Instead they gave him some money and told him to "get the hell out of town." He not only went, but stole Russell Clark's new automobile for his transportation.

The Michigan City gang robbed the American Bank and Trust Company, of Racine, Wisconsin, on November 20, 1933. For their transportation they used a blue Buick with yellow wire wheels. It was about 2:30 P.M., when Makley and Dillinger entered the bank, followed a short distance behind by Pierpont and Clark. Makley went up to a teller window and told Harold Graham, assistant cashier, "Hands up." Unfortunately for Graham, he was a little hard of hearing and told Makley to go to the next window. Makley, infuriated, fired at him and Graham fell with a bullet in his arm and side. When he hit the floor his knee hit the alarm bell.

As the bandits were scooping up the cash, two officers answered the alarm, but Clark got the drop on one as he entered the bank. Then Makley fired at the other, Sergeant Wilbur Hansen, and he fell to the floor, his machine gun crashing across the room.

The gang left with $28,000, the machine gun, and four hostages. Near the edge of town they dropped two of their hostages, but they carried the other two, a man and a woman, all the way to Saylesville, where they tied them to a tree.

The Chicago police got a tip that the Michigan City gang also owned a green convertible. They had left it at an auto repair shop on Catalpa Avenue, to have a fender straightened. The garage owner told them he would not be able to get to it, and suggested they take it to a place at 5320 Broadway. Then he phoned the police and reported the incident. It was December 14, 1933, and Patrolmen Martin Mullen and Frank Hopkins got the call to go to the garage and wait for the owner of the car. They were later joined here by police Sergeant William T. Shanley.

When 4:00 P.M. arrived it was time for a police shift change so Sergeant Shanley told the two officers to return to the station, and tell the desk sergeant to send him two from the new shift. They left, and Sergeant Shanley settled down to wait.

Just about 4.05, Red Hamilton and his girlfriend returned to pick up their car. Sergeant Shanley stepped up to Hamilton and asked him, "Is this your car?"

"No," Hamilton replied, "it belongs to my wife," and he pointed at his girlfriend. She promptly pulled out a piece of paper and handed it to Shanley.

Hamilton reached to his pocket, but Shanley told him, "Keep your hands out of your pockets." He then began to search Hamilton, placing most of his attentions upon his pockets. Hamilton pulled a gun from his shoulder holster, and shot Shanley twice.

Patrolman Frank Hopkins had just returned, determined to stay with Sergeant Shanley until the others arrived. He got back just in time to see Hamilton run off, leaving his girlfriend behind. It was too late to catch Hamilton, but he did grab Miss Elaine Dent Sullivan Burton DeKant.

Police Sergeant William T. Shanley, a father of four, was a winner of the *Chicago Tribune's* Hero Award, for a past performance. He was the 13th policeman to be killed in line of duty in Chicago, in 1933. Hamilton's girl friend was released without charge, when she convinced the authorities she had no idea Hamilton was a crook.

With this narrow escape by Hamilton, the entire gang went on a hair dyeing spree, and then fled to Florida, to bask in the sun for awhile. Here Dillinger is supposed to have called his arch enemy Matt Leach, to ask how the manhunt was coming along. It is very doubtful that he did, however, for long distance calls were very easy to trace in those days.

With police all over Chicago pulling raid after raid, it was only a matter of time before they turned up something. On a tip that the gang was located in a Paris, Illinois, hotel, Matt Leach, with the cooperation of the Illinois authorities, sent a team of his men to check it out. The only member of the Michigan City gang they found was Edward Shouse, who had returned from the West Coast, still driving Russell Clark's car.

He was staying in the hotel with two girlfriends when he was surprised by the police. In the confusion that followed, one of the officers accidently shot one of his fellow members to death in a crossfire. Shouse was taken without further resistance.

December 21, 1933, Captain John Stege and his special detail rushed to an apartment in the fashionable Rogers Park district, on a hot tip that the gang was hiding there. They charged into the building only to be met with a blast of fire.

Immediately the officers leveled their machine guns and raked the place with a withering barrage. Keeping up the rapid fire, the police, instructed to "shoot to kill," stormed the barricaded flat.

As they advanced into the apartment, the guns from within

fell silent. Piled up in a corner of the parlor were three men, all dead. They had been struck several times each, while none of the officers had been injured. So sure were the officers that they had killed Dillinger and two of his hoodlum buddies, that the news was released to the press.

In reality, as a routine Bertillion examination showed, the dead men were Sam Ginsburg, an escaped convict from the Michigan State prison at Jackson; Charles Tilden, alias Talleman, of Streator, Illinois, and an escaped inmate of Joliet penitentiary; and Lewis Katzewitz of Streator, Illinois, also an escape inmate of Joliet.

Found in the apartment were 20 bullet-proof vests, three machine guns, half a dozen shotguns, and a large array of pistols. Though this wasn't the Michigan City gang, it was quite apparent that this group, known as "The Jews," had been ready to start a crime wave of their own.

The "Special Squad" that had knocked off this bunch was a group of officers of the Chicago Police Department, who had been put together especially to get the Michigan City gang, and more specifically John Dillinger. They had special equipment, and were ready to go anywhere at any time.

Now the newspapers were calling the Michigan City gang the "Dillinger" gang. This was started as a favor to Matt Leach, who hoped to cause dissension among the gang members. He knew only too well that John Dillinger wasn't the leader, but merely a junior member. The newspapers cooperated, but the cry was taken up across the nation, and soon the "monster" Matt Leach had created, rose up to bite him.

The Michigan City gang had been lolling on the beaches in Daytona, and now decided to head North again. They made a date to meet first in Tucson, and then go on to Chicago. Dillinger and Hamilton, however, decided to return to Chicago first and see if they couldn't pick up a little extra money.

January 15, 1934, three men drove up close to the First National Bank of East Chicago, Indiana, and parked. Two of the men got out, one carrying a trombone case, and they entered the busy bank. It was about 2:45 P.M., just before closing time, and everybody was rushing.

Suddenly Dillinger laid his trombone case down, and with a flourish brought out a submachine gun. Then in a loud, clear voice he yelled, "All right—this is a stickup. Everybody move toward the back of the bank."

Walter Spencer, one of the bank's vice presidents, was on the phone at the time, talking to a bank official in Indian Harbor. When the bandits, both carrying machine guns, motioned to him, he told his party, "It's a holdup," then he broke the connection. At the same time he also pushed an alarm, which signaled the police a block and a half away, but did not sound inside the bank.

Hamilton, who had kept his machine gun under his overcoat, now was using it to herd everybody back toward the bank vault in the rear. When Patrolman Hobart Wilgus, the first to answer the alarm, entered the door with his pistol drawn, he found himself faced by two machine guns. He dropped his pistol and was also forced to the back of the bank.

Dillinger collected $20,426.60 in a large sack, and then, looking out through the glass front windows, he saw another uniformed officer and three plain clothes detectives. The detectives he identified by the pistols in their hands.

Taking Wilgus and Spencer as hostages, they came out the front of the bank. Patrolman William Patrick O'Malley saw an opening and fired at Dillinger, hitting him several times. Dillinger staggered, but was not seriously hurt as he was wearing a steel vest.

He cut loose with his machine gun and hit O'Malley in the leg. As O'Malley collapsed toward the ground, Dillinger's gun continued to chatter, and O'Malley dropped in a heap, mortally wounded.

Now desperate, the bandits made their way toward their car, and safety. Hamilton pushed Spencer away from him and sprinted forward, but just then one of the officers fired directly at him, and he staggered and fell. Dillinger, also without a hostage, went back and picked up Hamilton. He wasn't so concerned about his buddy as he was about the fact that he had the money. While he dragged Hamilton, who still clutched the money bag, toward the car, he kept the other officers at bay with short bursts from his machine gun.

Getting into the car, later described as a blue Plymouth sedan, with Ohio license plates, they fled. Taking the small back streets, they drove back to Chicago. Captain Matt Leach immediately ordered eight officers, stationed at Tremont, to the scene.

Chicago squads hurried to the southern part of Cook County, to watch for Dillinger's approach, but the gang had made good their escape. Now John Dillinger had killed his first man, and Matt Leach wanted him for murder.

Dillinger dumped Hamilton with a doctor, and headed for Tucson.

iv

Tucson lies at an altitude of 2,400 feet above sea level, surrounded by mountains, and it is a land where sunshine is almost
perpetual. It is also the county seat of Pima County, about 60
miles from the Mexican border, and the terminus of a Mexican
railroad.

The Michigan City gang was to rendezvous here around January 22, for additional rest and relaxation. The place was ideally
situated for a sudden dash to the Mexican border, if the need
should arise. It is possible that the gang even toyed with this
idea. They had the money and the armament to get more, if
they ran short.

Charles Makley arrived in Tucson on January 9, and he was
the first of the gang to get there. He registered at the Congress
Hotel, a three-storied building located, appropriatly enough, on
Congress Street. He immediately left in search of a girl he knew—
a local singer.

The following day Russell Clark and Opal Long arrived. They
had also driven up from Florida, and Clark moved in with
Makley, while Opal Long got an adjoining room. Since Makley
had been kicking up his heels in Tucson and knew the ropes,
Clark and Opal joined him in the night life.

When Harry Pierpont and Mary Kinder arrived from Florida it
was the 16th of January. They had taken their time in driving up,
and were in no hurry to join the others in the festivities, so they
rented a cabin in a tourist court, just on the edge of town. Pierpont
was driving a new 1934 Buick, and he was enjoying the good life.

John Dillinger and Evelyn "Billie" Frechette arrived at Tucson
on the 21st of January, and like Pierpont they also checked into
a tourist court. They too had been having fun and enjoying life.

Dillinger had met Evelyn in Chicago while she was working in
a night club. The two of them had hit it off right away. "Billie"
Frechette was French-Indian, from the Chippewa Indian Reservation at Neopit, Wisconsin. She was married to George "Spark"
Frechette, who was now in Leavenworth serving a 15-year sentence for bank robbery.

Early on the morning of January 22nd an oil overflow in the
furnace room of the Congress Hotel caused a fire, and necessitated
the immediate evacuation of all the occupants. Makley and Clark
departed their room so fast they left behind them all their luggage. The bags also contained their guns and money.

Once they got safely outside they began to worry about their belongings. According to various written reports they gave two firemen $2.00, $12.00 or $50.00 to bring their luggage out. Anyway the sum was large enough to make the firemen happy, and the luggage was saved.

The following day William Benedict, one of the firemen, saw pictures of the gang in a detective magazine, and recognized Makley and Clark. He called the Tucson police, who started to do a little detective work.

The police located a cab driver who had taken two men and their luggage to a house on North 2nd Avenue. Four officers— Detective Sergeant Chester Sherman, Dallas Ford, Patrolman Frank Eyman and Mark Robbins, a bureau of identification man— staked out the house, and waited. In just a few minutes the door opened and Makley came out with a woman; they drove into town.

The officers followed them to the Grabbe Electric and Radio store, where Makley was preparing to buy something. Sherman, backed by Eyman and Ford, entered the store and placed Makley under arrest.

Makley pretended amazement, and claimed he was J. C. Davies, just up from Jacksonville. He offered to prove it if they would only take him back to his house where he kept his identification. The officers dropped him off at the police station, and then they returned to the house.

They decided they didn't need their identification expert, Mark Robbins, anymore, so they traded him for Patrolman Kenneth Mullaney. The uniformed officers, Eyman and Mullaney, went around back, while Sherman, in plain clothes, took the direct approach straight up to the front door. Ford, also in civilian clothes, remained discreetly out of sight, covering Sherman.

Sherman knocked on the door and when Opal Long opened it he waved an envelope in her face. He told her he was looking for Mr. Long. Clark had slipped into the back room, but now he came toward the front door.

When Sherman saw him he drew his service revolver, but Clark quickly grabbed it with both hands. Sherman tenaciously clung to it so Clark, a much heavier man, yanked him inside the house and wrestled him toward the bedroom. Here Clark clung to Sherman's gun with one hand while the other searched vainly beneath a pillow on the bed for his own. He didn't know that Opal had moved it to a safer place.

Ford, suspicious, opened the front door but before he could get

in, Opal slammed it on his hand, breaking his finger. In spite of
his surprise and pain he forced his way in, flinging Opal aside.
He rushed into the bedroom where he clouted Clark on the head.
This made Clark mad, so he clouted Sherman on the head with
his own gun. About this time Eyman and Mullaney entered the
back; they both clouted Clark on the head so he gave up.

A while later Pierpont and Mary Kinder pulled up outside the
now-empty house. Leaving Mary in the car, Pierpont mounted
the stairs toward the front door. Half way up he saw blood on
the steps, and without changing his facial expression, he did an
about face. Jumping into the car, he and Mary drove away.

All this did not go unnoticed by a neighbor, who had been
watching the house since the last fracas. He promptly copied down
the license number, and phoned it to the police. Two patrolmen,
Jay Smith and Earl Nolan, who had been joined by Frank Eyman,
spotted the wanted Buick and pulled it over near South 6th Street.

Patrolman Frank Eyman gave Harry Pierpont some cock-and-
bull story about having to have a safety sticker on his windshield.
He got into the rear of Pierpont's car, and offered to direct him to
the nearest police station where he could get one.

Apparently suspecting no skullduggery, Pierpont happily drove
Eyman downtown to get his sticker. All along the way he kept up
a lot of happy chatter, but he did adjust the rear view mirror so
he could keep his eye on him.

It wasn't until he was well into the police station that he saw
Makley and Clark's baggage, and knew he had been flimflammed.
He drew a gun, but five Arizona officers drew theirs quicker.
Searching him they found two more pistols—one in his belt and
one in his sock. "Three gun Harry," they called him laughingly.
But Harry Pierpont wasn't laughing—he was wanted for murder.

Flush with success, the officers decided to keep up their stakeout on the house, and await further developments. Officer James
Herron watched the house from across the street, while Mullaney
and Officer Milo Walker waited inside.

Soon a new Terraplane with Wisconsin license plates pulled
up. Inside were a man and a woman. John Dillinger got out and
started up the steps of the house; then he too saw the blood. When
he tried to backtrack to the car he found himself looking down
the barrel of James Herron's pistol.

Then Mullaney and Walker joined the party and they took into
custody a blustering "Mr. Frank Sullivan, traveling salesman from
Green Bay, Wisconsin." In the car was "Billie" Frechette, who
told them her name was Anna Martin.

Without firing a shot, a comparatively small police force had accomplished what the entire police departments of several states, and the city of Chicago, had been unable to do. They had captured the whole Michigan City gang, and their reputed boss, John Dillinger.

v

As soon as the news of the spectacular capture was released, the battle for custody began, with four states participating. The most demanding cries were from the states of Indiana and Ohio, which wanted them for murder. Indiana wanted Dillinger for the murder of Patrolman William Patrick O'Malley, and Ohio wanted Harry Pierpont, Charles Makley and Russell Clark for the murder of Sheriff Sarber.

Indiana and Ohio would utimately win out, but the legal manipulations took several days. Perhaps the most interesting event was the manner in which John Dillinger was moved from Arizona to Indiana. To say that Dillinger objected to this move is putting it mildly.

He was dragged, fighting and screaming, from his jail cell, on January 29, and taken to an airplane. Still fighting, dragging his feet, and screaming obscenities, Dillinger was pushed aboard a chartered plane, where he was chained to the seat. He was then handcuffed to Officers Nicholas Makar and Carroll Holley, with Officer Dale Myers at the controls of the plane.

Dillinger in effect was kidnapped from Arizona, with the Arizona Governor's approval, while his lawyer was preparing some delaying legal maneuvers. He was then taken to Chicago, and later transferred to the County Jail, at Crown Point, Indiana.

"Billie" Frechette and Opal Long were released from custody, but Mary Kinder, who was wanted for her part in aiding the Michigan City escaped prisoners, was held. She would later be delivered into the waiting hands of Matt Leach, who would take her back to Indiana by train. In less than a month she too was free.

When Dillinger arrived at Crown Point he was surrounded, not only by armed men, but by newsreel cameramen, reporters, and photographers, all yelling for information and poses. One of the more enthusiastic photographers yelled at Prosecuting Attorney Robert Estill, whose job it would be to put Dillinger in the electric chair, to put his arm around the criminal. Impulsively, and without much thought, he did as he was ordered, and Dillinger arrogantly put his arm on Estill's shoulder. The resulting picture would rock Indiana politics for a long time to come, and later it had a great deal to do with the ruining of several promising careers.

Dillinger was lodged in the Lake County jail, which was a three-story brick building, and between him and freedom were six barred doors, and 45 to 50 guards. With no gang to help him now, Dillinger knew that if he got out he would have to do it himself.

Dillinger was allowed a small pocket knife and he amused the guards, and the inmates, with his incessant whittling. He wouldn't show anybody what he was making, but he finally got the nick-name of "Whittling Johnny." No one ever imagined that the product of his hobby would buy his way out of jail.

The morning of March 3, 1934, it was grey and gloomy outside. It had been raining all night, and promised to continue through the day. At 9:00 A.M. Sam Cahoon, an elderly turnkey, opened the door leading to the cell block, to let a work group in to clean up.

Suddenly Dillinger shoved a "gun" into Cahoon's stomach and forced him to open his cell. He then ordered Cahoon to call Deputy Sheriff Ernest Blunk back to the cell block. Sam Cahoon, in keeping with jail regulations, was unarmed. Dilling was bluffing; his "gun" was made of wood. Still and all, that wooden gun in the hands of the "great" John Dillinger looked as deadly as a machine gun, so Cahoon called to Blunk.

Blunk, completely unaware that anything was amiss, came back to see what Cahoon wanted. Dillinger pointed his "deadly" little wooden pistol at him, and the Sheriff's hands shot up and his mouth flew open. Then Dillinger closed his hands around Blunk's pistol—a real one.

Now he was in complete command, and all the bluff was gone. Dillinger turned to his cell mate, Harry Jelinek, who was in on a robbery charge. and motioned to him. "Come on, Harry, let's go."

Jelinek sneered at him. "Go to hell. I wouldn't walk two feet with you!" Another inmate, a Negro named Herbert Youngblood, who was being held for a Gary murder, offered to join him, and Dillinger motioned him out. Then he locked Cahoon in his cell, and relocked the cell block doors.

Blunk was forced to show them where the stairs were, and to open the door. When they reached the first floor, Blunk then tapped on the glass in the door and told the turnkey there to open it. As soon as it was opened, Dillinger and Youngblood surged through, taking the turnkey prisoner also.

Dillinger took the second turnkey to the jail office, where he intended to lock him up. In the office the delighted Dillinger found two submachine guns lying near the window. He immediately checked to see that they were loaded, then pocketed Blunk's gun, substituting the machine gun for it. He gave the other to Youngblood, and they were on their way.

Still forcing Blunk before them, Dillinger and Youngblood made their way slowly and carefully toward freedom. First they entered the jail kitchen, where they encountered Mrs. Irene Baker, matron and cook. She looked up and exclaimed, "Good Lord, you're John Dillinger!"

He grinned at her sardonically and told her, "Be a good little girl and we won't kill you."

Then, still prodding Blunk ahead of them, they entered the jail garage, but all the cars were locked, and there were no keys to be had. Dillinger tore out all the ignition wires in each car, making them useless, then they stepped out into the open where they saw a public garage. Slipping down the alley, Dillinger entered the rear door, and motioned to Youngblood and Blunk to follow him. They had no trouble forcing Edwin Saager, a mechanic in the garage, to tell them which car was the fastest. Mouth agape, he pointed out Sheriff Holley's Ford V-8, which was standing nearby. Dillinger then ordered Blunk to take the wheel, while Youngblood forced Saager into the rear.

As they shot out of the Ford Garage, and spun off down the street, Dillinger turned to the nervous Blunk, "Listen, you son-of-a-bitch. Not so fast now. You hit it up to about 35 or 40 miles an hour and hold it. If anyone chases us we can take care of the situation."

They drove over country roads until they were approximately 20 miles west of Joliet. Here the car slid on the muddy roads, and came to rest in a ditch. It took them almost 40 minutes to get the car back on the road. Then Dillinger made Edwin Saager put chains on the tires, before they proceeded any further.

As Saager recalled, "He didn't appear to be in any great hurry. He just kept whistling, 'I'm heading for the Last Roundup.'" This was a popular song of the day. While they were all standing around watching Saager, he proudly showed Youngblood and Blunk his wooden gun. He was quite happy about it, and laughed as they stared in disbelief.

About three miles east of Peotone, Illinois, Dillinger, who had been watching the countryside with interest, told Blunk to pull up. "This looks like a forlorn neighborhood—no damn telephone wires anywhere." Blunk stopped the car, and he and Saager got out expecting to be shot any minute.

"This is as far as you are going, boys," Dillinger told them, ominously and deliberately cruel, "The colored boy and I will take it from here." Then he smiled and gave them each a dollar for "carfare," a cigarette, and then shook their hands. Turning to Youngblood he told him to get into the back, and they drove away.

The wooden gun—made of two blue steel safety razor blades, a piece of broomstick, the handle of Dillinger's safety razor, and some black shoe polish—had bought Dillinger his freedom. There would be many recriminations, many accusations, and much wailing and gnashing of teeth, but "Whittling Johnny" was gone.

All was not victory for John Dillinger, however, as he had just committed the biggest mistake of his career. This would not only cost him his freedom, but his life. A flyer, issued a few days later by the Division of Investigation, U. S. Department of Justice (the FBI), stated it with simple eloquence:

Wanted—John Dillinger, with alias Frank Sullivan. The United States Marshal, Chicago, Illinois, holds warrant of arrest charging John Dillinger with feloniously and knowingly transporting Ford V-8, four door sedan, motor number 256,447, property of Lillian Holley, Sheriff, Lake County, Indiana, from Crown Point, Indiana to Chicago, Illinois, on or about March 3, 1934.

Not once during his lawless career had John Dillinger run afoul of the laws of the Federal Government. All his crimes had been against city and state governments, while the FBI compiled a list of his activities, and watched and waited. Then he violated the Dyer Act, by transporting a stolen vehicle across a state line. If he had stopped at the Indiana line, walked across, and stolen another car in Illinois, he would have avoided Federal pursuit.

vi

Dillinger's playmates, Harry Pierpont, Charles Makley and Russell Clark, had been turned over to the Ohio authorities, and were languishing in the same jail they had delivered Dillinger from. They were dressed in their pajamas, and were in a rather gloomy state of mind.

When they heard of Dillinger's electrifying escape, the three immediately discarded their pajamas and put on their street clothes. Their attitudes changed from one of sad, sour hopeless-

ness to ones of happy expectations. They were that sure that
Johnny would be along soon to get them out of jail.

Sheriff Don Sarber, son of the Sheriff Pierpont had killed in
this same jail, had other ideas about his father's killers getting
away. The jail at Lima had become a garrison, with searchlights
on the roof, sandbags in front, and armed patrols all over town.

As soon as Dillinger got to Chicago he immediately phoned
his attorney, Piquett. He needed money, and Piquett was that
kind of lawyer. He was known throughout the underworld as a
fixer.

Louis Phillip Piquett was a short man, of stocky build, with a
dark complexion, baggy eyes, and a head of hair that looked like
a sheaf of porcupine quills. He was a self-made man, who had
taught himself law. After several failures he had managed to pass
the Illinois bar examination. He had run the gauntlet from
ambulance chaser to City Prosecutor of Chicago.

Finally booted out of this job, he had become a fixer for the
highest bidder. He was the fellow who could find you a hideout,
arrange for plastic surgery, arrange to have hot money exchanged,
or perform just about any other service crooked money could buy.

Here in Chicago Dillinger was determined to form a gang—
and he was in a hurry. He needed money, and he needed it
quickly. He had dreams of perhaps heading for Mexico, where
he could lie low for a while, until he heat he generated had
cooled. Never once did he seriously consider trying to free his
old buddies from the Allen County jail in Lima.

Sheriff Holley's Ford V-8 had been found, abandoned, in front
of 1057 Ardmore, on the North Side of Chicago. The police staked
it out, but no one came near it, and it was finally removed for
further examination.

Sheriff Lillian Holley, who had twin 18-year-old daughters, was
serving out the term of her late husband. He had been murdered
while performing his duties. She had laid her career on the line
when she refused to let Dillinger be transferred to the Michigan
City Penitentiary. Now, she too, would become one of the side-
effect victims of John Dillinger.

Dillinger, joined by Billie Frechette, moved to St. Paul, Minnesota, where they felt safer. The city was run by Harry Sawyer,
who assured them of his mantle of protection. For a price he
was more than happy to have Dillinger in his town.

Here Dillinger gathered about him another gang, this time his
own, consisting of his old friend Red Hamilton, who had some-

what recovered from his wounds; Baby Face Nelson; Homer Van Meter; Tommy Carroll; and Eddie Green. Green was not a full-time member, but acted as their advisor, helping with their plans, securing arms and ammunition, and arranging hideouts for them through Harry Sawyer.

They immediately began laying plans for the robbery of the Security National Bank, of Sioux Falls, South Dakota. The secret here was to hit banks at great distances, then scurry back to the safety of St. Paul. By leaving the local banks alone, they kept the heat off, and insured their own safety. Eddie Green drew up the getaway routes, and did it so skillfully that they could drive all the way from Sioux Falls to St. Paul, without passing through a single city.

The car they were to use was a big, new green Packard; Eddie Green and Red Hamilton had stolen it from the Jay Brothers Motor Car Company the day before Dillinger made his Crown Point escape. Walking into the company parking lot, they had taken the car and kidnapped the two attendants. The gangsters later released them, unharmed, but warned them against making identifications.

It was 10:00 A.M., March 6, 1934, and the selection of a jury for the trial of Harry Pierpont had begun. It was being held in a courtroom only yards from the jail where Pierpont had brutally murdered Sheriff Sarber. As Pierpont sat in the courtroom, hand-cuffed and wearing leg irons, the court house itself fairly bristled with guns and armed men, watching for Dillinger.

The jail next door and the entire town of Lima had the air of a fortress. National Guard troops were everywhere, and armed patrols scouted the streets looking for unusual or suspicious cars.

John Dillinger, however, was concerned only about John Dillinger. With his gang he was three states away, just entering the Security National Bank and Trust Company in Sioux City. With him were Homer Van Meter, Eddie Green, and Baby Face Nelson.

Outside the bank and across the street stood Red Hamilton, with a machine gun tucked under his overcoat. Guarding the car was Tommy Carroll, also armed with a machine gun. Between the two of them they could put up a pretty good enfilading fire.

Dillinger yelled as loud as he could, "This is a holdup!" Then much to his chagrin Baby Face Nelson added, "If any of you want to get killed, just make some move." Dillinger was the leader of this gang and he didn't like the idea of Nelson putting his two cents worth in; but he didn't say anything. Next time he'd leave this pompous little runt outside.

There had been no casing of the bank—Dillinger didn't have time for such foolishness—so from this moment forward they would play it by ear. Then the alarm bell started clanging on the side of the building, and Nelson jumped as if he had been shot. Swinging his tommygun in an arc, he spat, "I'd like to know who the hell set off that alarm!"

Outside Hamilton was having his troubles with curious people. As one bunch gathered too close for comfort he swung his machine gun on them and yelled, "Get back or I'll blow daylight through you." They moved back, but they didn't leave. Curiosity was stronger than self-preservation, it seemed. Eyes peered at the bank, and at Hamilton from windows, doorways, and from behind telephone poles. This was the first time a bank had ever been held up in Sioux City.

In the bank there were over 30 customers and employes, and Nelson jumped up on a marble table so he could cover all of them. Looking out of the plate glass window of the bank, he saw Hale Keith, an off-duty motorcycle officer, approaching the building.

Without a moment's hesitation, he fired right through the window, shattering it, and brought Keith to his knees with bullets in his abdomen, his thigh, and his wrist. Then, jumping up and down like some kid at play, he yelled, "I got one. I got one!" Dillinger and the others were too busy grabbing money, to notice his exhibition.

After the gang had sacked up some $49,000, they started to move out, taking ten hostages to surround themselves with as they headed for the door. The several officers who had answered the alarm were unable to fire for fear of hitting the hostages.

When they reached the car they released all but five of the hostages. Leo Olson, the teller, and four women employes—Emma Knabach, Mildred Bostwick, Alice Blegen, and Mary Lucas—were forced into the car; the gangsters then drove away.

About a mile from town the car slowed and they made Olson jump out—the car was too crowded. Then they sped up again, and one of the bandits threw roofing nails out on the road to discourage pursuit.

When three cars, filled with officers, drew too close, the car stopped again, and two members of the gang got out and fired their machine guns at them. This caused the officers to swerve off the road, and sprinkling more nails on the highway, the criminals took off again.

About four miles out the Packard started sputtering, and the gang had to pull up. Just about this time a farmer, driving a Dodge, came down the road and they flagged him to a stop. Then they took his car, and left him, the women, and the Packard, and roared off to the south.

Later they swung east into Iowa, north into Minnesota, and finally pulled up safely in Minneapolis, right in front of Eddie Green's apartment. Inside, they divided the loot. The results were disappointing to Dillinger. There would have to be more robberies.

The jury in Lima, after deliberating for only 55 minutes, found Harry Pierpont guilty of murder in the first degree, with no recommendation of mercy. Sentence would be deferred until later, but ultimately he would be sentenced to die in the electric chair at the state penitentiary in Columbus, Ohio.

March 12, 1934: the First National Bank of Mason City, Iowa, sat fat, and serene. Its vault bulged with almost a quarter of a million dollars. In the lobby, up high, sat a bank guard, Tom Walters, in a bulletproof cage. From his vantage point he could see every part of the bank, and from here he could fire tear gas shells into the midst of any ambitious bank robbers.

Into this setup rode the "greedy seven"—Dillinger, Nelson, Van Meter, Green, Hamilton, Carroll, and John Paul Chase, Nelson's protégé. As usual they hadn't cased the bank. This time Dillinger, as he had vowed, left Baby Face Nelson on the outside, guarding their car in the rear of the bank. Chase remained at the wheel.

Dillinger, Van Meter, Green, Hamilton, and Tommy Carroll entered the bank, with Carroll taking up a position near the front door, his machine gun hidden under his overcoat. This time when Dillinger sang out, "This is a holdup," there were no smart comments from other members of the gang.

Then Carroll saw one of the tellers look up behind them, and he too glanced up and saw Tom Walters's little cage. For the next few minutes he really enjoyed himself, firing his machine gun at the openings in the cage each time Walters tried to lob out a teargas shell. In spite of this, Walters did manage to fire enough to bedevil everybody, including the customers and employees. Someone heard Dillinger later remark, "If we had known we were going to run into this stuff, we wouldn't have tried it."

One of the women employees managed to work her way, unnoticed, to the back of the bank, and looking out of the window she saw a little fellow in a cap standing below. "Hey!" she yelled, "Do something. The bank is being robbed!"

Nelson looked up and pointed his machine gun at her, "Ain't that the everloving truth," he replied. Then he almost doubled up with laughter, as she shrunk back.

All wasn't fun for Nelson, however, as the inevitable crowds began to gather and surge forward. Curiosity seems to make even the most intelligent of people rather stupid. To keep the curious back, Nelson fired short bursts from his gun in the direction of the crowds, but even with bullets singing around them they refused to quit and go home.

During this period of guard duty and harassment, R. L. James, secretary for the School Board, strolled toward Nelson, completely unaware of the bank robbery in progress. Suddenly Nelson turned on him and fired, shooting his legs from under him.

Inside the gang was getting more nervous all the time. Most of them were crying from the teargas; Carroll was still shooting at the guard in his cage; outside Nelson was shooting at God knew what; and now the alarm bell on the side of the bank had started clanging. Because of this they decided to leave with what they had, and get to safety. Their sacks held $52,344, but they left behind almost four times that amount.

Then as they were heading out the door someone shot Dillinger in the shoulder, but it didn't slow him down. Red Hamilton, always unlucky, also got a shot in the shoulder. With their hostages they ran around to the rear of the bank and loaded into the car. The hostages were placed along the sides, on the running boards. Then someone yelled, "Hang on," and the car spun out of the alley.

The police followed the gang to the edge of town, but there the gang stopped and made a stand. This forced the officers to pull off into a side road. Then the gang sprinkled nails on the street, abandoned their hostages in the shivering cold, and escaped.

Back in St. Paul there was more to worry about than splitting the money. Dillinger and Hamilton were both in a great deal of pain from their wounds, and needed medical attention badly. Pat Reilly, a former mascot of the St. Paul Ball Club and now a flunkey of Sawyer's, took both of them to Doctor N. G. Mortensen, his family physician and also the city health officer.

While the doctor was not a member of any gang, or in the

habit of treating hoodlums, he could do little with so many guns around him. He treated them, and so great was his fear of Dillinger and his gang, that he decided not to report the incident.

In Port Huron, Michigan, on March 16, 1934, four officers, led by Sheriff William L. Van Antwerp, went to a store in the predominantly Negro section of the town. They had received a tip that a Negro there was brandishing a gun and bragging about his recent escape from jail.

When Herbert Youngblood came to the door he denied the allegation. However, when the officers tried to enter, he opened fire. He managed to seriously wound Undersheriff Charles Cavanaugh and Deputy Howard Lohr. Then he shot Sheriff Van Antwerp in the arm just before he himself was cut down.

Youngblood, Dillinger's assistant in the Crown Point jail escape, died a few minutes later with one shot in his heart and three in his abdomen. Undersheriff Charles Cavanaugh also died later of his wounds.

Around the 20th of March, John Dillinger and Billie Frechette set up housekeeping at 93 South Lexington Avenue, in the Lincoln Court Apartments. It was only one block from the spot where Edward G. Bremer had been kidnapped by the Barker-Karpis gang the month before. Here they lived as Mr. and Mrs. Carl T. Hellman; and here they seemed to have an almost endless procession of visitors.

They tried to avoid attracting attention, but their efforts merely succeeded in attracting more. It was the case of the curious caretaker. His name was Daniel Coffey, and he began to make the Hellmans his hobby. He noted that they always left by the rear door, never the front, kept their shades drawn, and absolutely refused to let him in to make necessary repairs. St. Paul was full of hoodlums, and Coffey was convinced that he had a whole nest of them here.

He voiced his opinion to the patrolman on the beat, who told him to call the station. He called the station, and before any of Harry Sawyer's men could get wind of it, the FBI was notified of Coffey's suspicions. There was nothing definite, so the item was placed on the investigation list.

At 10:30 A.M., March 31, FBI agents R. C. Coulter and R. L. Nalls, accompanied by City Detective Henry Cummings, arrived at the Lincoln Court Apartments. Agent Nalls stayed outside to guard a Ford sports coupe belonging to the people in the suspected apartment.

Agent Coulter and Detective Cummings went to the door of number 303 and knocked, then Coulter darted around into the rear hall to cover any attempt of escape by that route. The door was opened by Billie Frechette, who asked Detective Cummings what he wanted. He told her he would like to speak to "Carl." She told him Carl wasn't in, and asked him who he was. He replied, "the police," and with that she slammed and locked the door in his face.

Agent Coulter was also having his problems. He stopped a man in the hallway and asked him who he was. Homer Van Meter, who had just dropped by for a little friendly visit, told him he was a soap salesman, and started to retreat down the rear stairs.

Agent Coulter followed, intending to press the man with more questions, but Van Meter had had enough conversation, and he turned suddenly, firing his pistol at him. Couter returned the fire, retreating back up the stairs, while Van Meter made his way through the cellar and out into the front yard. Here he jumped into a passing truck, snatched off the driver's cap, and forced the man to drive him to safety.

Cummings heard the shooting and hammered on the door. Suddenly from inside he heard a curse, and as he moved aside the door was splintered by machine gun fire. Then Dillinger came charging out, but Cummings had retreated around the bend in the hall.

Dillinger, with Billie at his back, and still manning his chattering machine gun, retreated down the rear stairs. At the bottom she ran to a three-car garage where they had a new Hudson parked. Getting behind the wheel, she backed the car out as Dillinger stood in the alley with his machine gun slowly sweeping the open space on Goodrich Avenue. Just as he jumped into the car Detective Cummings managed to shoot Dillinger in the leg.

Agent Nalls had heard the shooting from his post out in front, so he immediately fired several shots into the tires of the coupe he was guarding and came up to the front door on the run. As he mounted the front stairs, heading for the third floor, Van Meter came out from the cellar. They never saw each other.

The car Dillinger and Billie made their escape in had been purchased from the William Poothoff Motor Company, at 216 Bates Avenue, St. Paul, by a Mr. Carl T. Hellman. He had traded in a Chevrolet coupe and paid a difference of $1,717.81 in cash. The car was a new Hudson sedan, with yellow wheels, a yellow stripe, and Minnesota license plates B–317-241. An immediate alert was put out, but by then Dillinger and Billie were in Minneapolis, pulling up in front of Eddie Green's place.

Behind them in the apartment they had left two automatic rifles; a .38 caliber automatic, with 20-shot magazine clips; two steel vests; a photograph of Dillinger in a sailor uniform; and a slip of paper with a telephone number on it.

When Dillinger and Billie arrived at 3300 Fremont Avenue, in Minneapolis, Eddie Green had already been alerted by Homer Van Meter. Eddie immediately got Dillinger a doctor, and then they all hurriedly cleared out of the apartment.

By the time the FBI arrived at Eddie Green's place, led there by the telephone number found in Dillinger's apartment, the occupants had fled. It was evident that the departure had been sudden, as they had left behind them a few ammunition clips, some ammunition, and lots of Green's luggage.

It was March 24, and while the jury was still out deciding Russell Clark's fate, the judge used this time to sentence both Harry Pierpont and Charles Makley to the electric chair. The sentence was to be carried out Friday, July 13, 1934. Then the Clark jury came in with its verdict of guilty, but with a recommendation of mercy.

The FBI staked out the apartment at 3300 Fremont Avenue, and waited for someone to come and pick up Eddie Green's luggage. The stakeout paid off on April 3, when two Negro women, Alma Powell, and her sister Ruth, arrived to "pick up Mr. T. J. Randall's things."

That same afternoon the FBI agents posted themselves inside Alma Powell's house at 778 Rondo Street. As they watched through the windows in the front of the house they observed a Terraplane sedan draw up just across the street. In it were a man and a woman.

Eddie Green got out of the car and started across the street toward the house. Then, according to witnesses, the FBI agents started firing and Green fell to the street, mortally wounded. They explained later that Green had made a menacing move toward his hip pocket. It was clearly evident that it was dangerous for a hoodlum to reach for his handkerchief. Green carried no gun.

Bessie Green, Eddie's wife, ran screaming from the car and

knelt beside her dying husband. She was taken into custody, and Green was rushed to a hospital, where he was put under a heavy guard. Before he died, eight days later, he spilled everything he knew.

Curiously, on Saturday, March 31, 1934, a grand jury that had been in session in St. Paul, investigating crime in the city and possible collusion between the police department and the criminal element, issued to both the City and the Police Department a clear bill of health. The grand jury stated that it had found no justification for any charges that an excess of crime existed in St. Paul. It also reported that it found no evidence of collusion between police and the underworld, and no evidence of excessive graft. Harry Sawyer laughed with glee when he read this.

From Minneapolis Dillinger and Billie Frechette went to Mooresville, where John enjoyed a pleasant visit with his family and friends. Apparently he walked around town with immunity, shaking hands with the good people, then left. No one reported his presence to the authorities. The FBI arrived just behind him, but got little or no cooperation from the Mooresville citizens.

Then Dillinger and Billie drove to Chicago, where he planned to hide out for a while and let his wounds heal. But the FBI was hounding his every move, and agents seemed to drop in regularly on any of his friends they could discover.

Monday, April 9, 1934, John Dillinger had a date to meet with another hoodlum friend at a saloon, located at 416 North State Street. He let Billie out while he parked the car, and she went in and was immediately arrested by the FBI.

After having walked halfway back to the saloon, Dillinger apparently sensed something was wrong. He turned and went back to the car, jumped in, and drove away. Later he called his attorney, Piquette, and told him to check and see if Billie had been arrested. If she had he was told to represent her.

The Dillinger gang had lost a lot of their weapons and steel vests, so Dillinger and Homer Van Meter decided it was time to replenish their supplies. Early on the morning of April 13, Officer Judd Pittenger of Warsaw, Indiana, was accosted on the street by the duo. At gun point they forced him to let them into the city hall, where they broke into the arsenal and stole two revolvers and three bulletproof vests.

Reports of John Dillinger and his activities came into the FBI and the Indiana State Police, as well as the Chicago Police, from all over the country. Some of the reports were so silly that they gave birth to the following item which appeared in *The Chicago Tribune*:

Mr. Dillinger was seen yesterday looking over the new spring gloves in a State Street store in Chicago; negotiating for a twelve-cylinder car in Springfield, Illinois; buying a half-dozen sassy cravats in Omaha, Nebraska; bargaining for a suburban bungalow at his home town of Mooresville, Indiana, and shaking hands with old friends; drinking a glass of soda water in a drugstore in Charleston, South Carolina; and strolling down Broadway swinging a Malacca cane in New York. He also bought a fishing rod in a sporting-goods store in Montreal and gave a dinner at a hotel in Yucatan, Mexico. But anyhow, Mr. Dillinger seems to have kept very carefully out of London. Berlin, Rome, Moscow, and Vienna. Or at least if he did go to those places yesterday he was traveling incog.

viii

The gang had split up and scattered, but they made a date to meet at a summer resort in northern Wisconsin—a resort which stayed open all year round. The name of the resort was "The Little Bohemia Lodge," and was owned and operated by Mr. and Mrs. Wanatka, immigrants from the Bohemian province of Czechoslovakia. It was located deep in the Wisconsin woods, on Star Lake near Mercer.

The lodge itself was a large two-storied affair, facing away from the lake. There was a small beach running along the lake-front. Nearby were a few three-room cabins, built to handle any overflow from the main lodge during the rush season.

About 1:00 P.M. on April 20, a car that contained Homer Van Meter, Pat Riley, and Marie Conforti stopped at the lodge to check it out. They had lunch and then explained to the owner that there would be a larger party of their friends arriving later in the evening. Mr. Wanatka was delighted, as this was the off season, and he assured them they would be given the best rates available.

That evening two cars arrived at the lodge, carrying Dillinger, Hamilton, Pat Cherrington, Tommy Carroll, Jean Delaney, Baby Face Nelson, and his wife Helen. They all climbed out and went into the Lodge, chatting and carrying on like a group of tourists. Their baggage was later brought in by two employees of the lodge, Frank Traube and George Baszo, who wondered what was in that baggage. Each one of the bags felt like it was filled with rocks. Of course they were really filled with machine guns, rifles, and ammunition, which did make a heavy package.

In the evening, after a leisurely dinner, the Dillinger gang, which by now was on first-name terms with the owner and his wife, decided to play cards. Mr. Wanatka joined in the friendly little game, and the evening promised to be a social success. He was hardly prepared for the sight of the two pistols in shoulder holsters that Dillinger presented to him, as he reached for the pot.

A little later Wanatka excused himself from the game and went into the kitchen where he searched through some old newspapers. Here he found a picture and description of Dillinger. Then he knew he was right. Back at the table, a few minutes later, he began to spot guns on the other "tourists."

The next morning Wanatka told his wife of his findings, but they did nothing. That afternoon (Wanatka later said) he asked Dillinger if he could see him in his office, alone. When they were in the office with the door closed he faced Dillinger with the truth and the criminal admitted who he was.

Wanatka then said he told Dillinger that he didn't want any shooting in his lodge. His whole family was there, and all his money was tied up in that place. Dillinger then assured him that all they wanted was peace and quiet, and the last thing they wanted was any shooting.

Because of this, the Dillinger gang allowed Mrs. Wanatka to drive to Manitowish to visit with her brother and her brother-in-law, Henry Voss. Voss owned the Birchwood Lodge, about two miles down the road from Little Bohemia. It was to him that she confided their problem, and he promised to report it to the police.

It was Voss who telephoned the police in Milwaukee, and who, upon their advice, then called the FBI. He reported to agents that the whole Dillinger gang was ensconced at the Little Bohemia Lodge. He finally talked to Melvin Purvis, who had checked on Mr. Voss's reliability. He assured Voss that the FBI would be along shortly.

Purvis then asked him for the location of the nearest airport, and Voss told him that the nearest one would be in Rhinelander, which was over 50 miles from Mercer. Voss was then told to proceed to Rhinelander and await the FBI. He was also told to wear a white handkerchief around his neck for identification.

FBI agents then left from Chicago, and from their office in St. Paul. They arrived in Rhinelander about 6:30 P.M., April 22,

1934. Purvis immediately looked for Henry Voss, and he came running up, with the white handkerchief fluttering around his neck.

There was no car rental in Rhinelander so the agents were forced to commandeer five privately owned automobiles. Then they started out on the long, bitter cold trip to Little Bohemia. Before they got there, two of the cars broke down, and the agents who were riding in them had to ride the runningboards of the other three. As they rode on, their hands almost froze to the metal sides of the cars, while they struggled with their guns.

About two miles from the lodge all lights on the cars were turned off, and the convoy proceeded very slowly. The lodge itself was built about 400 yards off the main road, and there was just a single-lane driveway leading to it. Because of this the FBI parked their cars across the drive, completely blocking it, and went the rest of the way on foot.

Henry Voss had filled in Melvin Purvis as much as he could regarding the lodge and its cabins. He described the lake and its beach, the trees, and the surrounding grounds. He forgot to mention a barbed wire fence running along side the lodge, the watch dogs, and a few other minor details.

As the agents were fanning out among the trees, preparing to surround the lodge, Mr. Wanatka's two collie dogs, Shadow and Prince, started barking. At the same time John Hoffman, 28, a filling station operator from Mercer, Eugene Boiseneau, 35, and John Morris, 59, from the nearby CCC Camp decided to leave.

Mr. Wanatka's two employees, Baszo and Traube, walked with them to the porch, and watched as they got into a 1933 Chevrolet coupe, with Hoffman taking the wheel. They then turned up the volume on the car radio, which blared with dance music, and started to drive away. By now the two dogs were barking like mad, but Baszo and Traube tried to quiet them.

Suddenly out of the darkness came a barrage of bullets and the side window of the coupe disappeared. Hoffman, his right arm shattered, stopped the car, jumped out, and went running off for the lake as fast as he could. He didn't know who was shooting but he made up his mind to put as much distance between himself and them as he could.

Morris, sitting on the other side, came out of the car with two bullets in his hip, and two in his shoulder. In shock and on the verge of collapsing, he struggled up the steps of the lodge and fainted inside.

The only one who didn't move was Boiseneau, who had been sitting in the center. He couldn't move—he was dead.

From the FBI's point of view, agents were converging upon a lodge where it had been definitely established that the Dillinger gang was hiding. Suddenly two watch dogs started barking, giving their secret approach away. Then five men appeared on the porch of the lodge, and three of them immediately went down the steps and got into a car. The agents called as loud as they could for them to halt and surrender, but the three men ignored them and started their getaway in the car, so they had opened fire.

The Dillinger gang was now fully alerted, and upstairs they poured down a deadly fire. Then running down stairs, they all crawled out a rear window, and headed for the lake. The women ran into the basement where they would remain for the rest of the night.

At the lake Dillinger, Van Meter, Carroll, and Hamilton turned to their right and escaped along the lake side. In the darkness Carroll got separated from the other three, and would make his way out of the woods, alone.

Baby Face Nelson delayed his flight, in hopes of getting a clear shot at a couple of the agents, but when they returned his fire, he changed his mind. When he got to the lake, he had no idea which way the others went, nor did he care. He turned to the left, and went off on a trip of his own.

Back at the lodge Pat Riley and Pat Cherrington, who had been on a mission for Homer Van Meter in St. Paul, were just returning. Riley turned into the drive to the lodge, and the first thing he saw was the agents' cars blocking the way. He quickly switched off his lights, put the car into reverse, and took off with a shower of bullets crashing after him.

Then Melvin Purvis got word that Baby Face Nelson had just killed Special Agent W. Carter Baum, and seriously wounded Special Agent Jay Newman and Constable Carl C. Christensen. He sent agents to check it out.

The net result of the raid on the Little Bohemia Lodge was the capture of Marie Conforti, Helen Gillis Nelson, and Jean Delaney, the death of Special Agent W. Carter Baum, the killing of Eugene Boisneau, and the wounding of Constable Carl C. Christensen, Special Agent Jay Newman, John Hoffman, and John Morris. For the FBI it had been a bitter victory.

Dillinger, Hamilton, and Van Meter made their way through the woods to another resort. Here they kidnapped Robert Johnson and stole his automobile, and then made him drive them out of the area. Tommy Carroll also found another resort, where he silently stole a car and drove himself to freedom.

Baby Face Nelson's escape was more harrowing, longer, and more involved. (See Chapter 7.)

A cry went up across the nation for the resignation of Melvin Purvis, who bore most of the brunt of this fiasco. In the face of so much clamor he would tender it, and it would be refused by J. Edgar Hoover.

Perhaps the unkindest cut of all to the FBI was the comment in Will Rogers's syndicated column, commenting on the Little Bohemia Lodge fiasco—"Well, they had Dillinger surrounded and was all ready to shoot him when he come out, but another bunch of folks come out ahead, so they just shot them instead. Dillinger is going to accidentally get with some innocent bystanders sometime, then he will get shot."

The following day Dillinger and Van Meter were racing toward St. Paul, Minnesota, in Mr. Robert Johnson's car. They had released him, unharmed, and he had reported the theft of his car to the police. In the back seat of the car lay Red Hamilton, who was bushed and had decided to take a nap. Van Meter was driving and Dillinger was just sitting beside him watching the scenery go by.

Deputy Sheriffs Norman Dieter and Joe Heinen had been assigned to a spot near Hastings, Minnesota. Here they were told to be on the lookout for members of the Dillinger gang. They had also been given a good description of the car Van Meter was driving. They were bored with the assignment, because "everyone knew" that the Dillinger gang would never head this way—then Van Meter went speeding by.

The two deputies took off after the car with the wanted Wisconsin license plates. When it started to pull away from them, they opened fire. Van Meter, the better driver, with wide experience in evasion tactics, managed to outmaneuver and lose the officers. On the rear seat Red Hamilton lay moaning. One of the officers' shots had entered the back of the car, and tore into Hamilton's stomach.

According to a later confession given by Helen Gillis Nelson, Hamilton died in Aurora, Illinois where he had been taken for medical attention. The gang had tried to enlist the services of "Doc" Joseph P. Moran, but he refused to have anything to do with any member of the Dillinger mob. Hamilton died before they could get him to another doctor. Significantly Dillinger made no threats of reprisals against Moran, but tried to ignore the entire matter. Moran had powerful friends, Hamilton didn't.

Mrs. Nelson said that Red Hamilton's body was then taken to a nearby gravel pit, where John Dillinger poured can after can of lye in his face and on his hands. He was trying to thwart any later identification of the body. She said Dillinger looked down at Hamilton's body, and quipped, "Sorry to do this to you, old buddy, but I know you'd do the same thing for me."

On April 30, 1934, the ever-busy FBI turned up H. S. Lebman, a San Antonio, Texas gunsmith. He admitted to the agents that he had delivered five machine guns and other weapons to Jimmy Williams for delivery to the Dillinger mob in St. Paul. Jimmy Williams was a pal of Tommy Carroll's.

Early in May, Mrs. Eddie Green pleaded guilty to a charge of harboring a wanted fugitive, her husband, and received a 15-month sentence. Then on May 23, the jury in the trial of Evelyn "Billie" Frechette and Doctor May deliberated seven hours before convicting them both. Doctor May's nurse, Mrs. Salt, was acquitted. The judge immediately sentenced both Frechette and May to two years in a federal prison and fined them $1,000.

A couple of days later Dillinger's "jack-of-all-trades" Attorney Louis Phillip Piquett, made arrangements for Dillinger to have his face altered, and his fingerprints erased. The operation was performed by Dr. Harold B. Cassidy, Dr. Wilhelm Loeser, and James Probasco, on May 28, 1934.

During the operation Dillinger swallowed his tongue, and his heart stopped beating. But the good doctors, faced with losing a rather large fee ($5,000) could not allow this. They yanked his tongue out of his throat with a pair of forceps, and with artificial respiration and novocaine, they brought him back.

Then, as if nothing had happened, they removed a couple of moles from between his eyes, covered up a dimple in his chin, pulled his cheeks up, and managed to change his appearance somewhat.

When Dillinger saw himself in a mirror he blew his top, because his face was in such a puffed condition. They managed to convince him that this was an expected result, and that his face would return to normal in a couple of weeks. "You'll look fine after that," the doctors assured him.

So convincing was their argument that Homer Van Meter decided to let them perform an operation on him. But when they had finished, he too was very unhappy with the results. While he raved and ranted about the mess they had made of his face, Baby Face Nelson watched happily. He and Van Meter had just one thing in common—they hated each other passionately.

While all this was going on, the governors of Illinois, Indiana, Michigan, Minnesota, and Ohio signed a reward proclamation, putting a price of $5,000 on Dillinger's head.

Also the three women who had been captured during the Little Bohemia raid were sentenced to a year and a day. Federal Judge Patrick T. Stone then suspended the sentence, and granted 18 months probation. He was to say later that he had released them in the hopes they would lead the FBI to their men. They did indeed join their men, but nobody thought to follow them.

June 1, 1934, Pat Cherrington and Opal Long were arrested at the old Chateau Hotel, at 3838 Broadway, and both were charged with harboring John Dillinger. Pat Cherrington was sentenced to two years in the Federal Reformatory for Women at Alderson, West Virginia, while Opal Long got six months in the city jail at Minneapolis.

June 4, 1934, Joseph Fox, one of the original ten who had escaped from Michigan City Penitentiary, was picked up in Chicago, and returned to the penitentiary, where he received an added sentence for escaping. Since he was already serving a life sentence, this didn't bother him too much.

June 7, 1934, Tommy Carroll and Jean Delaney stopped at a filling station and garage in Waterloo, Iowa, to have some work done on their car. The mechanic, while working on the car, discovered some weapons and an extra set of license plates in the rear, and became suspicious. When Carroll and Jean left for a while he called the local police.

Detectives P. E. Walker and Emil Steffen, of the Waterloo police, staked out the garage and waited. A little after noon, Carroll and Delaney returned to pick up their car. The detectives stepped out and called for Carroll to put his hands up. Carroll reached for his gun, and fell with five bullets in him. The gun was still in his hand.

June 27, 1934, Harry Copeland received a sentence of 25 years for his part in the Greencastle bank job. Later Pat Riley would be arrested, tried, and receive two sentences of one year, nine months and fourteen days—sentences to run consecutively.

ix

On June 30, 1934, Adolf Hitler had Ernst Röhm, Kurt Von Schleicher, Frau Elizabeth Von Schleicher, and Heinrich Kalusmer assassinated. Also, John Dillinger, Homer Van Meter, Baby Face Nelson and John Paul Chase held up the Merchants National Bank, at South Bend, Indiana.

It was about 11:30 A.M., a Saturday and just prior to closing time, when a Hudson bearing Ohio license plates and containing four men parked at the corner of Michigan and Wayne Streets. On this corner stood the Merchants National Bank.

Chase remained in the car as a lookout, and Baby Face Nelson took up a position near the rear to control all the approaches with his machine gun. John Dillinger and Homer Van Meter slipped inside and announced in the old familiar way, "This is a stickup, everybody, hands up, please."

When the people didn't react fast enough to suit him, John Dillinger let loose a burst of machine gun bullets into the ceiling. From here on out he would be certain that the people would listen and obey.

Outside Nelson was already having his problems. Patrolman Harold Wagner, who had been directing traffic nearby, heard Dillinger's temper tantrum, and came on the run to see what was happening. Nelson shot him dead with one burst from his machine gun, while Chase smiled approvingly at his hero.

As Nelson was chattering away with his machine gun outside, Dillinger and Van Meter were grabbing all the cash they could find. The take wasn't as much as they had hoped for, but Dillinger's idea that casing a bank was a waste of time still prevailed. They were still playing it by ear and there were mutterings of discord in the gang.

When Dillinger and Van Meter came out of the bank with their hostages, Nelson was more than ready to leave. They forced the hostages to take a place on the running boards, then they slowly drove away.

Officers had converged upon the scene, and as soon as the getaway car started off they began to shoot. They succeeded in shooting Delos N. Coen, a cashier, in the left leg and Perry G. Stahly, a bank official, in the side.

Detective Harry Henderson, who had just arrived, was certain he had hit the driver of the car, Homer Van Meter. But he suffered only a minor head wound. Changing cars on the west

side of town, the gangsters dropped their hostages, and fled in
a Pontiac with Indiana license plates. They left behind them one
dead man and five wounded. They had the enormous sum of
$28,000 to divide four ways.

x

July 21, 1934, a Saturday, two members of the East Chicago,
Indiana, police called Melvin Purvis and told him they had a hot
tip on the whereabouts of John Dillinger. The two officers were
Captain Timothy O'Neill and Sergeant Martin Zarkovich.

A meeting was arranged in a hotel, located in Chicago's loop.
There they told Purvis that a woman by the name of Anna Sage
had approached them to make a deal. She said she knew where
John Dillinger was staying, and she would finger him for them,
if the FBI would help her with a problem she had with the
government.

Another meeting was set up, this time to include Anna Sage.
She was a rather large woman, with a round face, black hair, and
snapping black eyes. She had plucked her eyebrows, and drawn
in new ones with an eyebrow pencil. She had a distinctive "for-
eign" look about her, and told her story, through thin red lips,
with a thick accent.

Anne Sage had run a bawdy house and had been caught. Since
she was not a citizen of the United States but of Romania, she
was under a deportation order. In exchange for Dillinger she
wanted the FBI to intervene with the immigration authorities,
and she wanted the $15,000 reward the various governments had
posted.

Purvis told her he could not guarantee that she would receive
the full amount of the reward, as that would depend upon the
circumstances of his capture. He would, however, put in a good
word for her with the immigration authorities, but here again he
could guarantee nothing.

This was about what Anna Sage had expected, so she agreed
to cooperate with them. She told them that John Dillinger had
taken up with a girlfriend of hers—a waitress named Polly Hamilton. He had a date with her the following day and the three of
them were going to the movies. The last time, she said, they had
gone to the Marbro theater in West Chicago. She would call
Purvis's office when she had something more definite to go on.

All that night and the next morning the FBI made its preparations, and all members of the special "Dillinger Squad" had been put on alert. Captain O'Neill and Sergeant Zarkovich of the East Chicago police were also working hand in hand with them, as they had a special interest in this particular case. Then everyone sat back to wait for a phone call from Anna. At 5:00 P.M., the telephone in Purvis's office rang.

It was Anna Sage and she seemed in a hurry. "He's here; he's just come. We are leaving in about five minutes. We will go to either the Biograph or the Marbro." With this she hung up, leaving a stunned Purvis staring blankly at the dead phone. He immediately notified Special Agent Sam Cowley, who would be in charge of the operation.

This was the first mention of the Biograph theater, and while they had fully reconnoitered the Marbro and mapped all its exits and approaches they knew nothing about the Biograph. Hurriedly Cowley ordered agents sent to the theater to make a hasty assessment of the layout.

They decided they would have to cover both theaters simultaneously, so Special Agent Charles B. Winstead and Sergeant Zarkovich rushed to the Marlbro, while Special Agents Melvin Purvis and Ralph Brown, raced to cover the Biograph. Special Agent Sam Cowley and Captain Timothy O'Neill remained with the main body of FBI agents and two other East Chicago officers, ready to go to either the Marbro or the Biograph.

While Purvis and Brown sat in their car, they strained their necks trying to see everybody coming or going in the direction of the Biograph theater. Suddenly they spotted Anna Sage—wearing a red dress, as she had promised. With her were John Dillinger and another woman they could not identify.

Purvis nodded to Brown, and he raced to the telephone and called Sam Cowley: "Dillinger has just arrived at the Biograph with two women; the identification is absolute." Cowley then called the Marbro and called off the stakeout there.

Dillinger was wearing dark glasses, a sailor straw hat, grey trousers, and no coat. He was also sporting a small, full-lip mustache, which they could clearly see as he stared up at the marquee and read, *Manhattan Melodrama*. He then went over and purchased three tickets, and they went into the theater.

A couple of agents entered the theater later and tried to locate Dillinger, but the place was packed and the light was very bad. Not wishing to unduly alarm Dillinger, and cause a possible shootout with all these people around, they quietly left.

For two hours and five minutes, with the temperature just a little below 100 degrees, young men loitered outside the theater. They smoked cigarettes, looked in shop windows, girl watched, and did just about anything they could think of to remain inconspicuous..

Passersby cast inquisitive glances in their directions, probably wondering why in the world people would be out on the steaming streets this time of evening, wearing button-up coats.

Two East Chicago policemen, in plain clothes, were stationed just to the north of the theater. Melvin Purvis had been stationed at the door, as he knew Dillinger by sight. He was to light his cigar as soon as he was certain of the identification.

To the south side of the theater, Sam Cowley had placed two of the East Chicago policemen, and two special agents. Special Agent H. E. Hollis and Special Agent Ralph Brown stood near a car, chatting and watching.

Across the street were Special Agent Sam Cowley—who was in charge—Zarkovich, O'Neill, and five FBI agents. There were other agents scattered about, covering every conceivable exit. Now all they had to do was wait, and watch that cigar in Purvis's mouth.

The young lady in the ticket window was becoming increasingly suspicious of all these men hanging around the theater. She called the manager and told him so. He, fearing a possible robbery attempt, called the Chicago police, who dispatched a car.

When Cowley saw the marked Chicago police car, he immediately sent an agent to tell them to "get the hell out of there." When the agent explained the situation to the officers in the car, they moved on out of sight, and the tension lessened just a bit.

At 10:40 the movie was over, and people started coming out. Then John Dillinger, now called Public Enemy Number One, came out with a woman on each arm. He looked right at Melvin Purvis, but took no interest in what he saw. Then they turned to their left, toward Anna Sage's apartment, and started off down the street.

Melvin Purvis struck a match and tried to light his cigar, but his hand shook so badly he couldn't do it. It didn't matter, though, for the agents had seen his motions.

Anna Sage suddenly dropped back behind John Dillinger and Polly Hamilton. She didn't want to be anywhere near him when the fireworks started. Polly Hamilton, who wasn't in on the plot, continued on down the street with Dillinger until she saw a man with a gun. She nudged Dillinger, and then she, too, ducked away.

Almost at once John Dillinger became aware of the trap that had been laid for him. And oh, how Johnny did run! He had just turned into a nearby alley and was tugging at the gun in his hip pocket when the bullets struck. He was dead when he hit the ground.

One bullet tore through Dillinger's side, and another, the fatal one, entered his back as he fell forward, and came out his right eye. Altogether he had four bullets in him. The fatal bullet was later credited first to Melvin Purvis—who had ripped the buttons off his coat in his haste to get his gun out—Agent-in-Charge Sam Cowley, and finally to Special Agent H. E. Hollis.

While credit for the fatal bullet is interesting, it is not really important. The important thing was that John Herman Dillinger was dead, and his depredations were over. In his bumbling way, he had become a national figure, and the news would be flashed around the world.

An ambulance was called to take two women, slightly wounded by stray bullets, to the hospital. While this was going on the morbid stood around looking down at the fallen hoodlum. People bent down and dipped their handkerchiefs into his blood, to keep as souvenirs. At the mortuary they would file by for hours, and an estimated 15,000 people would stare at John Dillinger's body, which had been propped up for their benefit.

This insignificant hoodlum, who had never done one decent thing in his entire life—who had robbed, maimed and even killed— would have a funeral entourage of an estimated 5,000 "decent" citizens. Letters would be written to editors of the various newspapers, lamenting the "unnecessary" death of John Dillinger. Bleeding hearts would exclaim in horror over his "murder." It is not recorded that a single one of them stopped to think of William Patrick O'Malley, and the possible thoughts he might have had on the matter.

John Herman Dillinger was buried in the Crown Hill Cemetery, on the outskirts of Indianapolis, Indiana. There would be some loud voices later raised, from several quarters, who would resent having this two-bit hoodlum buried in the same hallowed ground as President Benjamin Harrison, James Whitcomb Riley, three vice presidents, and two governors. But his father's will would prevail.

On July 24, 1934, at 3:15 P.M., the body was lowered into its grave. A guard was then posted over it to protect it from grave robbers. Later the cemetery would have the entire area of the grave covered with concrete to prevent future desecration.

xi

James Probasco, who had presided at the plastic surgery performed upon Dillinger, was arrested on July 25, 1934. The following morning he dived out of the 19th-floor window of the Bankers Building, where the Chicago FBI headquarters was located.

Anna Sage fled to California, where she remained incognito. She later received a $5,000 reward for her assistance in bringing John Dillinger to his just end. Though the FBI did try to mitigate her case with the immigration department, they had no real authority in the matter, and she was later deported to her native Romania, where she died in 1947 of a liver disease.

From a St. Paul waitress, police learned that Homer Van Meter was in town, and had been there for about two weeks. The relatives of Opal Meliga, alias Opal Mulligan, became suspicious of her boyfriend and insisted that the police be notified. Following this lead, the police staked out her home on University Avenue.

Thursday, August 23, 1934, at 5:12 P.M., Homer Van Meter appeared, strolling down University Avenue toward his girl's home. Tom Brown, head of the Bertillon Department of the St. Paul police, told Chief Frank Cullen that this was their man.

Police Chief Cullen, with Detectives Jeff Dietrich and Thomas McMahon, jumped out of their police car, and shouted to Van Meter to stop and surrender himself. Van Meter was in no mood for surrender, however, and he took off in a loping run, drawing his pistol.

While many spectators watched, Van Meter ran into a blind alley between Madison Street and Aurora Avenue. There he turned, like an animal at bay, with his gun in his hand, but before he could get off one shot the police opened up with machine guns and shotguns. Homer Van Meter dropped like a rock, with over 50 pieces of lead in his body.

Dr. Wilhelm Loeser, Dr. Harold B. Cassidy, Louis Piquette, and Arthur O'Leary were arrested and charged with harboring a fugitive wanted by the United States Attorney General.

Much to the disgust of the government, Louis Phillip Piquette, pleading his own case and insisting that he was only protecting the rights of his client, John Dillinger, was acquitted. Dr. Wilhelm Loeser, who had been paroled from Leavenworth, was returned to finish out his three-year sentence. Dr. Harold B. Cassidy and Arthur O'Leary received suspended sentences because they had cooperated with the government.

September 23, 1934, Charley Makley and Harry Pierpont, taking lessons from their old buddy, whittled out two realistic-looking guns from soap. To these they added such stuff as parts of a fountain pen, tin foil, shoe blacking and other odds and ends. Then they tried to bluff their way out of death row at the state penitentiary in Columbus, Ohio.

Surprisingly enough they managed to get through two doors, slug one unarmed guard, and free Russell Clark. But they then ran into a guard who wouldn't be bluffed, and he turned in an alarm. Frustrated, Makley and Pierpont tried to batter down the third door with a wooden stool, while the terrified Clark ran back to his own cell.

In a few moments reinforcements arrived, and seeing the "guns" in Makley and Pierpont's hands, they opened fire, wounding both of them. Charles Makley died a short time later, from his wounds, but the less fortunate Harry Pierpont recovered.

Harry Pierpont went to the electric chair on October 17, 1934, paying for his brutal murder of the unarmed Sheriff of Allen County, Jess Saber. His parents and his girlfriend, Mary Kinder, sat nearby in a cheap hotel, waiting to claim his body for burial at Leipsic, Ohio.

The end of Baby Face Nelson, Helen Gillis Nelson, and John Paul Chase are detailed in the next chapter.

In June 1935, Louis Piquette would be tried again, this time for harboring Homer Van Meter, who had never been a client of his. He was found guilty, but being a lawyer, he instituted a series of delaying appeals. Finally, on May 9, 1936, he entered the Federal Penitentiary at Leavenworth on a two-year sentence. He was paroled on June 11, 1938, and pardoned in January 1951. In December 1951, he died while trying to get reinstated as a member of the Illinois Bar Association.

••7••

Mrs. Gillis's Little Boy Lester

In the history of American crime, there has been no single individual more vicious, or who got more of a thrill from killing, than Mrs. Gillis's little boy Lester. Once a small child, with a cherubic face, he eventually grew into a bantam-sized, hoodlum-killer, with a baby face. At full growth he would never tower above five feet, five inches.

Lester was born in Chicago, Illinois, December 6, 1908, of Belgian immigrant parents. His father died while he was still very young; thus he was denied the needed guidance and companionship only a father can give to a son.

Lester's mother, Mary Gillis, had to work very hard to provide for him and his sisters. As an unskilled worker, she earned very little money, and the children had to fend for themselves during the day.

Lester grew up in the packing and stockyard district of Chicago. This was a rough slum neighborhood, ruled by a local mob of young toughs known as the Five Points Gang. They were a kind of local crime wave, and stole from practically everybody.

With his small stature, baby face, and the meek-sounding name of Lester, he had to learn the art of self-defense at an early age. One look at him, and the members of the Five Points Gang wanted to start a fight with him. He fought back, and soon became most proficient with the "poor boy's equalizer"—the switchblade knife.

It was about this time that he met a pale, pimpled-faced young kid with a leaky heart, and the impossible name of Francis Albin Karpoviecz, who was also unacceptable by the Five Points Gang. This young man interested Lester, so the two of them teamed up. Lester taught the young Lithuanian all he had learned about stealing cars, and stripping them. Then the sickly kid got sicker, and had to leave Chicago. Lester was alone again. He didn't mind really, for he would get used to the loneliness. He didn't trust anyone, and felt that he needed help from no one. Yet, his ostracism by the members of the Five Points and other gangs did cause him some resentment, and increased his bitterness.

When his legs failed to grow to the length demanded by society, and his delicate features failed to mature, he became even more incorrigible. Mary Gillis had lost complete control of her son, and he of himself. His temper became so ferocious that members of the Five Points Gang came to fear him.

In 1922, Lester was arrested for auto theft while attempting to sell some of the accessories he had taken from the car. His vicious attitude toward the arresting officers, and his complete refusal to cooperate, earned him harsh punishment.

He was sentenced to an indefinite term at the St. Charles Reform School. Then, in April 1924, he was surprisingly enough paroled for "good behavior." In September of the same year, he was back as a parole violator. In July 1925, he was again let out on parole—apparently in an expense-cutting maneuver—but he was returned again in October.

Not ones to give up easily, the authorities again paroled him, in July 1926. Now old enough to be sent to the penitentiary if he misbehaved again, he would not return to the school.

Lester never once looked upon these years in the reformatory as lost ones. He had spent the time getting an education from its inmates. He had real professionals as teachers; this was his education, and he made the most of it. He learned new methods of stealing cars, how to blow a safe, and even held debates with the older boys about the merits of bank robbery, as opposed to burglary.

When he left the Reformatory, Lester hung around his mother's house, on Marshfield Avenue, for a time. He was 18 years old now, but he never gave serious thought about getting a good formal education, or looking for a job. He was going to live the good life, with plenty of money, girls, cars, and excitement.

Mary Gillis gently tried to hint to her son that he should get a job and help out a little with the expenses. His sisters came right out and told him that he was a dead beat, and that he should help pay his way. Lester, however, was unimpressed.

Finally, disgusted with their incessant "nagging" Lester left Chicago, and started roaming across the country. He had stolen a car for transportation, and held up lonely filling stations for his expense money.

He lived in Reno, Nevada, for a short while, getting a job (his first) as a chauffeur for a small time gambler. Here he saw the easy money flowing across the gaming tables; but it eluded him. Still, he saw how the big gamblers, and the little gamblers, were living, and he wanted to live that way too. He was no professional gambler, though, he knew this, so he continued his travels Westward, looking.

He drifted into the Los Angeles area, where he settled for a while, and tried his luck at bootlegging and rumrunning. All it took was a small investment, and a lot of nerve; Lester had both. This occupation paid quite well, and no one seemed concerned with his small stature or his baby face.

Still the big money was eluding him, so he decided to move up north into the San Francisco Bay area. San Francisco was a wide open seaport town, where prohibition was just a nasty word. Up and down the Embarcadero, out on Market Street, and throughout Chinatown, swanky speakeasies drew large crowds, and the booze and money flowed.

Bootleggers and rumrunners here were making good money, with little or no interference from authorities. This was just what Lester was looking for: A wide open town, with plenty of opportunities for an enterprising young hoodlum.

By the end of 1928, Lester had earned enough money to return to Chicago in style. He was most anxious to show everybody in his old neighborhood, and particularly the members of the Five Points Gang, just how much of a big shot he had become.

His return was sweet, and many people were impressed with the lavish way he threw his money around. Unhappily for Lester, the old Five Points Gang had changed; it was now controlled by an entirely new crop of delinquents who had never heard of him. Still, they were impressed, and so was a petite Polish girl who worked in the local five and ten.

Blue-eyed Helen Wawrzyniak was indeed five feet, two. She weighed about 94 pounds. She was a brunette, very pretty, and only 16. But she knew what she wanted, and now it was that strutting, swaggering, pint-sized Lester Gillis.

Against the violent objections of Helen's parents, they were married, and he spent lavishly to make her happy. Then they settled down for a while in Chicago, where he tried to make a go of things. But Lester didn't inspire much confidence with the local gangs, and he could seem to make an inroad into the Chicago Underworld.

Disgusted and disappointed, Lester packed up his new bride and moved back to the West Coast. They settled in the small village of Sausalito, on the east side of Golden Gate, the entrance to San Francisco Bay.

Here and in the Bay Area, Lester tried to reestablish his once flourishing bootleg enterprise, and pulled several small-time robberies in the meantime, to pay the rent. It was in San Francisco that he was picked up by the police for carrying a gun. A short time later he was arrested again, this time on suspicion of holding up a gas station, but was released without prosecution.

Through various criminal activities, he and Helen managed to put together a bundle, and then they felt the call of home. There were two children in the family now. Ronald was born in 1929, and Arlene was born the following year. Lester Gillis, who was now using the name George Nelson, hadn't wanted any children, and they were proving a nuisance to both himself, and Helen. So, when they got to Chicago, they unloaded both of them on their grandmother, the long-suffering Mary Gillis.

Here Arlene would stay, and eventually would come to know her mother only as "Aunt Helen." Ronald would later be sent to Bremerton, Washington, where he would live with a married sister of Helen's. Neither of the children would ever come to know their father.

Things were always a bit rough for "George Nelson," because he just didn't look like the bad man he wanted so desperately to be. His tough talk and egotistical boasting sounded like the crow of a bantam rooster to most of the hoodlums he wanted to work with.

Eventually Nelson did find a couple of bank robbers who were more desperate than they were choosy about the help they hired. He was given a minor role as a lookout and wheelman in the robbing of a bank in Spring Grove, Illinois.

His cut of the take was niggardly, but he now had a foot in the door and he could properly call himself a "bank robber." This, to him, was the most important part of the operation. And, sure enough, the boys called for him again, and he helped them loot the First National Bank of Itasca, Illinois. Things seemed to be looking up for George Nelson, and Helen was also elated.

Time passed, then Nelson and a couple of other hoods hit the bank in Hillside, Illinois. Nelson, feeling cocky, shot a bank guard. The guard wasn't killed, but the news media screamed for vengeance; so the three of them divided the $6,250 in loot, and separated.

With this fabulous wad, the Nelsons went on a spending spree that wouldn't stop until they ran out of money. Helen bought jewels, furs, exotic perfumes, and all the clothes she could carry. They also purchased a Ford V-8, and wined and dined in the most fashionable speakeasies in town. Then suddenly there was no more money, and George Nelson had to go back to work.

The newspapers, reporting on the Hillside bank job, with its subsequent shooting of the bank guard, described one of the hoodlums as "a young man with a baby face." Now some of his acquaintances began to call him "Baby Face Nelson," and although it had a distinct ring to it, he didn't like it one bit. Helen calmed his ruffled feelings, however, and told him she thought it was kind of cute. He grew to hate this name passionately.

Helen had bought some of her jewelry at a small shop just off Michigan Avenue. At that time, Nelson had learned that it was owned and operated by one old man. So on January 15, 1931, Nelson entered the store, and told the old man "This is a holdup."

On the way out, his pockets filled with loot, Nelson walked into the arms of the police. They, too, had been impressed with the store's vulnerability to robbery, and had staked out the place. While Nelson had been casing the store for a hit they had been casing him, and when he made his move they made theirs.

Booked in the station downtown, as Number 5437, George Nelson, alias "Baby Face Nelson," alias Lester M. Gillis, was charged with armed robbery. At the jail, during a routine lineup, someone remembered the story about the baby faced bandit, the Hillside bank job, and the shooting of the guard.

Witnesses were brought in, and Nelson was positively identified as one of the three bandits who had held up the bank. His refusal to cooperate by naming the other hoodlums went hard on him, but he couldn't help that. He knew that if he became a "stoolie" it would upset all his future plans for a career in crime.

On July 15, 1931, he was found guilty, and the judge gave him the maximum sentence of from one year to life in the Penitentiary, and he entered Joliet on July 17, 1931.

Living in Joliet was miserable to say the least, and with his rebellious nature, Nelson did nothing but antagonize both guards and inmates. He was in one fight after another, and was placed in solitary for long periods of time. This only served to make him more defiant, and more vicious, if that was possible.

During the waning days of 1931, Nelson tried to escape, but the attempt failed miserably. All it got him was an additional sentence, and again brought him to the attention of authorities.

These authorities, in reviewing his case, discovered that he matched the description of one of three holdup men in a bank robbery in Itasca. This identification, and news stories, led authorities into the habit of referring to him as "Baby Face Nelson."

Nelson, now formally accused of the Itasca bank job, was taken from Joliet Penitentiary, and placed on a train to Chicago. Upon arrival there, he was transferred by automobile, to the DuPage County Jail at Wheaton, Illinois, to await trial.

The trial took three days, and he was again found guilty of bank robbery, and sentenced to from one to twenty years in the state penitentiary (Joliet). Now he knew he would never get out of prison unless desperate measures were taken.

On February 15, 1932, he was put aboard the Rock Island Special, in leg irons, and handcuffed to his guard. Then they headed back to Joliet. They debarked from the train in downtown Joliet, and his guard hailed a cab to take them to the penitentiary.

Strange as it might seem, this action was not unusual, as guards had standing instructions to take cabs if a prison car was not waiting for them. This, authorities believed, reduced the possibility of escape, which would be compounded by loitering around the depot awaiting an official car.

Nelson, still handcuffed to his guard, and still wearing the cumbersome leg irons, entered the cab first. This placed him right behind the driver, with the guard on his right. As soon as the door of the cab was closed, and the cab started away from the curb, *Nelson pulled a gun!*

He disarmed his guard, and then placed his pistol to the back of the cab driver's head. He instructed him to drive out of town, and to avoid attracting any attention, otherwise, Nelson assured him, he'd be a dead hero. Then he turned his attention to his guard again, and ordered him to remove the irons.

The nervous driver started speeding toward the outskirts of Joliet, and Nelson warned him to slow down. He told him, "I'll blow your damn head off, if you don't slow this cab down!" The driver slowed down, and the three quietly cruised into the suburbs, where Nelson noticed a cemetery on his left. It was a nice quiet and secluded place so Nelson ordered the driver to pull over and get out.

The guard got out first, prodded by Nelson's pistol, and Nelson knocked him unconscious with a rap on the head from his gun.

Then Nelson led the terrified cab driver deeper into the cemetery and told him to turn around. Scared witless, the driver started to run, but Nelson also struck him down with his pistol.

Nelson then stripped the cab driver of his hat and coat, put them on, and drove away in the cab. No one had been killed, but the driver did catch pneumonia from lying on the frozen ground, and the guard awoke with a bad headache.

How Baby Face Nelson got his pistol was never established, though there have been many theories. It could have been slipped to him, as he brushed against someone on the crowded train, or delivered to him as he and the guard walked down the station platform. Both the guard and the cab driver were cleared of any suspicion of complicity in the escape.

One thing was certain—Helen Nelson had somehow gotten a gun to her husband. He had no gang, and with the exception of Helen there was no one who cared if he stayed in prison or not. He didn't have enough money to buy a friend or his freedom.

From this moment on Nelson would never see the inside of a jail or prison again. Yet the police would come to know him as Lester Gillis, Alex Gillis, Lester Giles, Big George Nelson, Jimmie Nelson, Jimmy Burnett, and of course, Baby Face Nelson.

Nelson fled back to San Francisco, where he used the name of Jimmy Burnett. Here he again entered the waning trade of rum-running and bootlegging. For a while he worked at these occupations industriously, trying to earn enough money to send for Helen.

ii

Most of the criminal activities in and around San Francisco were syndicated by a gang under the direction of a hoodlum named Joe Parente. Parente's operations covered most of the San Francisco Bay area, but stretched as far south as the San Joaquin Valley.

"Burnett," because of his past bootlegging connections, was allowed to join the gang, which was then engaged in many diversified activities, and earned enough money to send for his wife. She arrived, bringing their daughter Arlene with her. She told Nelson she had done this to throw off suspicion, and that a kid would make them appear more like a regular family. Though this made good sense, Nelson didn't like the idea.

While working for Parente, Nelson met two other characters

who would later play their part in the drama of his life. One was a two-bit hoodlum called Fatso Negri, who was not too heavy in the brain department, but more than made up for it elsewhere. He would do anything for a buck, and this made him valuable for use as an errand boy.

The other was a tall, dark-eyed, dark-haired bootlegger named John Paul Chase. He was destined to become Baby Face Nelson's lieutenant. Chase's parents were native Americans, and had come to California from Omaha, in 1901. That same year their son was born, and they gave him the patriotic name of "John Paul."

Before Chase could finish grade school he quit and went to work ranching, farming, and also held a job as a chauffeur for a Reno gambler. Later he got a job as a machinist's helper in a railroad shop, but in 1926 he was fired, and this ended his career as a working man.

Chase became a bootlegger, and with his suave manner, and small, trim mustache, was also something of a ladies' man. He was ambitious, industrious, and anxious to make a lot of money, but he lacked the brains or intelligence to funnel this energy into the proper channels. What John Paul Chase had need of was a leader.

He became strangely attracted to this short, baby-faced character, who strutted around as if he were six feet tall. His interest increased sharply when "Burnett" confided in him that his real name was Nelson, and then told of his escape from the law, and of his many bank robberies. Perhaps he laid it on a bit thick, but he thought he might be able to use this charming, none-too-bright, hoodlum in the future.

Chase had heard of Baby Face Nelson and was smitten with a kind of hero worship. He would sit around and listen to "Big George," as Chase called Nelson, while he bragged of his past glories, and told of his grandiose plans for the future.

Things were going real well for Burnett, but one day poor, dumb, Fatso Negri, reading his favorite detective magazine, came across a picture of Baby Face Nelson. The accompanying article told of Nelson's fantastic escape, and mysterious gun.

Any rational hoodlum would have quietly called the article to Nelson's attention, and then let it go at that. But not Fatso. He took an extreme delight in showing it to every hood he knew, and all at once everybody in the area seemed to know that Jimmy Burnett was really Baby Face Nelson. The Nelsons fled.

In Vallejo, California, there was a seemingly respectable hospital, which was really operated by and for criminals. For an extremely high fee the gangster could have bullets removed, his fingerprints erased, or even his face changed.

The hospital was owned and operated by a retired bank robber, safe blower, and burglar, Thomas C. (Tobe) Williams, whose real name was Thomas C. Cohen. He was known throughout the West Coast, in the underworld, as "The Goniff from Galway."

Helen Nelson entered the hospital here for a serious operation, and it was performed successfully by an underworld doctor. Nelson, as he sat around fidgeting, decided to have a small operation himself, so he had his fingers burned with acid to get rid of his fingerprints. The operation, of course, was a dismal failure, and it cost him a bundle.

When Helen could travel, Nelson began to make plans. He wanted to form his own gang so as a beginning he offered a position to John Paul Chase, who accepted immediately. His first assignment was to purchase an automobile that couldn't be traced.

Then Nelson, Helen, and Chase drove across the country to the city of Minneapolis, where they rented an apartment. From this base of operations, Nelson hoped to form a gang, fan out across the Middlewest, and hit some of the fat little farm banks. In the meantime he and Chase hit the bank in Brainerd, Minnesota in October 1933, and got their first big money: $32,000.

The two of them split the money down the middle, then settled back to enjoy it. With $16,000 apiece, they didn't have to work for a while. In those depression days, this sum of money was a fortune.

Repeal came suddenly on December 5, 1933, and thousands of hard-working bootleggers, rumrunners, hijackers, and other allied professionals were thrown out of work. Many of these would be forced to find other ways to make a dishonest buck.

For reasons which have always remained vague, on March 4, 1934, Baby Face Nelson shot and killed Theodore W. Kidder, 35, a paint salesman. Kidder worked for the National Lead Company in St. Paul.

Kidder was with his mother-in-law, and they had just come from attending a children's party in Minneapolis. Although the police did not find out why Nelson killed him, they did have an excellent description of him and the car, with its California license plates. Kidder was Nelson's first recorded murder victim.

In the days that followed, the story was splashed across the nation's newspapers, together with a picture of Baby Face Nelson. Also included was a complete description of the Ford sedan, with its tag number: 6-H-475.

The seemingly senseless killing aroused the people in the Twin City area, and the newspapers played it up, but then it was suddenly bumped off the front page by another, more exciting story. The day before, John Dillinger had pulled his sensational escape from the Crown Point jail using a wooden gun, and the details were just now being released.

Running scared the Nelsons and Chase fled from Minneapolis to Bremerton, Washington, where they hid out with Helen's sister for a time. Here Nelson read about the escape of John Dillinger, but it made no impression upon him. He didn't know Dillinger, and had no personal interest in the whole affair.

Intuition told Nelson that it was time to move again. He feared the authorities might trace them here, so they drove down to Reno where he and Chase both had friends. In Reno, the hoods greeted them with open arms. They needed the help of the two hoodlums.

A couple of the local boys were in real trouble, and were most anxious to get rid of a witness before he could testify. They asked Nelson and Chase if they would help. The pay was high and they needed money, so Nelson agreed to take the contract.

Nelson did the actual killing, while Chase drove the murder car. After they had disposed of the body, Nelson decided the car was too hot so he instructed Chase to drive it to San Francisco and get rid of it. They made a date to rendezvous later in Chicago.

Chase took the car to California, where he disposed of it, and the Nelsons then took a train to Chicago, where they awaited Chase's return.

iii

While in Chicago, Nelson bumped into Tommy Carroll, who had worked with him on a couple of bank jobs. He told Nelson that a friend of his, one John Dillinger, was hiring gun hands.

This was big news for Nelson, for John Dillinger was now the talk of the land. He was really big time, and Nelson knew that he himself was still small potatoes. He believed that this man could open a whole new future for him, so he told Carroll he'd like to meet him.

Huddled around a table in a hideout in Chicago were Dillinger, Red Hamilton, Homer Van Meter, Eddie Green, Tommy Carroll, and Dillinger's latest girlfriend, Billie Frechette. The men were in the middle of planning a bank hit when Nelson arrived.

The proposition was simple, and the offer curtly made. Dillinger needed another man for the bank job, and he wanted to know if Nelson was interested in joining them. The split, he told Nelson, would be equal shares for all. Nelson agreed at once, and then joined them in the planning.

The only member of the gang who had worked with Dillinger before was Red Hamilton, but the rest had agreed to follow his orders. Carroll, Van Meter, and Billie Frechette knew Nelson from past experience, and none of them liked him. Nelson didn't like anybody but Nelson, so this presented no problem.

March 6, 1934, the Dillinger gang arrived in Sioux Falls. As soon as they entered the Security National Bank and Trust Company, someone set off the alarm. This robbery meant a great deal to Nelson, and he was sure it would go off without a hitch with the "great" John Dillinger leading them. Nelson had also been fooled by the Dillinger publicity.

Now Nelson's temper took over, and he nearly threw a fit. Employees and customers later reported that he raved and ranted, and told them of the terrible things he was going to do to that "son of a bitch who set off that alarm." The only trouble was he never did find him.

A little later, while the other members of the gang were grabbing the money, the maniacal little killer shot Hale Keith, an off-duty motorcycle cop, seriously wounding him. Then he did a kind of "Lindy-Hop" around the bank, eyes glistening, and screaming "I got one of them! I got one of them!"

In all probability, if Dillinger or others in the gang had witnessed any of these shenanigans, this would have been Nelson's last job. This business of holding up banks was a serious one, and they couldn't tolerate any nuts.

Taking their hostages, the gang, with its loot, wheeled out of town and headed back to Eddie Green's apartment in Minneapolis.

When it came time to count and divide the loot, Eddie Green started to officiate. The sight of this infuriated Nelson, who violently disliked Green. Impulsively, Nelson snatched up a machine gun laying nearby, and pointed it at Green, demanding to know who the hell had made him the official counter.

Dillinger, not wanting any dissension in his newly formed gang, told Eddie to let Lester count it. "It'll come out just the same," he assured Green.

So Nelson, like a petulant child, and spitefully taking his time, eventually divided the loot of $49,500 into six neat piles. Out of

Nelson's split would come a smaller one for his protégé, John Paul Chase, money for expenses, such as weapons and bullet proof vests, and protection money.

No one was in more of a hurry for money than John Dillinger, so the gang was again called together on March 12, and they hit the First National Bank of Mason City, Iowa, the following day.

Nelson had a ball here, as they decided to leave him on the outside, stationed near the rear door of the bank. While here, he took a particular delight in firing bursts from his machine gun at the crowds of curious people. It was one of these playful bursts that cut the legs from under R. L. James.

Tommy Carroll, who had been posted across the street from the bank, couldn't find a thing to shoot at during the same time that Nelson, at his post in the rear, had used almost a full drum of ammunition.

Upon leaving, a sniper managed to shoot both Dillinger and Hamilton in the shoulder. The take was also only $52,000, and it should have been a lot more, according to the newspapers. Nelson began to wonder if the "great" John Dillinger was as great as he had once thought. As far as he was concerned both bank jobs had been dismal failures.

With two of the gang wounded, the members voted to split up for awhile. This would give Dillinger and Hamilton time to heal their wounds, and allow the rest of the gang time to seek rest and relaxation. Nelson found no argument with this decision.

Returning to Chicago, Nelson picked up Helen, and parked John Paul Chase. Then they headed to Milwaukee, away from the others, so they could really enjoy their ill-gotten gains. Meanwhile, Dillinger and Billie went to St. Paul, where they moved into the Lincoln Court Apartments.

Secure and safe in Milwaukee, Nelson and Helen read, with mild interest, the latest news from St. Paul. It was March 31, 1934, and the FBI had caught up with Dillinger at his Lincoln Court address, and with a St. Paul detective had tried to take him. There had been quite a gun battle, but John, Homer, and Billie had escaped. One of them had been wounded, however, for there was blood on the scene. Nelson wondered, idly, who it was.

Then, on April 3, the FBI shot and killed Eddie Green, in St. Paul, and Nelson laughed about this. "Now," he told Helen, "that SOB won't be dividing any more money."

Next came the arrest of Billie Frechette and Doctor Clinton

May, who had been enlisted by Green to treat Dillinger. They
were charged with harboring a fugitive.

Still feeling safe, Nelson tickled his wife, Helen, by going
around the apartment, whistling and singing, "Those FBI agents
are breaking up that old gang of mine." He was cocksure of himself, and had never given the FBI a serious thought.

On April 17, Nelson got the word, through Chase, that Dillinger was gathering the gang together and wanted to see him.
He had been spending his funds freely, so he was ready to go back
to work. Helen went with him, then dropped off in Chicago.

In Cicero, the gang presented a sad sight. Dillinger was limp-
ing, and his shoulder was still sore. Hamilton had never fully recovered from his shoulder wound, and didn't seem to be interested
in anything. Homer Van Meter and Tommy Carroll were both
followers who couldn't lead a gang, and nobody was willing to
follow Nelson, whom they all believed to be a neurotic.

Under the circumstances, someone suggested that they all
go to a resort in northern Wisconsin for a rest, and then later,
maybe, they could come up with an idea for a job. The place was
called Little Bohemia, and was primarily a summer lodge. It was
located on Little Star Lake, not far from Mercer. Since it was a
summer lodge, but open in the winter, they were sure of having
it all to themselves.

iv

While the rest of the gang settled down in the main lodge
building, the Nelsons preferred to keep to themselves. The owner
had a few separate three-room cabins nearby, so they took one
of these.

Mr. and Mrs. Emil Wanatka were delighted to have so many
free-spending guests in the off season. Mr. Wanatka had remained
open in hopes something like this would happen. He was carrying
a heavy mortgage on the place, and could use the extra money.

His happiness soon changed to terror when he finally figured
out who his guests were, and he got word to the FBI. On Sunday
night, April 22, 1934, the agents surrounded the lodge, and before
long a full-fledged battle was in progress.

Nelson and Helen were in the main building when the shooting
began, and Helen ran into the cellar with the rest of the women.
Dillinger, Hamilton, Van Meter, Carroll, and Nelson all escaped
through a back window, but the sounds of battle stimulated

Nelson's interest so he circled the lodge, hoping to get a clear shot.

According to Melvin Purvis, Special Agent in Charge, Nelson did spot him, and churned up the dirt in front of him with his machine gun. But when the agents returned the fire, Nelson fled.

While Nelson was having his fun, his comrades were churning up some dirt of their own, but with their feet. When they reached the banks of the lake, they turned to the right and escaped along the shore. By the time Nelson got there everyone had gone, and he turned to the left.

He stumbled along the left bank of the lake for a while, but he soon got winded. Living the easy life of wine, women and song, he wasn't in the best of condition. Finally he cut away from the lake, and crossed through the woods.

Presently he came upon a store operated by Mr. and Mrs. Alvin Koerner. They also ran the telephone exchange for the area. Nelson ran inside, wild-eyed, and waved his tommygun at Alvin Koerner.

Nelson's words were curt and to the point: he wanted to know if Koerner owned a car. Koerner, his eyes glued to the waving machine gun, said there was a car outside, but it didn't belong to him. "To hell with that," Nelson spat, "get out there and get in —we're going to take a ride."

Outside Koerner tried to reason with Nelson but Nelson told him, "Get in and shut up, I gotta think." Just as they had gotten into the car and Nelson had switched on the lights, they saw another car coming. He immediately shut the lights off, and told Koerner to keep quiet.

In the other car were a local constable, Carl C. Christensen, Special Agent Jay Newman, and Special Agent W. Carter Baum, of the FBI. Christensen was showing them the way to Koerner's store so they could call the FBI field headquarters at Rhinelander for more agents.

Nelson just sat there calmly waiting for the other car to arrive. He was fingering the machine gun in his lap nervously, and thinking dark thoughts. He had had just about enough of being chased, and was about to lose his vicious temper. He wasn't thinking about getting away now, but only about getting even.

When the car got close enough so Nelson could see the pistol in Agent Newman's hand, he opened the door of the car and began to spray the FBI car with a deadly fire. Agent W. Carter

Baum had a machine gun in his lap, but he never got a chance to use it.

According to Christensen, he tried to duck down behind Baum, and Newman tried to duck down behind him. Baum fell out of the car, then he got up, and tried to run but fell across a fence. He had been hit in the throat. Then Newman was hit in the head by a bullet and he rolled out.

Christensen then jumped out of the car and started to run, but Nelson's bullets slammed him to the ground. Christensen was very bitter in his story, as he said, "I tried to crawl to Baum, who had fallen across the fence. I could still hear him breathing, but he died before anyone got there. They let us lie there about an hour before anyone dared to come!"

Then Nelson jumped into the car the officers had driven to the scene, and sped away into the night, leaving behind him two badly wounded men and one dead one. Special Agent W. Carter Baum, 29, died, draped across a fence. Christensen had eight bullets in him, and Special Agent Newman had been shot in the forehead, but both would live.

Koerner, who had jumped from the car, raced into his store. Here he immediately telephoned the police in Mercer and reported what had happened. They, in turn, got in touch with the FBI, who eventually got agents to the scene, but it was too late.

Nelson drove the car as far south as Squaw Lake, where it quit on him. Then he fled into the woods on foot, but having no sense of direction, he headed north to the vicinity of Lac du Flambeau.

Here he stumbled upon the hut of an old Indian called "Catfish," a full blooded Chippewa. Still carrying his machine gun he convinced Catfish to act as his host for three days. The old Indian had no idea who he was, but tolerated him and his weapon.

When Nelson decided that it was safe enough, he left the Indian Reservation, and made his way to the small town of Fifield, in Price County. Here he stole a car, and sped back to the safety of Chicago.

In Chicago he called Chase and sent him on errands—buying food, guns, ammunition, and a bulletproof vest. He remained in the hideout, where he kept his ear glued to the radio. Before long he had a pretty good idea of the situation. All of the gang had gotten away, but Helen—his Helen—Marie Conforti, and Jean Delaney had been captured. He felt the loss of Helen rather strongly for the moment, for he was beginning to get a little scared.

The next day Dillinger and Van Meter were speeding toward St. Paul in a stolen sedan, with Red Hamilton asleep on the back seat. Two officers recognized the car from a description they had, and started out in pursuit. When Van Meter speeded up they fired at the car, and a lucky shot entered the back seat, then entered Hamilton, mortally wounding him.

On April 30, 1934, three policemen recognized Baby Face Nelson, Chase (who they thought was Hamilton), Van Meter and Harry Fox. They pursued them and finally cut in front of Nelson's car; but before they could make their move, Nelson was out of the car with a machine gun in his hand.

Getting the drop on the three officers, he ordered them out of their car. As the driver emerged, Nelson beat him to the ground, then ordered the other two to start running.

The two officers, their hands still raised, started off up the highway, and Nelson cooly raised his machine gun and took deliberate aim at their backs. Both Chase and Van Meter pleaded with Nelson not to shoot; they told him they were already too hot as it was.

Nelson lowered the gun, but he was plainly disappointed. Then to vent his pent up anger, he suddenly whirled and blasted the police car with his machine gun, shooting out most of the glass, and disabling the automobile.

Bad news came on June 7, when Nelson heard on the radio that Tommy Carroll had been killed in a shootout with Detectives Emil Steffen and P. E. Walker, of Waterloo, Iowa. He hadn't particularly liked Carroll, but the killing hit too close to home. Then came the good news: Helen, Jean Delaney, and Marie Conforti had been sentenced to two years, then let off with probation. In less than a day, Helen joined Nelson in Chicago.

During the waning days of June, Chase brought the news that Dillinger and Van Meter were planning to rob the bank in South Bend, and wanted their help. According to Van Meter, who was the expert in such matters, this bank held enough money to put them all on easy street for a long time.

v

On June 30, 1934, the quartet hit the Merchants National Bank of South Bend, with Dillinger and Van Meter performing the actual robbery, while Nelson and Chase remained on guard outside.

Dillinger, showing the strain of past events, sent an angry burst from his machine gun into the ceiling of the bank. Nelson, had he seen this, would have been proud of John. But he was too busy with his own problems to take notice.

A jewelry store owner, Harry Berg, heard the machine gun fire, and peered out of his shop window. When he saw Nelson with his gun, he instantly knew what was happening, and decided to become involved. He came charging out of his store with a pistol in his hand. Taking careful aim, he fired at the unsuspecting Nelson, and Nelson spun from the impact of the bullet. His steel vest had protected him, and he was only bruised.

As he recovered from the impact of Berg's bullet, his temper took over, and he poured a torrent of bullets at his assailant, who prudently ducked back into his store. The shots shattered the shop's front window, and a ricochet bullet plowed into the leg of Jake Soloman, a customer. Another citizen, Samuel Toth, who was sitting in his automobile across the street, was struck in the head by a stray bullet. Then Patrolman Harold Wagner showed up, drawn by the noise of the shooting, and Nelson promptly killed him.

While Nelson was trying to look in all directions at once, a most extraordinary thing happened. A 16-year-old high school boy took a high flying leap and landed on Nelson's back! Around and around they went, with Nelson's machine gun spitting out sudden death. At last he shook off his tormentor, and then fired his remaining shots at him. The kid fell against a store window, shattering the glass, and one of Nelson's bullets passed through the palm of his hand, and he fainted.

By now Nelson was in a dour mood, and he must have reflected briefly upon the wisdom of following this man Dillinger. His gun was empty and he had no idea who would attack him next.

When Van Meter and Dillinger came out of the bank with several hostages, Nelson was more than ready to leave this crazy city. A gun battle with a jewelry store owner and a wrestling match with a school kid was about all he could take in one day. He felt no emotion over the killing of Patrolman Wagner.

They all loaded into the car, placing hostages on each running board. Then law officers came from everywhere, and everybody started shooting. The police succeeded in shooting two of the hostages, and they wounded Van Meter slightly.

Fleeing the town with their $28,000 in loot, they left behind one dead policeman, and five wounded citizens. The bank robbery had been a total failure as far as Nelson was concerned. The gang split up at once, with Dillinger going back to Chicago, Van Meter to St. Paul, and Chase to Gary, where he had a girlfriend. Nelson picked up Helen and they went to a hideout he had arranged in Barrington, Illinois.

Then the inevitable happened, and on a muggy Sunday night, in Chicago, the FBI and East Chicago, Indiana, police caught up with the "great" John Dillinger, and killed him. Dillinger didn't even get a shot off.

Nelson didn't feel any remorse over the death of Dillinger, whom he now rated as a third-class bum. He did feel anxiety, for now he became the FBI's Public Enemy Number One. Now he would have all those Federal Officers on his trail.

Mrs. Gillis's little boy Lester had come a long way since the days of the Five Points Gang. He was now the most wanted man in America, and he felt an overpowering sense of doom.

He was the leader now, and he decided to see if he couldn't supervise a bank job without it turning into a disaster. His bank jobs would be thoroughly cased before he pulled them. To hell with this "playing it by ear." That was just plain foolishness!

Nelson knew that he would have to leave this part of the country soon, so he made plans to return to the West Coast. They would need money—plenty of it, Nelson said—so he sent Homer Van Meter, who had accepted his leadership, north into Minnesota. His assignment was to look over the fat little banks in the Iron Range district. He was to see if he could locate two banks that they could hit in the same day.

Van Meter looked over the field, but he wasn't too happy with the prospects. The roads left much to be desired. They were narrow, twisted affairs, which made it too easy for the law to set up roadblocks. He thought it better to stick to the flat country, so he headed to St. Paul for a look-see, and to visit his girlfriend.

It was August 23, 1934, and the gang was about to lose another member. Four St. Paul officers recognized Van Meter and called him to surrender. He took off, sprinting down the street, and into an alley where they killed him. For all practical purposes, this finished the Dillinger gang.

With this new development Nelson decided the time to leave the Chicago area was now. To hell with money. He rounded up Chase and Helen, and they started Westward.

Traveling the country roads, they made their way to Reno, being careful not to exceed the speed limits in the states they crossed.

Helen always rode in front, while Nelson or Chase ducked down in back. This made them look like a couple out for a drive.

In Reno, Nelson looked up an acquaintance, Frank Cochran, a garage owner and airplane pilot. He told him their troubles, and Cochran got them a secluded cabin, where they enjoyed the fishing and hunting. Another acquaintance, Henry O. (Tex) Hall, a Reno gambler, promised to keep them informed of any police or FBI activity. It wasn't long before he sent word by Chase that Reno was filled with FBI agents who were questioning everybody.

Leaving at once, they fled to California, where they headed for the criminal hospital in Vallejo. Tobe Williams wouldn't even let them come in the door. He handed Nelson a thousand dollars and told him to keep going; he was too hot to handle.

Frightened, the trio gingerly threaded their way back towards the Chicago area. It was the only place they had left to go.

The underworld wanted Baby Face Nelson out of the way as much as did the police and the FBI. He was bringing too much heat down on their heads. The FBI was everywhere, peering, prying and probing. It was getting so a hard-working hoodlum couldn't ply his trade without an FBI agent stepping up to him to ask if he knew where Baby Face Nelson was hiding. Crime was a business, and Nelson was bad for business. He had to go.

vi

Somewhere along the way back to the Chicago area, an informer saw the Nelsons and Chase. He notified the FBI, and also gave them a description of Nelson's car, and the license number.

All FBI agents in the Chicago area were immediately alerted to be on the lookout for a Ford V-8, bearing Illinois license plates Number 639–578. Agents were also watching a house in Barrington, where Nelson had hid out after the South Bend job.

On November 27, 1934, one of the agents watching the highway leading to the house saw Baby Face Nelson drive by in a car. He immediately called the nearest FBI field headquarters for assistance. Two special agents, Thomas M. McDade and William C. Ryan, were sent to investigate.

Then, a one-in-a-million event happened, and Nelson's car passed the FBI car, which was headed the other way. Nelson grew suspicious of the car as soon as he saw it, and when they came abreast, he saw one of the agents straining to get a better look at him. That settled it. He yelled to Chase, "That guy in that car. He was a Fed. I'm sure of it, and we're going to take another look."

With this he swung the car around, and the agents found themselves being pursued by Nelson. Chase, seated in the rear, told Helen to duck, then he started shooting right through the windshield at the agents' Ford Coupe. They fired back, pulling on ahead; then they saw a turn-off, and took it. Stopping their car, they jumped out, took up defensive positions, and waited.

Nelson was cursing again as his Ford coughed to a rolling stop. "They hit something," he said, "the car has quit on me." Just at this moment another car came speeding up from the rear with Inspector Samuel Cowley and Special Agent Herman E. Hollis inside; they, too, were looking for Nelson.

They saw his stalled car, and immediately recognized him. Hollis slammed on the brakes, but the momentum of the car still carried it on ahead for about 40 or 50 feet.

Inspector Cowley and Agent Hollis got out of the car, and looked for cover. Cowley, with a machine gun, ran over to the roadside, where he took up a position in a ditch. Hollis, armed with a shotgun, elected to stay with the car.

Nelson yelled at Helen to get out of there, and he and Chase took up defensive positions. Helen ran out across a plowed field, then fell to the ground, covering her head with her hands.

The battle began at once, with Cowley and Baby Face Nelson dueling with machine guns. Hollis swapped shots with Chase, who was using a high-powered rifle. Suddenly Hollis was given a clear view of Nelson's legs, and he fired at them; Nelson staggered. Then, in pain and anger, Nelson fired a long burst from his machine gun at Cowley, who pitched forward on his face, but not before he fired again at Nelson.

Hollis, his shotgun empty now, threw it aside, and clawed at his pistol as he ran toward Cowley and the machine gun. Nelson, crazed from his wounds, staggered into the open and emptied his machine gun at Hollis, who spun around, and fell head on into the ditch, near Cowley.

With both FBI agents now dead or dying, Nelson turned his attentions toward getting away. He expected the other agents to return at any moment, so he yelled to Chase, "Get Helen, and let's get the hell out of here!"

They both knew their Ford was useless, so they all loaded into the Hudson Hollis had been driving. Then, as an afterthought, Chase got out again and went back to their own car and got a blanket and the remainder of their guns. He tossed the blanket to Helen, then slipped in behind the wheel, and they drove away from the bloody scene.

Special Agent Herman E. Hollis had been killed instantly, but Inspector Samuel Cowley was still alive. The entire battle, while savage and brutal, had lasted only a few minutes.

State Patrolman William Gallagher, who had stopped at a gasoline station, gave his version of the battle: "The cars stopped on the northwest highway about 500 feet west of state road 63. I sensed that it was a case of police authorities after hoodlums of some sort.

"As the agents advanced with drawn guns, instinctively I pulled out my rifle. When the shooting started, I started firing at the desperados. There were about fifteen people getting in my line of fire, and I had to stop. The people in the other machine got out too; swinging a machine gun, its muzzle flaring lead. Then, with the agents lying on the ground, they jumped into a machine and roared away." Just how Gallagher determined who were the "hoodlums," and who were the FBI agents, he didn't say.

On his way to the hospital, in Elgin, Illinois, Cowley was fully conscious, and kept insisting upon talking to Melvin Purvis. Just before they gave him ether for an emergency operation, he asked, "Did you get Purvis? I must talk to Purvis before I die." By the time Purvis got to the hospital, Cowley was unconscious, and was undergoing an operation.

Cowley regained consciousness three times following the operation, but he was unable to talk clearly. He died at 2:40 the following morning.

That same morning, Baby Face Nelson, with 16 slugs from Hollis's shotgun in his legs and thighs and at least one bullet from Cowley's machine gun in his side, also died. The machine gun bullet had ripped through his stomach, liver and pancreas.

Philip Sadowski, a Niles Center undertaker, protested that he needed more information. He had received a call at 7:55 A.M. from a woman who told him to go to Lincoln and Harms Avenue, and pick up the body of Lester Gillis. She refused to elaborate and hung up.

He then called Chief of Police Axel C. Stollberg, and reported the mysterious call. When he told the chief that the name of the dead man was supposed to be "Lester Gillis" Stollberg exclaimed, "My God, man, don't you know who that is? That's Baby Face Nelson!"

Stollberg immediately notified the FBI of the mysterious call. They dispatched 12 agents to check it out, as it was only 15 miles from the site of the battle, near Barrington. They found no body, but they did find a pile of bloody clothing, an empty money belt, and a laundry bag stamped with the name of a Chicago hotel, the Pratt Lane.

Slowly searching, in an ever-widening circle, the area had grown to almost 2½ miles. They were just about ready to give up the search when one of the agents shouted—he had found it.

And there he was, in a drainage ditch, where he had been dumped. His arms and legs were twisted, and his cherubic face contorted, giving grim testimony to the fact that he had died in intense agony.

In an attempt to bind the gaping wound in the little man's side, a crimson-soaked blanket had been wrapped around his middle. Under the blanket was a knotted handkerchief, which had been used in a hopeless attempt to stem the bleeding.

Baby Face Nelson sported a blonde moustache, and his finger tips were scarred by acid, but little difficulty was encountered in establishing his identity by his fingerprints. Also, most of the FBI agents had spent a great deal of time committing his face to memory, following Special Agent W. Carter Baum's death.

The following day, the stolen FBI Hudson was found on a Winnetka side street, where it had skidded into a muddy ditch. The body of the car had been severely damaged by bullet holes, and its steering wheel almost completely blasted away. It was a wonder that Chase could have steered the car at all. There was no report of any automobile having been stolen in Winnetka recently, so authorities decided that Helen and Chase had made their escape on foot.

The papers screamed the headlines that Helen Nelson Gillis was now the first woman to be listed as Public Enemy Number One. They also carried the story that orders had been issued to shoot her on sight. What the FBI had said was that it would not withhold fire because she was a woman.

A radio station, capitalizing on the bloody events, persuaded John Wawzynak, Helen's father, to go on the air with an emotion-filled plea for her to give herself up before she, too, was killed. It may have been a little overdramatic, and a bit on the sensational side, but it apparently worked.

Two days after the demise of her hoodlum husband, Helen surrendered to the FBI. She would eventually be returned to Madison, Wisconsin, where her original two-year-probation—following the Little Bohemia fiasco—would be revoked. Later she would escape a more severe penalty, by "ratting" on her husband's lieutenant, John Paul Chase.

On December 1, 1934, Baby Face Nelson was laid to rest in the St. Joseph's Cemetery, at River Grove, Illinois. Mrs. Gillis's little boy Lester would kill no more.

vii

But for Helen Nelson Gillis, John Paul Chase might have remained free. He was completely unknown to any police or federal authorities, as he had never been arrested in his life. Both the authorities and the newspapers were theorizing that the man with Baby Face Nelson had been John Hamilton (long dead), Tommy Touhy, or Alvin Karpis.

He had every reason to feel safe, so he took the name of Elmer Rockwood, and answered an ad in a paper, offering jobs for men to drive a convoy of cars to Seattle. Then he brazenly went to a police station, where he had his photograph made, got a chauffeur's license, and drove a car to Seattle, Washington, safely.

Cocksure of himself, Chase then backtracked to Butte, Montana, where he had $2000 stashed away in a safety deposit box. Here he telephoned a friend, the one who had rented the box for him, and asked him to get the money. The electrifying reply was that the box was under FBI surveillance, and that he had better clear out fast.

Now Chase knew that the FBI had, somehow, discovered his identity, and he fled the state in terror. Years before, he had worked for one summer at the California State Fish Hatchery, in Mount Shasta. Now, without a leader, and showing the lack of clear thinking, Chase showed up there on December 27, and applied for a job.

The FBI had done its homework, and they had the Fish Hatchery, along with every other place Chase had lived or worked, under surveillance. When Chase showed up in Mount Shasta, the FBI quietly took him into custody, without a shot being fired.

Tried for complicity in the murders of Inspector Sam Cowley, 35, and Special Agent H. E. Hollis, 30, he was found guilty. He was sentenced to life imprisonment, and sent to Alcatraz. As years passed, Chase mellowed, and became an artist, painting many oils. Later he was transferred to Folsom Prison, where he remained until his death.

Epilogue

Chapter 1

Kathryn Kelly got her wish, and she and her mother were eventually sent to Alderson, West Virginia, to the Women's Federal Penitentiary.

In June 1958, Kathryn and her mother, Ora Shannon, gained their release from prison on a $10,000 bond. They claimed that their constitutional rights had been denied them, and that they had not been properly represented by counsel. They had spent 25 years of their lives behind prison bars.

At the time of this writing they are still out on bail, and living in Shawnee, Oklahoma.

Robert K. G. (Boss) Shannon, who was also serving a life term at Leavenworth, had his sentence reduced to 30 years, and in 1944, he received a pardon from President Roosevelt, due to his advanced age and ill health. He returned to his ranch in Paradise, Texas, and died at the age of 79, December 25, 1956, in a hospital at Bridgeport, Texas.

Harvey J. Bailey, 76, gained his freedom from the Federal Correctional Institution at Seagoville, Texas, after a long legal battle, on July 24, 1961. His freedom was short-lived, however, for waiting for him when he walked out were Kansas authorities. They wanted him for leading the Memorial Day, 1933 escape from Lansing.

Albert Bates, old and broken in health, died in Alcatraz of heart disease, July 4, 1948.

Ben Lasha, one of Kathryn Kelly's attorneys, who was sentenced to 10 years for accepting part of the ransom money as his fee, was pardoned a few years later. He was reputed to be living in Denver, Colorado.

Mr. and Mrs. Charles F. Urschel left Oklahoma City, a short time after the trials, and moved to San Antonio, Texas.

On December 1, 1934, the Government announced that it had solved the Denver Mint robbery of $200,000 which had taken place on December 18, 1922. They said the automobile the robbers had escaped in was driven by Harvey J. Bailey.

Five men and two women—all of whom are now dead or in prison—were involved in the crime, which had baffled the best detective minds in the country for more than 13 years. They were:

James Clark, serving a life sentence in the Indian State Penitentiary, at Michigan City, for a bank robbery at Clinton.*

Frank McFarland, alias The Memphis Kid. Now dead.

Robert Leon Knapp, alias Robert Burns. Now dead.

Nicholas Trainor, alias Nick Sloan, whose frozen, bullet-riddled body was found in a residential garage in Denver, January 14, 1923.

Florence Sloan, also known as Florence Thompson, the "queen" of the mob, and the consort of Trainor. Now dead.

Margaret Burns, who posed as the wife of Knapp, or Robert Burns. Now dead.

The robbery of the mint was regarded as one of the most daring and ruthless crimes in the nation's history at that time. The bandits laid down a heavy barrage of gunfire, killing one Mint guard and pockmarking buildings in the vicinity. They struck in the forenoon of December 18, 1922, when a Federal Reserve bank truck had stopped at the Mint to obtain $200,000 in $5.00 bills. So sudden was the attack, and so complete the getaway, that no trace of the bandits was found until Nick Trainor's body was discovered in a garage more than a month later, preserved by the extremely cold weather.

The two women, Florence Sloan and Margaret Burns, were shot and burned to death in an automobile, near Red Wing, Minnesota.

Chapter 2

William "Jack" Killingsworth, who was kidnapped by Charles "Pretty Boy" Floyd, on June 16, 1933, was elected mayor of Bolivar, Missouri, in 1962, at the age of 64.

The younger brother of Floyd is now serving his seventh term in office as Sheriff of Sequoyah County, Oklahoma.

Jack Dempsey Floyd now lives in Richmond, California, with his wife and two children. His mother, Mrs. Ruby Hargraves Floyd, was last known to be living in Sallisaw, Oklahoma.

---

* Clark escaped from Michigan City, with John Dillinger's help, on September 23, 1933, but was recaptured.

Chapter 3

January 19, 1935, Edward George Bremer was taken to a house in Bensenville, Illinois, which he positively identified as the place he had been held captive in for so long. He would never forget the pattern of that wallpaper. The owner of the house, Edmund Bartholmey—who had also furnished the hideout for the gang during the kidnapping of William Hamm, Jr.—and 25 others were convicted and sent to prison for their part in the capers.

Harry Sawyer was also convicted for his part in the Bremer kidnapping and was sent to a federal penitentiary for life.

Volney Davis managed to elude the FBI for over a year after the kidnapping, but was finally arrested in Kansas City. Agents were flying him back to St. Paul, when the plane was forced down in a small town. Davis managed to knock his guard out and fled in a stolen car; but he was later recaptured. He was eventually tried in St. Paul, and sentenced to a federal penitentiary for life.

Chapter 6

Edgar Singleton, John Dillinger's first partner in crime, and the one who had started him on the way down the road to Public Enemy Number One, got drunk in 1937. He then sat down on the railroad tracks in Mooresville, Indiana, and was killed by a fast freight train.

John Dillinger, Sr., died in 1943, at the age of 79, after touring the country with a "Crime Does Not Pay Show," where he gave lectures about his son. He was buried next to his son, in the Crown Hill Cemetery at Indianapolis.

Matt Leach, who had dogged Dillinger's heels for so many months while head of the Indiana State Police, was fired on September 4, 1937. This was a direct result of his open and venomous feud with the FBI. He spent years writing a book about Dillinger (never published) in which he claimed that $7,000 was taken from Dillinger's dead body and given to the widow of William Patrick O'Malley. He also maintained that Dillinger was unarmed when he was shot.

Leach, returning from a television appearance in New York, was killed in an accident on the Pennsylvania Turnpike.

Robert Estill, the man who was to have prosecuted Dillinger,

and whose photograph with his arm around Dillinger created
such a furor, died in 1961.

Evelyn "Billie" Frechette and Mary Kinder joined traveling
"Crime Does Not Pay" shows, touring the country, telling about
their adventures with Dillinger and members of his gang, then
quietly dropped from sight.

In July 1935, Melvin Purvis quit the FBI, wrote a book entitled
American Agent, then organized the Junior G-Men for Post
Toasties, a breakfast cereal. Moving to South Carolina, he pub-
lished a newspaper, and was a Colonel in World War II.

After the war he returned to South Carolina, where he bought
a radio station. Then in February, 1960, he shot himself to death.
His wife, Roseann Purvis, of Florence, South Carolina, said the
shooting was an accident, but it was officially listed as suicide.
Purvis was only 56, but he had been in poor health for some time.

Chapter 7

Thomas C. Cohen, alias Thomas C. (Tobe) Williams, alias The
Goniff from Galway, who ran the Vallejo General Hospital, received a prison sentence of 18 months, and was fined $5,000, for
harboring Baby Face Nelson.

Henry O. (Tex) Hall, Reno gambler, and Frank Cochran, Reno
garage man and aviator, were convicted of harboring Baby Face
Nelson, and each got a year and a day in a federal penitentiary,
and a fine of $2,000.

Anthony Moreno, a San Francisco bartender, also received six
months in jail for conspiracy in the Nelson case.

Of the four, Judge Walter C. Lindley, presiding over the federal court in San Francisco, April 5, 1935, commented:

"No man can consider himself decent who aids, and gives
shelter or comfort to help the fugitive from justice; the gunman;
the gangster; the spume of humanity!"

Bibliography

A small book written in 1934 by Mrs. Emma Parker, Bonnie Parker's mother, and Nell Barrow Cowan, Clyde Barrow's sister, contributed a wealth of material. This will account for the large amount of personal facts; dialogue, and papers that make this chapter ("The Thrill Seekers"), the most documented in the book.

This book could not have been written without the availability of the works of hundreds of unknown reporters, who wrote the events as they were happening in the following newspapers:

The Tulsa World; The Tribune, Tulsa, Oklahoma

The Joplin Globe, Joplin, Missouri

The Kansas City Star, Kansas City, Missouri

The Daily Oklahoman; Oklahoma City Times, Oklahoma City, Oklahoma

The Pioneer Press; The St. Paul Dispatch, St. Paul, Minnesota

The Ocala Star Banner, Ocala, Florida

The New Era, Hot Springs, Arkansas

The Commercial Appeal, Memphis, Tennessee

The Arkansas Gazette, Little Rock, Arkansas

The St. Petersburg Times, St. Petersburg, Florida

Photographs: United Press International Photo (as applicable); Wide World Photos (as applicable).

Though there are very few books of authority on any of these criminals, with the exception of John Dillinger and the small book on the Barrow gang, the following listed books were of great assistance in researching for material and dates:

Alcatraz Island Prison, by Warden James A. Johnston, Charles Scribner's Sons, New York, 1949

American Agent, by Melvin Purvis, Garden City Publishing Co., Inc., New York, 1938

The Dillinger Days, by John Toland, Random House, New York, 1963

The FBI in Peace and War, by Frederick L. Collins, G. P. Putnam's Sons, New York, 1943

The Lawless Decade, by Paul Sann, Crown Publishers, Inc., New York, 1957

Persons In Hiding, by J. Edgar Hoover, Little, Brown & Co., Boston, 1938

Milligan (The Inside Story of the Pendergast Machine) by Maurice M. Milligan, Pub. Charles Scribner's Sons

Index

291